THE POWERS OF SENSIBILITY

THE POWERS OF SENSIBILITY

Aesthetic Politics through Adorno, Foucault, and Rancière

Michael Feola

Northwestern University Press
Evanston, Illinois

Northwestern University Press
www.nupress.northwestern.edu

Printed in the United States of America

10 9 8 7 6 5 4 3 2 1

ISBN 978-0-8101-3746-2 (paper)
ISBN 978-0-8101-3747-9 (cloth)
ISBN 978-0-8101-3748-6 (ebook)

Cataloging-in-Publication data are available from the Library of Congress.

Contents

Acknowledgments

As readers will know, writing a book is a long and often solitary affair. Many hours spent with dusty books. Late nights of staring at a screen. Revision after revision after revision. And yet, as solitary as the process may be, no intellectual work is conducted in a bubble. Every writer depends on the kindness of friends, colleagues, and strangers: the late night conversations, the nagging questions, the patient advice, and the moments of encouragement that unfailingly arrive exactly when they are needed. Every intellectual work bears witness to countless debts to both the living and the dead. And this book is no exception.

To begin, I would like to thank those at the University of California, Berkeley, who were present at the very inception of this project: Hans Sluga, Anthony Cascardi, Frederick Dolan, and the fellows at the Townsend Center for the Humanities. Above all, I bear a debt to my comrades in thought for those years. Benjamin Yost, Michael Holt, and Mark Pedretti merit particular mention for conversations that stretched far beyond the spaces and times of official scholarship—from the classrooms to the plazas to the pubs. These were the conversations that pushed me in ways I had not yet begun to imagine on my own.

As is the case for so many in the contemporary academy, my path after graduate school was circuitous—and I have many to thank on my various stops. I thank the Introduction to the Humanities program at Stanford University, where I worked with many inspirational scholars and teachers. A particular debt must be acknowledged to Kathleen Coll, Ellen Woods, Phaedra Bell, and Sarah Cervenak. At Duke University, I thank Michael Gillespie, Thomas Spragens, Peter Euben, Luc Perkins, Lindsey Andrews, and the excellent students in my graduate seminar on continental political theory. At Williams College, I was lucky to find company in Mark Reinhardt, Neil Roberts, James Mahon, and Kiara Vigil. At Lafayette College, I have landed in a supportive intellectual environment—particularly through the research assistance of my EXCEL scholars (Joshua Geesey, Juannell Riley, Timothy Elliott, and Alexander Shulman). I am particularly grateful for the support I have received from my colleagues in the Government and Law Department—especially Seo-Hyun Park, Liz Suhay,

Joshua Miller, Il Hyun Cho, and Helena Silverstein. In addition, there have been so many who have been helpful in ways that exceed any institutional connections: Wendy Brown, Robyn Marasco, Sam Chambers, Lawrie Balfour, Moya Lloyd, Bonnie Honig, Robert Blunt, Neha Vora, and Steve Belletto have all helped me in ways that they may or may not know.

There are some individuals who bear particular mention in helping this book become a reality. Tom Lay intervened at a crucial time, when all hope seemed lost. At Northwestern University Press, Trevor Perri has been a model editor, ever responsive and generous in his guidance. Jay Bernstein must be thanked for his willingness to take an itinerant graduate student into his intellectual world—a gift of hospitality all too rare in this profession. Above all, I bear a significant debt to Judith Butler, who has been unfailingly supportive at every step of the way. It is a testimony to her generosity that she is able to find time for her students, no matter the many demands on her time. The influence of these two thinkers on the study will be evident to the reader.

Of course, no book is completed without significant investments of time and energy—sacrifices largely borne by all those around them, who are forced to pick up the pieces of everyday life. Patricia O'Leary has been a constant source of support and motivation in my intellectual pursuits. Without her, I would not be. And, above all, I bear a debt to Joelle Newnam for her unfailing support, joy, and love. Every day, she inspires me to think and be better.

* * *

Chapter 3 represents a greatly expanded, revised version of my "Speaking Subjects and Democratic Space: Rancière and the Politics of Speech," *Polity* 46, no. 4 (2014): 498–519. A few paragraphs of chapter 1 were drawn from my "Difference without Fear: Adorno *contra* Liberalism," *European Journal of Political Theory* 13, no. 1 (2014): 41–60. And a few paragraphs of chapter 4 overlap with the themes of my article, "The Body Politic: Bodily Spectacle and Democratic Agency," *Political Theory* 46, no. 2 (2018): 197–217

THE POWERS OF SENSIBILITY

Introduction

Critical Reflections on the Aestheticization Thesis

One does not need to look far to recognize the tangled relations between aesthetics and politics. There is a long line of figures who have proclaimed the ability of art to save, deliver, awaken, or redeem society. And yet, few things raise so many hackles as the perceived encroachment of aesthetics into politics—or, in the now-canonical formula of Walter Benjamin, the "aestheticization of politics."[1] Even the briefest scan of the literature shows a wide array of indictments. From some quarters, this entanglement represents a kind of retrograde neo-romanticism. From another angle, it represents a movement of withdrawal: a turn to the consolations of art when public institutions betray the ideals they avow. And from a world-historical vantage point, it might represent a desire to flee modernity for a time when the good and the beautiful existed in untroubled continuity. No matter the significant differences in these challenges, what persists throughout is the sense that there has been some kind of improper admixture. Indeed, the force of this charge is evinced by its air of finality: in much critical discourse, once an argument has been tarred with the brush of "aestheticism," no further argument is needed to disqualify it from serious normative consideration.

In light of these concerns, it may be surprising that contemporary normative debates have seen something of a "turn" to the aesthetic.[2] Or, to render this tendency in more expansive terms, recent literature has expressed a renewed willingness to consider aesthetic contributions to political thought, when significant theoretical effort has been spent to keep these domains apart. To open this study, then, it will be useful to spend some time exploring these suspicions that there *is* some essential divide between these categories of experience. Only by getting clear on these anxieties will the stakes, potentials, and liabilities of this "turn" become manifest.

First, political appeals to "the aesthetic" face a burden of underdetermination, since it is hardly self-evident what specific sense of these terms is at stake. There is a familiar way to think of how art might serve political aims when used to express contents that cannot be spoken freely under present social conditions (whether the constraints be official or unofficial). Here it may be useful to think of Picasso's *Guernica*—a work that uses symbolic displacement to convey truths that were inconvenient, prohibited, censored, or difficult to convey through official political channels. If one follows this path (as many have), then there are robust debates on what art can do to memorialize a suppressed past, recapture forgotten truths, or problematize elements of social practice. Here, the task is not simply to track the history of art's social engagements. Rather, this form of cultural production yields important resources with which to reinvigorate civic discussions, displace the self-evidence of the everyday, or, in the terms of Claire Bishop, "witness what is structurally excluded from society."[3] Take the recent (2000) work by the Austrian artist Christoph Schlingensief ("Please Love Austria"), where he placed twelve "asylum seekers" (played by actors) into a shipping container that was perpetually monitored, and every day observers could vote out (in the style of reality television) one of the inhabitants, who would be returned to the deportation center. In this case, it was not only these bodies that were highlighted and made visible to the public, but likewise the nativist response to their presence—the racism, refusal, and xenophobia that represent the unavowable unconscious of national belonging.[4]

From this angle, it is necessary to account for how works of art have spilled out beyond the walls of the museum, so as to structure everyday interactions and build a material memory into the spaces of life. Schlingensief's container was not, after all, situated within the walls of a gallery, accessible only to ticket-paying customers, but rather in a public square, near the Vienna Opera House. Observers could gather around the container and peer in through the holes in the sides. The artist would climb on top of the container, beneath a banner that read "Foreigners Out," to shout provocations to those gathered around. To follow the lead of what has been termed the "social turn" in art practice, such works do not remain in elite forums of cultural consumption; rather, they enter into the life of the community in celebratory and disruptive ways. They shape social conversations or they force the public eye to rest upon uncomfortable questions—those topics swept under the rug by sanitized narratives regarding the community in question. Or, in their more radically participatory forms, such artworks stage alternative forms of sociality, forcing the audience to participate within social conversations, enter into the practice of authorship, or collaborate with strangers in ways unprepared by the atomization of late capitalist public culture.[5] These are events in which the easy distinctions of work, world, author, and audience are destabilized, and new social forms are themselves at stake.

There is a large literature on this expanded field of art production and circulation. These familiar approaches, however, miss the question that will animate this study: what could it mean when theorists apply patently aesthetic criteria *as* political resources? For instance, the young Hegel who proposes that the wounds of a rationalized modernity can be healed not through a discourse of cosmopolitanism, justice, or "the vacuity of the rights of man"—but rather through "the most beautiful shape to match the high Idea of absolute ethical life."[6] Or Friedrich Schiller, who claims that "if man is ever to solve that problem of politics in practice he will have to approach it through the problem of the aesthetic, because it is only through beauty that man makes his way to freedom."[7] In such cases, the suspicion is that some important category error is committed when one framework (the aesthetic) is brought to bear upon the other (the political)—something like attempting to checkmate your opponent by drawing a picture or playing the accordion. Indeed, from the textbook definitions of these spheres, there appears to be little overlap or ground for intersection. As my students often contend, it is easy enough to sketch a family resemblance between political life and ethics (both of which address how human subjects negotiate values to live with one another); and it is likewise plausible to construe a strong overlap between politics and economics (both of which tackle the question: who gets what, and on what grounds?). But, we are often told, important difficulties follow from attempting to link (a) a sphere of appearance, sensation, pleasure, and feeling with (b) a sphere organized around justice, power, distribution, and rights (a set of rough distinctions that will be complicated over the course of this study).

To raise such questions is not, of course, to deny some obvious connections between political practice and a regime of vision, perception, and sensation. In watching political commercials during campaign season, it would be difficult to ignore the significant contributions of aesthetic resources—all designed to grab viewers and solicit their investments for (or against) certain candidates or policy measures. As a wide range of theorists have noted, the art of political persuasion hardly reduces to the elaboration of reasons to convince citizens that certain policies will (or will not) meet their normative commitments. Rather, important work is performed at the pre-reflective level, in the cultivation of love, fear, anxiety, rage, crisis, resentment, loss, or hope—and the investment of these affects within certain candidates, populations, or policies rather than another. Even the quickest scan of political advertisements reveals a familiar rogues' gallery designed to produce such effects: crime, poverty, job loss, perversion, disease, global warming, abortion, poverty, terrorists, corruption, welfare cheats, higher taxes, weapons of mass destruction, or outsiders swarming across unsecured borders. And these explicit themes are redoubled by sophisticated editing techniques, ominous voice-overs, catchy slogans, and musical cues. For a concrete example, think of the notorious moment in 2003 when George W. Bush donned the trappings of combat and climbed out of a fighter jet on the decks of the USS *Abraham Lincoln,* to announce the end of combat operations in the Iraq War. In watching this episode, one could not help but note the visual rhetoric crafted to convey an image of hard, warrior virility—or the connections between masculinity, militarization, and nationhood. The crowd, the uniform, the helmet, the cockpit, the soldiers at attention all speak to a *mission accomplished* (a sentiment spelled out by the banner in the background, for those apparently too thick to grasp the trappings of a warrior returning from battle).[8] Such moments offer an insight into how aesthetic strategies work within the practice of a mediated, dispersed democracy, where the theater of politics so often takes the form of a television or computer screen. Perhaps it is useful to begin obliquely, then, through the rich spectacle of politics, with its pageantry, architecture, parades, songs, and flags—which is not, of course, to say that this visual rhetoric will succeed in its aims, that it will not misfire, that it will not be mocked or parodied or co-opted by those with a similar acumen for the symbology of power.[9]

To appeal to one of the thinkers at the heart of this study, such instances evoke the impetus toward display that Michel Foucault identified within a classical model of power. When the sovereign law is broken, the transgressor is not hidden away in the dark space of the dungeon. Rather, this body is to be broken and tormented in public, where the eyes of the assembled must confirm the authority of the crown, now restored, undamaged and undiminished.[10] It is in the absoluteness of bodily undoing that the absoluteness of sovereign power is likewise staged. This theatricality of power resurfaces in the violence visited upon dark bodies on the plantations of the antebellum South or the lynchings of the Reconstruction Era. In each case, power is expressed in its display—in producing effects that can (or must) be witnessed so as to maintain an order enforced by terror.[11] And the lessons of these spectacles work on multiple levels. As historians have argued, public lynchings did not just exert power upon those who threatened the order of white supremacy; rather, they aimed to reconstitute white solidarity in the face of urbanization, growing class divides, and the destabilizing effects of capital.[12] Or, put differently, these spectacles of power do not simply demonstrate a lesson about those who appear before the public eye. Rather, they also stage the meaning of those who watch, of the "we" that is meant to be forged in the common experience of viewing—we who are here, who behold, who are validated or changed or bonded in this experience of beholding (whether the lesson be one of dread, or triumph, or loss, or vengeance, or memory).[13]

Of course, to open in this fashion may appear to sidestep the core problem entirely. As the foregoing demonstrates, it is not difficult to identify a spectacular dimension to the practice of politics. The operations of state power do not simply work through commands and treaties and laws, but are staged through a variety of theatrical means. In a feudal regime, there are the thrones, the crowns, the seals, the scepters, the choirs, the banners, and even the colors reserved for the sovereign.[14] In more recent times, there are the monuments that structure public space, the halls of power that loom over the individual body, the walls and security checkpoints by which the state performs its sovereignty.[15] There are the symbols and flags and anthems by which an "imagined community" is reconstituted when the organic bonds of the nation (itself located within some bygone golden days) have lost their power for disenchanted subjects.[16] And it would be difficult to forget how the United States military explicitly appealed to the work of spectacle during the 2003 Iraq War—when American viewers were encouraged to tune in via cable news and witness either the "shock and awe" to be unleashed upon a recalcitrant Iraqi nation, or the "breathtaking" scenes (in Donald Rumsfeld's words) of "free Iraqis celebrating in the streets, riding American tanks, tearing down the statues of Saddam Hussein in the center of Baghdad"—scenes, it turned out, that were staged for the benefit of viewers back home.[17]

The task at hand, then, is not to collect and catalog the theatrical presentations of power, whether the jumpsuit of the prisoner, the ritualized "perp walk," the robes and wigs of the judiciary, or the militarized costumes of the riot police as they march through neighborhoods of color. Such a list would only confirm what is already known. And likewise, the analysis would operate through a haphazard, ad hoc collection of examples, torn from disparate cultural, historical, and social contexts. To bring greater rigor to these openings, the question at hand is not the descriptive issue (i.e., whether politics persistently deploys aesthetic measures), but rather the normative discomfort over the intersection of these regimes—a discomfort that stems from a specific narrative regarding the course of modernity. It is to this narrative (and its far-reaching reverberations for the practice of critical theory) that we will now turn.

* * *

One way to gain purchase on these anxieties is through the various cognates of "the aesthetic" that populate these debates.[18] One sense of the term "aestheticism" marks a historical development of aesthetic practice, through which it becomes increasingly autonomous, increasingly reflexive, and increasingly prone to refer only to itself. This is perhaps best represented by the modernist movement of "art for art's sake"—no longer operating at the behest of the state, the church, moral values, or communal solidarity. Such art need not serve the aims of civic binding, as the statue of the civic god may have done for the ancient polis; nor does it glorify the transcendent, absent god, as with the high church art of Christendom. This aesthetic movement instead offers a purification of artistic production, such that it pursues those virtues internal to the art world: the flatness of the canvas, the spatial presence of the sculpture, the tonal possibilities of the octave, the color that is itself a perceptual event (rather than a predicate of particular objects).[19] And if this is the case, then the aesthetic comes to offer a refuge *from* the frustrations and hardships of the everyday. As Max Weber puts it: "art takes over the function of a this-worldly salvation, no matter how this may be interpreted. It provides a salvation from the routines of everyday life, and especially from the increasing pressures of theoretical and practical rationalism."[20] Even if the subject can no longer invest in the nation (increasingly bureaucratized and distant) or the satisfactions of labor (now rationalized, monitored, and precarious), one can yet enjoy the pleasures of culture. In a more fraught sense, however, to "aestheticize" (whether aimed at "the political" or some other sphere of experience) means a movement in the opposite direction. It is not a reflexive withdrawal, but rather an expansionist gesture that extends beyond its proper boundaries to "colonize" other regimes of thought, value, and meaning. To articulate the problem in broad strokes, a theorist is often said to have aestheticized a problem when she or he *substitutes* aesthetic criteria (e.g., beauty, harmony, intensity, pleasure, play, and so forth) for traditionally practical notions (e.g., rights, obligation, equality, fairness).[21]

It would not be difficult to cite instances in which this latter dynamic has yielded untoward consequences. Perhaps the most oft-discussed would be the effort to construe the nation along the lines of an artwork, forged by the hands of a leader-artist—in which case, the statesperson is allowed a nearly unlimited license to impose order upon the unruly "material" of social life. There are significant precedents in the history of political thought, where metaphors of formation (conducted by a single figure, in the service of aims that he or she has determined) substitute for the negotiations of citizens crafting a life in common. Friedrich Nietzsche, for instance, invokes the formative work of the *Staatskünstler*, who takes a shapeless mass of individuals, each pursuing private aims, and forges it into something recognizable as a people.[22] This analogy between technical and social formation is, however, not limited to the pages of philosophers, speculating on possibilities far removed from the practice of actual politics. Perhaps the most notorious instance comes from the fascist experiments of the twentieth century—when both Mussolini and Hitler construed the work of the leader as a kind of artistry that would permit the nation to actualize its historical destiny. Here the aesthetic appeal turns on tropes of crisis and redemption. What is in danger of being lost or squandered can be recaptured through the leader's historical vision and techniques of statecraft. As Joseph Goebbels captures this position: "the statesman is also an artist. To him the *Volk* is nothing more than stone is to a sculptor. Leader and masses, that is as little a problem as, say, painter and paint . . . Politics is the plastic art of the state, as painting is the plastic art of color . . . Forming a *Volk* from the masses and a state from the *Volk*—that has always been the most profound purpose of politics."[23]

From a democratic vantage point, the stakes are significant. The statesperson-as-artist threatens a relationship in which individual subjects are not co-originators of a power submitted to collective scrutiny; nor, in Aristotelian terms, are they participants in the reciprocal process of ruling and being-ruled. Rather, they are objects to be administered and managed in the service of aims they have not, themselves, decided. Such agents are, in a word, tools or material, rather than citizens.[24] And yet, this emphasis on statecraft hardly exhausts the concerns that tend to swirl around the charge of "aestheticization." Indeed, there is a prominent literature that questions whether an expansionist aesthetic might introduce pathologies more broadly into the fabric of everyday life.

Take the composer Karlheinz Stockhausen, who reputedly described the attacks on the World Trade Center (2001) as "the greatest work of art that is possible in the whole cosmos." The limits of this study do not permit a full interrogation of this statement, particularly in light of Stockhausen's insistence that he has been misquoted, misunderstood, or cited out of context. And an adequate engagement with its content would require addressing how the planners of these attacks consciously chose targets for their spectacular connection to American military power and global circuits of capital.[25] Indeed, this turn to visuality has become a staple of militancy in the internet age—evinced in the now-ubiquitous videos of death, executions, and cultural destruction made available for instant viewing (each of which is indicted as more gruesome than the last).[26] For present interests, however, this intersection of terror and spectacle will be set aside to focus on the normative controversies that surrounded Stockhausen's comments. On even the quickest reading, the public outcry over this statement (eventuating in the cancellation of his performances) targeted something deeper than a judgment that misfired as incoherent or bizarre. Instead, the outrage stemmed from a deeper anxiety: that the very act of applying these norms to social life commits a fundamental wrong.

To press this sense of injury, it is often suggested that "aestheticism" does not simply privilege non-moral criteria for evaluation, in which case it leaves each speaker to pursue her or his stance upon the meaning of events. My friend might describe an act as beautiful, while I might describe it as virtuous (or vicious, or depraved, or noble, or whatever). To each his own, we might say to one another, and then head to the pub to talk about other things. Against any such easy pluralism, the standard charge is that an aestheticist stance requires particular vigilance, since it threatens to distort, at some phenomenologically primordial level, how agents experience acts, obligations, and events. This expanded role for the aesthetic seems to threaten a kind of creeping pollution—along the lines of the nonnative plant that will grow and multiply and crowd out the virtues that ought to populate here. As Nancy Rosenblum asserts, "aestheticism involves cultivating certain exquisite sensations and tastes, but more importantly bringing artistic criteria to bear on every experience. By submitting every action and relation to this imperative, aestheticism . . . does not respect the conventional division among pluralist spheres with distinct attitudes, obligations, and norms."[27] And to elaborate exactly what sort of harm is at stake, the persistent fear is that an unbounded aestheticism erodes the distinction between (a) beings possessed of some intrinsic claim to dignity, and (b) artistic materials (sound, color, paint, tone, etc.) to be manipulated and shaped according to no criteria other than how they elicit pleasure or thought on the part of an observer. In this connection, it is tempting to cite Oscar Wilde's Dorian Gray, when informed of the suicide of his lover: "I must admit this thing that has happened does not affect me as it should. It seems to me to be simply like a wonderful ending to a wonderful play. It has all the terrible beauty of a Greek tragedy, a tragedy in which I took a great part, but by which I have not been wounded."[28]

There is a rich literature on this sort of aesthete—the one who transcends the sphere of good or evil in order to experience the world as a spectacle that can make no claims upon him other than the aesthetic coordinates of beauty, ugliness, pleasure, intensity, or boredom. And yet, the bite of the reservation stems from how this stance is not limited to the villains, rogues, or antiheroes of screens and novels, but might rather enter into the cognitive, evaluative, and affectual resources that orient subjects in their everyday entanglements. In contemporary debates, these anxieties have found voice in the discomfort toward video games in which the user is interpellated into the position of the one who wields violence, scores points for death, and gains status for kills enacted with particular artistry or flourish. This is violence as a play-act, in which bodies are undone for sport, and the doer of violence is immunized from culpability or consequence. These concerns are, of course, not wholly new.[29] For instance, Filippo Marinetti famously described the Italian attacks upon Tripoli (1911–12) as "the most beautiful aesthetic spectacle of my life." In broader terms: "War is beautiful because it establishes man's dominion over the subjugated machinery by means of gas masks, terrifying megaphones, flame throwers, and small tanks. . . . War is beautiful because it enriches a flowering meadow with the fiery orchids of machine guns. War is beautiful because it combines the gunfire, the cannonades, the ceasefire, the scents, and the stench of putrefaction into a symphony."[30] This classic example permits the critical reservations to be rendered more precisely. When the aesthetic stance no longer recognizes values such as utility, compassion, or moral dignity, it threatens to substitute its own terms and criteria for those that provide normative moorings. This is the eye that roams at will, surveys its objects, and delights in appearances, but does not admit that its objects might press their own demands upon the spectator.[31] Under this gaze, even the torments of bodies can be considered (in Marinetti's terms) a symphony; all pain is redeemed by the pleasure it brings to those who watch.

To thicken the account, many such anxieties stem from the flood of images that structures social life in late modernity—and the sense that we are increasingly able to see things that should not be seen. Even if one might resist the strong prohibition that frequently attends these critiques (i.e., that there are some acts or events that simply *must not* be represented), they lend social substance to the "aestheticization" debates by tracking these dynamics back to a media-saturated public sphere. Where the promise is to abolish distance and bring the world near, we are told that the perpetual "thereness" of images yields important liabilities.[32] Once images of violence or atrocity become commonplace, the normative work they can do (e.g., to trouble conscience, inspire outrage, or motivate action) is sapped. As Susan Sontag puts this, "Once one has seen such images, one has started down the road of seeing more—and more. Images transfix. Images anesthetize."[33] Or, in terms more narrowly tailored to present interests, she argues "whatever the moral claims made on behalf of photography, its main effect is to convert the world into a department store or museum-without-walls in which every subject is depreciated into an article of consumption, promoted into an item for aesthetic appreciation."[34] For critics of this stripe, such images (no matter what their content) become normalized through their circulation and availability. They can be pulled up for a viewer to peruse while flipping through other websites, taking the bus, killing time, or watching television in the background. In the strongest terms, such images are not just normalized, but become objects of pleasure, excitement, or eroticism.

As familiar as these laments may be, it is necessary to be wary of their conclusions. For instance, more sensitive readers have responded that this analysis hardly seems to capture the historical work of socially committed photography—how images of attack dogs, scorched bodies, coffins shipped home from faraway battles, or abused prisoners of war have agitated and outraged their viewers into a wide set of actions.[35] And so, if the "anaesthesis" charge strikes an important cautionary note, it does not do justice to the impact of these images or the conversations they inspire as they circulate throughout civil society (a point that Sontag came to concede in later writings).[36] From these rejoinders, it is more accurate to speak of an essential ambivalence to images of atrocity. Where photographs of lynchings were made into postcards and distributed as souvenirs of the event, so too did they mobilize anti-lynching opposition. Or, in more contemporary terms, when videos of prisoner executions or the last words of suicide bombers are bought and sold in the marketplace, so too do they generate outrage against the groups that record and broadcast these violations. When we take seriously how such images *circulate*, then, they possess an indeterminacy that prevents them from fixing the meaning they will have, the conversations into which they will be inserted, the responses they will trigger, or the causes they might mobilize.[37] Already, this cautionary note flags one of the methodological commitments of this study: to take seriously the material practice of a political aesthetics—how it produces unplanned, unanticipated effects—and how it resonates in ways that cannot be domesticated by a theory that would simplify, sanitize, and reduce its meanings.

* * *

To gain full clarity on the normative discomfort concerning aestheticism, then, it is necessary to avoid locating its roots within some "everyday intuition" that there simply *is* a difference in kind between aesthetic and practical considerations. As much of the literature demonstrates, it is unfortunately easy to make sweeping claims about morality, politics, and aesthetics in the abstract—what they are, how they should relate, and what the costs of their admixture might be (each spoken in the singular, in the eternal present).[38] It is likewise easy to isolate something called "the aesthetic attitude" and draw conclusions about a stance that seems to exert some ahistorical pull upon human experience, sketching timeless patterns of evaluation, perception, and meaning.[39] As popular as this approach might be, it proves less helpful for untangling the contested and changing meaning of these terms (aesthetics, politics, morality) within historical forms of life, in which these spheres have played different roles and carried different meanings. Such an approach does not only suffer from a clear methodological weakness (e.g., there are ample reasons to resist ascribing normative force to intuitions, no matter how "natural" they may appear), but it would fail to engage the rather more sophisticated options available within ongoing critical debates. Indeed, there is one position in particular that merits elaboration, since it will prove significant over the course of this study: the Weberian narrative of modernity that has been pressed in a more patently normative direction by the work of Jürgen Habermas.

Though the diagnosis entails a knot of philosophy, linguistics, social theory, and historiography, the central intuition can be put in broad strokes. Where the classic rationalist tradition (e.g., Kant, Hegel, etc.) maintained faith in the unity of reason, unfolding itself in history toward the end of a rational society, the course of modernity has cast doubt on any such holistic story. Rather, modernity might be described as a process of value-differentiation: each of its constitutive spheres (i.e., the theoretical, practical, and aesthetic) develops according to its own proprietary logic (*Eigengesetzlichkeit*), which is typically taken to mean that the criteria internal to each must be purified of "foreign" influences if they are to avoid distortion. In this connection, Habermas proposes: "As soon as science, morality and art have been differentiated into autonomous spheres of values, each under one universal validity claim—truth, normative rightness, authenticity or beauty—objective advances, improvements, enhancements become possible in a sense specific to each."[40] It is this thesis of axiological differentiation (*Wertsteigerung*) that gives both methodological and historical substance to the concerns loosely detailed to this point. If the history of modernity is a process by which these conceptual spheres have been distinguished, then a number of pathologies follow from confounding their demands. Minimally, to introduce aesthetic considerations within political argument demonstrates that the speaker has insufficiently understood the problem under consideration and what kind of discursive strategies would be appropriate to resolve its difficulties. To muddy these lines reveals a cognitive, if not existential, confusion. And, to press this discomfort further, such a move is objectionable not simply because it "unsettles the equilibrium of the lifeworld's communicative infrastructure" (construed in some abstractly systemic terms). Rather, if these conceptual partitions are considered central features of rational discourse, then any such categorial blurring undermines those evaluative procedures that render practices and institutions more transparent to interrogation through the most developed standards available.[41] These suspicions permit a clearer rendering of the link that is presumed to lead directly from aestheticism to fascism: an "aestheticized" stance not only refuses the complex social differentiation of late modernity, but its emphasis on expression (or intensity, pleasure, play, etc.) threatens to subvert the rational basis for a democratic public sphere. Instead, as Lutz Koepnick addresses the pathologies of fascism, an aestheticized public sphere "mobilizes people's feelings primarily to neutralize their senses, massaging minds and emotions so that the individual succumbs to the charisma of vitalistic power."[42]

If one can readily admire the aims of this partitioning strategy, it contains a significant liability: this desire to sanitize and fix the boundaries between these regimes of thought, experience, and discourse threatens its own commitment to rational transparency. It threatens what Foucault termed the Enlightenment "blackmail"—these are the conditions that must be accepted as foundational, lest your thought founder in contradiction.[43] And because these conditions are foundational for thought (even if in a provisional sense) they cannot, themselves, be interrogated, scrutinized, or put back into play. This premise cannot be accepted without challenge. To put in schematic terms a rejoinder that recurs throughout this study, such partitions cannot be treated as brute "givens" for argumentation, since this would ossify an ongoing, historical process of negotiation into a rigid set of conditions for reason *as such*.[44] And similar liabilities follow from the more modest position: that these discursive partitions are historically derived conditions of practical argumentation and thus the rules that "we moderns" must follow in order to realize the emancipatory promise of modernity. Seyla Benhabib courts such a position when she argues that "processes of value differentiation also initiate traditions of discursive justification in independent value spheres. Modern science, for example, no less than theology and art criticism since the sixteenth century has developed methods and procedures for the assessment of validity claims in its domain. The cumulative logic of these 'sphere specific' processes of discursive justification cannot be simply subverted."[45] Immediately, the suspicious reader is inclined to ask what options this "cannot" takes off the table for critical examination. Does this prohibition block interrogation of how the resources of certain value spheres could complicate, trouble, and expand the potentials of other such spheres? Even if these distinctions are part of the formative history of modernity, have they been fully accomplished, once and for all, or do they persist in a situation of tension, slippage, and negotiation? These are just some of the important questions that cannot be asked when efforts to complicate or question these boundaries are met by ex cathedra prohibitions.

In the interests of space, I will articulate only a preliminary rejoinder that will be filled out in various ways over the course of the study. Although the history of fascism is rich with examples of a noxious aestheticization (i.e., where the guideposts of morality are discarded), such nightmare cases too often eclipse more nuanced strategies to link these regimes of value and experience. At present, one path will suffice: where the aesthetic is not used to submerge the normative concerns of politics, but rather highlights how prominent ethico-political vocabularies fail to live up to their own substantive ideals. This formula marks a guiding thread for the discussions to come. Though the chapters address the core theme in different ways, each explores how aesthetic rejoinders might throw into relief the foreclosed possibilities and unacknowledged consequences of those discourses that delimit what is officially recognized as political. Such aesthetic appeals reveal how the political is not limited to policies or institutions, but rather engages forms of sensibility, perception, and feeling that also represent a terrain for power, agency, control, and contestation. Accordingly, the arguments to follow call attention to the "excess" of politics—how it does not simply turn upon what can be said or thought in the space of citizenship, but rather what (or who) can be seen or heard—and what, conversely, is blocked from the perceptual field of civic life. And if there is such an excess, then possibilities that have come to rest within the aesthetic might provide important resources for political thought and agency.

Before leaping into the specifics of these rejoinders, it will also be useful to clarify some paths that will not be taken as the book proceeds. First, there is a standing tendency for critical debates to concentrate on the specific question of art, as a mode of cultural production—and how artists might (or should) contribute to the work of social disruption, enlightenment, or emancipation.[46] It is not necessary to reach so far back as the early romantics, for whom the artist possesses (or is possessed by) some promethean capacity to awaken a corrupt bourgeoisie, salvage the remnants of a mutilated nature, or deliver humankind from a rationalized modernity. Or, to draw closer to the conversations that will follow, Herbert Marcuse asserts that art retains a memory of those forms of happiness, eros, and sensibility that have been buried by a "one-dimensional" society.[47] As familiar as these arguments might be, the concerns of this study run beyond this specific mode of cultural production. Instead, the guiding question will be: what might be gained by invoking aesthetic modes of meaning, value, and experience (whether tied specifically to art or not) *as* political resources? Or, put differently, what is at stake when theorists make this gambit in order to complicate the categorial divisions of modernity and their effects for political thought? Accordingly, this study will not pursue the power of art to disrupt a calcified public sphere, memorialize historical injustices, or shock everyday sensibilities. Although the book will periodically engage themes and resources drawn from the art world, it will set its sights on a more expansive terrain: how the forms of experience, sensibility, value, and meaning characteristically associated with the aesthetic might expand or problematize the resources available to construe emancipatory agency.

To this end, many of the reflections to follow will intersect with recent debates on affect, reason, and politics. Where contemporary schools of rationalism persistently construe politics through a thin, discursive framework, significant normative questions rest at a more somatically thick level: how power fastens upon the affectual resources that mobilize action, frame deliberation, and open (or close) arenas for possible agency. Here the questions take both ontological and political shape. On the one hand, a politicized concern for sensibility offers a more robust accounting of how the subject inhabits a shared world of value, meaning, and obligation. It is through sensibility that a common is forged and citizens invest in shared histories—or how they might imagine different futures and different visions of common life. On the other hand, this concern for sensibility calls attention to a neglected site of power and its potential disruption. To this end, the "aesthetic" at stake must be read in the ancient sense of *aisthēsis*: the embodied subject whose perceptions of justice and injustice, right and wrong, noble and base are rooted at the richly sensuous level.

Secondly, just as this study will resist any ahistorical definition of its central categories, so too will it resist another persistent temptation in the literature: to base its claims within a dehistoricized phenomenology of aesthetic experience. Recent work by Elaine Scarry, for instance, distills normative possibilities from a broadly Kantian opening: the encounter with the beautiful places a set of imperatives upon the experiencing subject. And while the details of Scarry's argument far exceed the space available, she places significant weight upon beauty's demand for perceptual care. This is not an unsympathetic starting point. Indeed, as Theodor Adorno argues (to be treated in the first chapter of this book), there may be something peculiar to the perception of the beautiful within disenchanted times—what he terms "an obsession with the particular [*der Obsession durchs Besondere*]."[48] The eye that perceives beauty does not seek any instance of this type, but rather tarries with the object in its specificity—the rough edges, the sensuous husk, the slight dissymmetry, the variations in hue, the way the beloved bites his or her lip or blushes too quickly. What begins as a sympathetic argument for perceptual care toward the beautiful too quickly, however, leaps to the big normative conclusion: there is therefore some essential connection between aesthetic experience and a less violent habitation of the world. According to Scarry, "the fact that something is perceived as beautiful is bound up with an urge to protect it, or act on its behalf."[49] While it is easy to appreciate the ambition of this proposal, the thin, phenomenological basis for the argument yields significant unresolved questions.[50] Just why should *the* proper stance toward the beautiful be a form of protection or care? Why shouldn't the perceiving agent want to hold, possess, covet, consume, destroy, own, or profit from it? Why extrapolate from one subject's experience, in one historico-cultural moment, from one class-position, to construct significant conclusions regarding "the" claims of beauty itself? Are there not significant questions of education, training, and social class that must be asked here?[51] And the difficulty can be pressed a bit harder to challenge whether beauty *as such* has any normative implications whatsoever. Might there not be competing experiences of its claims, leading to tensions, ambivalences, and contradictions in the conclusions that might be drawn?

For such reasons, this study will resist any effort to locate an essential saving power to aesthetic characteristics *as such*—whether this be aesthetic predicates, aesthetic experience, or the ostensible potencies of art. Given the mutability of each of these categories, any such effort risks ossifying a contested and unstable set of historical possibilities into some mystified essence of the practice that transcends history or context. Or, in terms offered by Gabriel Rockhill, it runs the risk of a "talismanic" approach, where the aesthetic is granted some timeless, quasi-magical power to intervene, repair, and transform the world (a power that is typically left ungrounded and uninterrogated).[52] Rather, the chapters to follow will attempt to untangle a more focused problem: what led a set of theorists to construe political agency through aesthetic resources when traditional models of emancipation have lost (or are losing) their exclusive claim on the Left imagination? There are a number of moving parts in this statement that should not be missed. First, the study will observe a strongly historical delimitation. Where inquiries into "the" aesthetic and "the" political (or the moral, the ethical, etc.) can too often take an abstract, assertoric tone, based within ostensible necessities built into these categories as such, this study will root itself within a historical crisis in agency and power—that is, when long-standing investments in systemic, revolutionary overthrowing have come under scrutiny. For instance, appeals for revolution in the "grand style" might fail to recognize how power works in micro-political (rather than institutional) ways; they might be oriented toward aims of social reconciliation, when such an ideal has proven false or dangerous; or they may be chastened by how the great communist experiments slid into murderous projects of state fascism. In broadest terms, then, the guiding question of the study will be: what is the aesthetic meant to offer in what are perceived as "dark" political times, when power seems to insinuate itself into ever more crevices of social life?[53] Or, to bring out what remains "living" in the arguments to follow, what might aesthetic resources contribute to ongoing efforts to think agency that are poorly served by the "official" discourses of politics?

To address these questions, this study will move in four major steps that reflect importantly different approaches to critical theory—where it should aim, how it should operate, and what kind of politics might be at stake. The first chapter begins at a particularly controversial moment: Theodor Adorno's diagnosis of the "fully administered society" in which art is privileged as one of the last vestiges of an "undamaged life." There is a familiar vision of Adorno, where he succumbs to pessimism over the course of modernity and instead takes refuge in the aesthetic domain. On this reading, Adorno turns his back on both politics and reason to find consolation in the non-discursive, arational domain of art. As the chapter argues, however, this common narrative distorts both Adorno's thought and what contemporary critical debates might learn from aesthetic modes of thought, value, and experience. More specifically, the chapter argues that a more careful reading reveals a rather more productive engagement with the rationalist tradition—one that uses the aesthetic to salvage possibilities for reason buried by a disenchanted modernity. And the final sections of the chapter step beyond the closure of Adorno's texts in order to suggest important ways that these remainders of reason might inform democratic practice. Where much critical attention tends to concentrate on his detailed accounts of art and aesthetic production, the chapter argues that aesthetic modes of sense-making (i.e., a willed attentiveness to those things that clamor for attention and yet find no purchase within existing canons of reason) can fruitfully inform the messy conversations of civil society. Where standing economies of discourse persistently foreclose some claims, social positions, and voices, Adorno's thought suggests ways to shelter such claims within an expanded field of justice.

The second chapter engages the late turn in Michel Foucault's thought, where he proposes that emancipatory resources might be found in an "art" of the self. As the literature demonstrates, this proposal has left Foucault's readers with a series of unresolved questions and suspicions that it departs from the concerns for power and domination that long defined his thought. Worse yet, critics have charged that this aesthetics of the self represents a kind of narcissistic "dandyism" that erodes subjects' ties to others and undercuts their ability to collaborate in forms of agonistic counter-power. Instead, such agents turn inward to conduct private experiments with their wants and desires. As the chapter argues, however, there are ample reasons to resist this conclusion. At the very least, these transformative "arts" of the self represent a way to mitigate the effects of normalizing power for those whose needs and pleasures and desires do not fit tidily within what has been recognized (and enforced) as the norm. And there is a deeper way that this approach might contribute important resources for thinking political agency. Even readers sympathetic to Foucault's aims tend to indict his model for its ostensibly individuating tendencies—how it locks the subject into his or her own private concerns and undermines possibilities for association. And yet, a nuanced approach to Foucault's late texts and lectures reveals that intersubjective entanglements may be necessary for these transformative arts. These are not isolated selves, absorbed in their private experiments; rather, these projects demand alternative social *worlds* to shelter and bind their experience into something recognizable as counter-knowledge.

Chapter 3 engages Jacques Rancière's intervention within this linkage of the political and the aesthetic. As this introduction has detailed, it is common for scholars to return to Walter Benjamin's now-canonical analysis: the aestheticization of politics is a staple of fascist modernity, which erodes possibilities for a rational politics. Rancière begins with a stark rejoinder to posit that "politics is aesthetic in principle." As the chapter elaborates, one way to unpack this thesis is through his effort to describe politics as a challenge to everyday economies of seeing, hearing, and feeling. Politics is a practice of disruption, designed to undo those "machines of vision" that condition who belongs where, what can be "seen" in the light of justice, and who is authorized to share in the exercise of power. More specifically, politics addresses one of the core "wrongs" that follows from everyday economies of sensibility: how some are not *seen* as full members of the community and are thus not *heard* as offering the full, authoritative speech of citizenship. Ultimately, this approach suggests forms of agency that could undo invidious economies of vision and speech. These are subjects who refuse their "proper place" and act in excess of the possibilities allotted for them. They insert themselves into public conversations and upend the established order of communication. As the chapter will elaborate, Rancière might offer the strongest rejoinder to a persistent suspicion toward an "aesthetic" politics: if it does not lead to fascism, it nonetheless represents a withdrawal from the agitational work of politics. At the heart of Rancière's vision is a strongly *praxical* commitment. And yet, the chapter argues that he would need to take more seriously the aesthetic resources he highlights if this vision is to succeed on its own terms.

The final chapter brings together a number of the strands that have run throughout this study in order to hazard a more fully elaborated position that I term an aesthetics of democratic agency. There is a familiar point of reference in the work of Hannah Arendt, for whom the work of politics is not a question of institutions, laws, or treaties—but rather a sphere of appearance. To appear to one's fellow citizens is what distinguishes the political from private life. Where references to Arendt are standard in the literature on aesthetic and politics, the debates that occupy this study reveal a position with more normative bite. The question is not simply whether appearance is the condition of politics, but rather how appearance might itself be the object of contestation, agency, and struggle. To draw from a number of threads developed over the course of this study, the sensible register of politics raises a number of distinct questions: what kind of agency is available to those who do not yet appear within the space of citizenship? How might these invidious economies of vision be disrupted in order to enter the space of visibility? And is visibility *as such* necessarily a good? In order to address these questions, it is necessary to reach more deeply into the sensuous resonance of power, into how power fastens upon what it is possible to see, hear, and feel. The deepest challenge behind this "aesthetic" politics, then, rests within a point that is raised in different ways and in different directions by each of the chapters to follow: if power can access the subject at the sensible registers of vision, hearing, and feeling, then so too must political agency work at this level. At stake is not simply the historical question (why did a set of theorists turn to the aesthetic in "dark" times?), but an urgent, contemporary question: how is it possible to conceive and invent forms of agency to disrupt the most visceral installations of power? And how do these tactics help to reimagine what political work is and can be?

1

Adorno

Aesthetic Rescue and Reparative Justice

It will be productive to begin this study with the thought of Theodor Adorno, since he is typically treated as a unique cautionary tale in the debates that swirl around an "aestheticized" approach to political life. Here, the charge is rooted within his perceived refusal of the central aims of critical theory. In 1937 Max Horkheimer wrote that a critical theory must be "a force to stimulate change" within the world.[1] That is, the vocation of theory is to intervene within social life—by transforming consciousness, challenging false narratives of the world, and inspiring subjects to remake the world so as to serve their genuine interests. Critical theory is not just a theory about the world; rather, it offers an intervention within social life, designed to stimulate its recipients to bring about a rational society. In *Minima Moralia*, however, Adorno asserts that "there is nothing innocuous left" in the societies of industrial modernity.[2] Late capitalism promises to abolish want, and yet it deforms needs, wishes, and motivations. Subjects are increasingly channeled into patterns of aggression and use-value. And in one of the few moments where Adorno addresses a positive course of action, he concludes that "the only responsible course is . . . to conduct oneself in private as modestly, unobtrusively and unpretentiously as is required, no longer by good upbringing, but by the shame of still having air to breathe, in hell."[3]

The question is, of course, what can be concluded from these passages. There is a standard story in the literature: such moments demonstrate that Adorno succumbed to a deep pessimism toward modernity and abandoned engagement in favor of a "strategy of hibernation."[4] Within the "network of guilt" (*Schuldzusammenhang*) that defines late modernity, there are no longer meaningful avenues for political emancipation. The sole refuge for nonviolent relations has come to rest within the artwork, which offers "the negative appearance of utopia."[5] In all, this style of reading could be put in a rough paraphrase of a Heideggerian formula: only an artwork can save us now.[6] Rather than the plaza, the factories, or the streets, undamaged experience is found by withdrawing into the museums and the parlors and the concert halls, where well-dressed patrons enjoy the fruits of culture, shielded from the rabble and din and heartbreak outside.[7] Because aesthetic experience offers satisfactions, meanings, and pleasures that can no longer be found in social practice, it can substitute for any meaningful transformation of a world that frustrates, uses, and damages those who sustain it.[8] This is the classic vision of withdrawal: Nero who fiddled while Rome burned.

At this point, it is easy to understand some characteristic reservations. Axel Honneth, for instance, proposes that "Adorno's premises leave critical theory with both dogma and resignation."[9] And Douglas Kellner doubles down on these charges to argue that Adorno offers only "a politics of resignation and despair and cannot account for struggles against advanced capitalism."[10] Such evaluations were not limited to the rarefied debates of high theory. Rather, the student Left in Germany expressed similar frustrations, culminating in the "bare breast incident"—where student activists stormed the stage during a 1969 lecture, declared Adorno "dead as an institution," and shed their clothing to indict his perceived unwillingness to offer the theory necessary to guide practice toward emancipatory aims.

This verdict is often mapped upon a second set of concerns typically associated with Jürgen Habermas—that Adorno's investment in aesthetic modes of thought and production symptomatizes a deeper error: a stark departure from the rationalist tradition of social theory. Here, the difficulty is meant to follow from an inadequate diagnosis of modernity. Because Adorno is thought to overlook the forms of rationality embedded in discursive communication, he instead equates reason *as such* with instrumental control and mastery.[11] And to push this reading to its standard conclusion, it is this "deep" pessimism that leads Adorno to seek refuge in the aesthetic domain.[12] Because the very roots of rational thought are polluted, the possibility of a domination-free social practice can be salvaged only by discarding reason entirely and leaping into some nondiscursive Other of thought.[13] At this point, the dossier reaches its conclusion: it is no accident that Adorno turns his back on questions of social emancipation and embraces instead the solace of art. This is not a matter of character or personal frustration with the messiness of political action; rather, he is forced into this "arational mysticism" due to his indictment of reason *simpliciter*.[14]

As familiar as this diagnosis may be, this chapter will argue that it is short-sighted in at least two important ways. On the one hand, this reading represents an inadequate account of what Adorno has to offer for a critical theory of late modernity.[15] On the other hand (and more broadly), it represents a foreshortened approach to what ongoing debates might draw from aesthetic modes of thought, reason, and value. Although the foregoing has detailed the ostensible "problem" of Adorno, it typically doubles as an indictment of aesthetic regimes of experience. Where emancipation demands an investment in worldly action, the aesthetic (we are told) offers a privatized form of consolation, more appropriate to the polite world of galleries and concert halls. Or the critical assumptions can be put in different terms. Where politics demands the seriousness of reason, the aesthetic is persistently figured as some nonrational domain of sensation, pleasure, play, or intensity. Accordingly, this chapter will operate on both narrow and broad registers. At the very least, it aims to contest a familiar version of a thinker that we all take to know already—and whose limits are also meant to be known. In doing so, however, some unexpected resources will be raised for broader discussions of power, politics, and sensibility. More specifically, the chapter will propose that these aesthetic entanglements can inform the practice of citizenship so as to mitigate some characteristic forms of democratic violence. What this ultimately means is that the argument will pursue a promissory note that is hinted at by Adorno, but systematically left underdeveloped in his own texts. To do so, it will be necessary to take the possibilities of his thought and push them into the messy world of democratic practice.

* * *

It would not be difficult to raise difficulties for the standard interpretation. To open with a stark thesis: Adorno's sustained engagement with aesthetic resources does not simply discard reason (and thus the normative core of the critical theory tradition), but rather pursues those possibilities of reason that have been suppressed and damaged through a disenchanted modernity. To access this reparative project, it is necessary to ask some preliminary questions. Why describe a disenchanted reason as damaged? And how are these damages expressed in normatively substantive terms?

The canonical source for these questions is the critical history that Adorno and Horkheimer detail in *Dialectic of Enlightenment*. Although the text offers an unwieldy mixture of historiography, mythology, philosophy, sociology, and economic theory (among other things), the core of the argument offers a challenge to a familiar Enlightenment narrative. The history of social rationalization is often represented as a narrative of emancipation—as that which (a) frees human life from the darkness of superstition and ignorance, and (b) unlocks the productive capacities of nature so as to meet human needs. And yet (to cite the Weberian resonance of the text), the process of enlightenment is fundamentally ambivalent.[16] As the first lines of the text propose: "the Enlightenment has always aimed at liberating men from fear and establishing their sovereignty. Yet the fully enlightened earth radiates disaster triumphant."[17]

Though the text pursues this claim in a dizzying number of directions, the clearest path highlights the abstractive tendencies of enlightened thought. As a long line of philosophers have recognized, there is a significant distance between the object of thought—the sensuous intuition given to cognition—and the concept by which it gains cognitive value (to invoke a brief and inadequate set of epistemological distinctions). Where the former is sensuous and specific—characterized by features that define it, and it alone—the concept evacuates these specificities and defines the object instead by those features it shares with other instances of its class. To take an obvious example, the shoe I am wearing is riddled with particularities. The smell of the leather as mellowed by usage. The scars of misadventures. This seam that never quite fit. The heel that has begun to cave. The eyelet worn smooth from the rubbing of the laces. As an exemplar of the category "shoe," however, it is evacuated of these particularities and instead defined by broad predicates: black, leather, lace-up. Friedrich Nietzsche famously describes this tendency as follows:

> Every word immediately becomes a concept, inasmuch as it is not intended to serve as a reminder of the unique and wholly individualized original experience to which it owes its birth, but must at the same time fit innumerable, more or less similar cases—which means, strictly speaking, never equal—in other words, a lot of unequal cases. . . . No leaf ever wholly equals another, and the concept "leaf" is formed through an arbitrary abstraction from these individual differences, through forgetting the distinctions.[18]

This dynamic is one significant strain of what Adorno comes to call "identitary" reason. Where thought identifies, it abstracts from the sensuous particularity of its objects. It translates these singular moments into predicates that transcend context. It leaves behind all those idiosyncrasies that would block translation into cognitive currency for those with no access to the particular object at hand. And, when pursued sufficiently far, this push to abstraction yields the mathematized approach to the real that characterizes the modern scientific project. What matters from this perspective is not the heft of the object as I hold it, how it absorbs or resists the warmth of my hand, or the textural variations as I run my finger across its surfaces—but rather, those characteristics that can be communicated without loss or variation: mass, height, depth, and so forth. The abstractive tendencies of the concept are here pushed to their furthest degree, permitting the equivalence of quantity to substitute for the messy particularity of objects. In the hyperbolic terms that define *Dialectic of*

Enlightenment, "abstraction, the tool of enlightenment, treats its objects as did fate . . . it liquidates them."[19]

Yet here it is necessary to move carefully. Where Nietzsche identifies a dynamic of falsehood at the heart of the concept, Adorno instead isolates the mastery and control exerted over the objects of thought. In sharper terms, his concern is for the *damage* that disenchanted reason inflicts upon its objects. It is this emphasis that moves the argument beyond a familiar romantic lament on the alienation of thought from the material world.[20] As Adorno proposes: "this kind of rationality exists only in so far as it can subjugate something different from and alien to itself . . . it can exist only by . . . leveling it and by defining it in its alterity as something that resists it and, we may even go so far as to say, something that is hostile to it."[21] The broader implications of this claim become legible by tracking this "subjugation" to the historico-philosophical project associated with philosophical modernity.[22] Though the philosophical provenance far exceeds present space, Adorno's argument targets the grammar of self-grounding that Kant placed at the heart of an idealist modernity: to be enlightened is to accept no authority other than reason. Instead, the binding power of reason must be relocated within norms legislated by thought and reflectively recognized as such.[23] When set against this idealist background, the charge of damage can be rendered in more philosophically rigorous terms: ultimately, this logic of autonomy erodes the possibility that particulars could be recognized as sources of claims, external to the sense ascribed to them. Instead, disenchanted reason *legislates*. It translates its objects into the concepts, predicates, and qualities by which it *makes* sense of the given.[24] To acknowledge an "outside" to the concept would be to admit a heteronomy at the heart of experience—a dependency upon all that thought is not.[25]

Upon registering these strains of the argument, it is possible to grasp some of the stakes behind this analytic of concepts and objects. If the authority of reason is located within the legislative exercise of thought—if cognitive and normative authority are situated in what can be reproduced through symbolically attenuated means—then this means that significant registers of experience can no longer be recognized as authoritative. It is these remnants of meaning that Adorno terms the nonidentical [*das Nichtidentische*]—a figure that will mobilize the argument of this chapter. The nonidentical are those contents that cannot be reduced to the terms of disenchanted thought and thus cannot be accommodated with its grammars of meaning or authority. It is the material body upon which thought depends, but cannot acknowledge as the source of rational claims. It is the sensuous particularity of the object, pared away in favor of those terms that can be quantified for maximal communicability (mass, size, quantity, etc.). It is the way that a glass of a certain whisky carries memories of a time and a place, with voices and conversations, tears, loves, and laughter with concrete others—associations that possess no salience for a scientized model of knowledge. The nonidentical, in some sense, means to mark the way that every object *means* in ways that cannot be translated seamlessly into conceptual terms.[26] In the terms of *Negative Dialectics*, nonidentity is based within "the untruth of identity, the fact that the concept does not exhaust the thing conceived."[27]

As much critical literature demonstrates, it would be tempting to conclude that this neologism flags the ineffable dimension to the objects of thought—the way that every experiential given exceeds discursive redemption.[28] Though here it is useful to attend more carefully to Adorno's renderings. As he proposes, "what is, is more than it is. This 'more' is not imposed upon it but remains immanent to it, as that which has been pushed out of it [*als das aus ihm Verdrängte*]. In that sense, the nonidentical would be the thing's own identity against its identifications."[29] The language of this passage makes it difficult to reduce the argument in the suggested fashion. It is not simply that these remnants are inexhaustible from the standpoint of the concept (in which case, Adorno would offer little more than a warmed-over nominalism, translated into a tortured German syntax). It is not only, in the words of Joseph Winters, that "the world is . . . always pregnant with meanings and possibilities that slip through and evade our extant horizons and conceptual frameworks, prompting us to interpret and engage this world in new ways."[30] The diagnosis of nonidentity is ultimately stronger than a framework of ineffability can convey: these contents are *stripped* of their authority when conceptual mattering attains hegemony within the official discourses and forms of reason. They are the remainders of serious thought, the experiential "noise" to be pared away to get to what really counts from the standpoint of the concept. To give this point more bite, the nonidentical is not just some excess of meaning that cannot be captured by the rough, cognitive tools applied to them; rather, this "noise" is produced by a form of conceptual mattering that (a) reduces the range of what can be rationally cognized, and (b) refuses the authority of that which cannot be accommodated within its terms. As the rest of this chapter will argue, this remainder not only represents the core damage of an abstract reason, but also stands at the heart of any potential reparation.[31]

* * *

To develop this reparative argument, it is necessary to ask what happens to these contents once they lose purchase within the official languages of reason. Does their claim fade away or live on in attenuated form? And is there any meaningful social content to the diagnosis that would redeem Adorno's provocative language of domination and violence?[32] Thus far, the reconstruction has largely centered on the relationship between thought and those "moderate-sized specimens of dry goods" that J. L. Austin famously described as the objects of epistemology.[33] The account has invoked leaves, shoes, animals—all objects that contain specificities unredeemed by the abstractions of conceptual thought. More pointed normative considerations arise, however, by taking seriously the systemic resonance of the argument (itself reflecting a significant strand of Marxian theory).[34] That is, this form of reason does not simply hollow out the sensuous core of object-relations; rather, it comes to organize a damaged social practice. In the terms of *Dialectic of Enlightenment*: "it is not merely that domination is paid for by the alienation of men from the objects dominated: with the objectification of spirit, the very relations of men—even those of the individual to himself—were bewitched."[35]

The question, of course, must be how these allusions can be expressed in substantive terms. At least one of these normative strains reflects a familiar Marxian argument. As detailed, the concept operates by eliminating the sensuous particularity of objects and assigning cognitive value to what they abstractly share. More specifically, the concept *works* by making sensuous particulars interchangeable. Members of a given class gain their meaning by belonging to this class and subtracting out all that impedes this translation. A dog is a dog is a dog, regardless of its fur, its scars, its fears, the way that it plays or the sound of its bark.[36] It is this abstract logic of equivalence that Adorno situates at the heart of a more recognizably normative dynamic: the capitalist colonization of the lifeworld. Once the particularity of objects no longer possesses rational authority, all beings (turnips, sex acts, televisions, labor power, gemstones, human organs, or whatever) can be measured through the money form and rendered exchangeable.[37] Only then can sensuously distinct things be translated into the abstract value-grammar of capital, where "all that is solid melts into the air."[38]

If the foregoing highlights the logical structure of an expansionist market, Adorno's diagnosis presses further, to identify how these abstractive dynamics damage even the positive ideals that orient social practice. For instance, he persistently claims that "equality itself becomes a fetish"[39] within "false life."[40] The most familiar register of this charge is Adorno's account of mass culture, in which individuals have their tastes leveled, their hopes and dreams channeled in the same directions, their forms of expression standardized, and their desires directed toward the same goals.[41] Although individuality is the highest fetish of late capitalism, it is imagined and actualized through the prefabricated options of the culture industry. At other moments, the argument presses a normatively deeper point—how a push toward equivalence has likewise infected even the positive moral ideals of modernity. In *Negative Dialectics*, for instance, Adorno asserts that "law is the primal phenomenon of irrational rationality. In law the formal principle of equivalence becomes the norm."[42] Under conditions of disenchantment, a logic of abstraction comes to define core, practical institutions. Normative authority is withdrawn from the particular and protections are instead situated within the abstract categories of "the citizen" or "the human."[43] And this overbid on the moment of universality extends beyond an institutional standpoint, to erode the substance of moral experience. To respond to the particular, to adopt a stance of empathy or compassion, is to court a feminized sentimentality. The "proper" claim of particularity instead migrates within the intimacy of private life—one of the last preserves of non-instrumental relations (if compromised and partial) within a disenchanted modernity.

This is an incomplete list of the social pathologies that Adorno tracks back to disenchanted reason. Even this rough guide, however, yields two important provisos—one that reflects the ground covered to this point, and another that leads to the aesthetic considerations that will occupy the remainder of this chapter. First, though the argument typically turns upon a detailed set of epistemological terms, the dynamics identified cannot be filed away as an episode within the ivory tower or the conference room. Rather, these practices of reason provide the resources through which agents situate themselves in relation to others and how they construe their ties, obligations, and responsibilities. They inflect the values by which subjects give reflective shape to their lives and delimit what kinds of appeals can claim their thoughts, desires, and willing.[44] In sum, social economies of authority condition what can *matter* to the subject.[45] Secondly, a caveat will clear space for the argument to come. While these critical texts indict a totalizing set of social damages, their hyperbolic rhetoric cannot be read literally without distorting Adorno's genealogical caution.[46] To give this cautionary note some positive content, the damaging character of reason is not an ahistorical given or an accomplished fact, but rather something that has come to be—and thus could yet be otherwise if other potentials of reason (now buried and devalued) could be salvaged.

* * *

At this point, readers are often left in a bind. Where Adorno painstakingly details the normative pathologies of late modernity and tracks their damages into the deepest crevices of social life (ranging from movie posters to footgear, marital relations, and doorknobs), his reparative efforts are perceived to take a peculiar direction. There are virtually no discussions of organized insurrection, political parties, or a revolutionary class that will take back the instruments of production.[47] Rather, it is the aesthetic sphere that is persistently invoked as a preserve of emancipatory meanings and sensibilities. In *Dialectic of Enlightenment*, for instance, the apocalyptic diagnosis is interrupted by the concession that "only authentic works of art were able to avoid the mere imitation of that which already is."[48] And the posthumous *Aesthetic Theory* pushes this thesis in a stronger direction when it proposes that art is "the imaginary reparation of the catastrophe of world history."[49] These are, put lightly, ambitious claims. In a thoroughly darkened time, when capitalism has remade the world and the revolutionary aims of Marxism have proven complicit with fascism, the artwork represents one of the last vestiges of meaning without violence. Stronger yet, works of art "are the unconscious schemata of that world's transformation."[50]

To understand how the aesthetic can do this kind of normative lifting, it will be useful to begin in an odd place—Adorno's distance from one familiar intersection of art and politics. Bertolt Brecht, for instance, situated the political potencies of art within its capacity to defamiliarize features of the everyday, such that they demand renewed thought and interrogation. Here the "estrangement effect" of art is meant to snap the viewer out the "second nature" of social practice, where institutions appear as the immutable furniture of the world. Though generated through social choices, these practices (e.g., gender relations; the institution of wage labor; the normalized performance of sexual identity, etc.) are mystified as eternal or natural facts, beyond the reach of transformation. And for a "committed" art, it is precisely this self-evidence that is problematized when social practices are presented in grotesque, parodic, exaggerated forms that make them "strange" and question-worthy. Take the following examples:

Hans Haacke's works that thematize the connections between the art world and the interests of capital

Barbara Kruger's superimposition of text upon photos, designed to problematize the dynamics of desire, violence, and power that characterize everyday social forms

Martha Rosler's collage pieces, which highlight the linkage between the consumer culture of the United States and the violence that its government exerts abroad

Carrie Mae Weems's presentation of African American bodies so as to bring out the violence that inflects their social experience.

There are many more possible instances. For Adorno's readers, however, much of the difficulty stems from how he resists this approach and privileges instead the works of aesthetic modernism—those that resist any such referential function, in order to interrogate the possibilities internal to a given artistic medium (e.g., the flatness of the canvas, the twelve-tone articulation of the octave, etc.). Indeed, the difficulty rests deeper yet. It is not simply that Adorno situates an important normative content within aesthetic modes of thought and production (rather than things like party mobilization, revolution, or direct-action strategies), but that he refuses any allegiance to empirical struggles or movements. As he responds: "the political positions deliberately adopted by artworks are epiphenomena and usually impinge on the elaboration of works and thus, ultimately, on their social truth content. . . . Real partisanship which is the virtue of artworks no less than of men and women, resides in the depths where the social antinomies become the dialectic of forms."[51] Though much of the passage targets the commitments of socialist realism (where revolutionary art is meant to represent proletarian consciousness), the broader point can be put quickly. It is not by expounding some socially edifying message that art could disrupt the "administered society."[52] Rather, it is necessary to look to the work's form to grasp its emancipatory potentials.

From such moments, it would be easy to conclude that the standard reading of Adorno is correct: he ultimately embraces the consolations of an elite art, distanced from social ills, such as systematic poverty, endless war, or economic exploitation. Though the artwork's form permits it to mirror the "truth" of an unreconciled world (i.e., its tensions, contradictions, and dissonance), it is difficult to see how this formal emphasis does any meaningful social work beyond the walls of the gallery or the concert hall. As Terry Eagleton contends, "it is possible to read his work as a retreat from the nightmare of history into the aesthetic . . . It is the most easily caricatured side of his thought: Beckett and Schoenberg as the solution to world starvation and threatened nuclear destruction."[53] A more patient engagement, however, reveals some normative bite when set against one of the core features of "false" life detailed above: a deep grammar of fungibility, where objects are emptied of sensuous meaning and rendered equivalent with other such abstractions. Automobiles, sneakers, vegetables, gems, labor, firearms, care, and even human bodies can be translated into the abstract cycle of monetary exchange, in which the sole distinguishing factor is "how much." One path to the artwork's critical weight, then, follows from this background—the fact that every such work makes a claim to meaning that could not be made any other way.[54] As Adorno proposes, the artwork "does not remain a dull particular for which other particulars could be substituted, nor is it an empty universal that equates everything specific that it comprehends. . . . It is only through the nonfungibility of its own existence and not through any special content that the artwork suspends empirical reality as an abstract and universal functional nexus."[55]

This is perhaps the quickest route to the reparative argument: works of art complicate disenchanted reason by demonstrating that a bare particular could lodge an authoritative claim that follows from its unique arrangement of line, color, sound, texture, or word.[56] The artwork seizes the recipient and demands her attention, even when its claim cannot be fully expressed in discursive terms or translated into the value grammar of a disenchanted modernity. As Jay Bernstein puts the point, authentic works of art "demonstrate that sensuous particulars can *mean*, can be hypnotic objects of attention, apart from and in defiance of any form of identifying mechanism other than the one their sheer presence insinuates."[57] And the experiential modality by which this claim is registered is what Adorno terms "the shudder" (*Erschütterung*)—the cognitive and sensible reflex of a non-reified experience of meaning. In the shudder, the subject experiences the limits of disenchanted thought; she or he registers the claims of the sensuous, even when these claims are not *thinkable* within a dematerialized reason.[58] Although this moment is crucial for the practical argument, some caution is required. It is tempting to assimilate the argument to an avant-garde position where the artwork erupts into social space, shocks its recipients, and thus produces a new public with new senses, new tastes, and new sensibilities.[59] Such an artwork does not speak to a given audience, so much as *generate* one anew. And yet, the phenomenology of the shudder does not permit such a reduction. The artwork does not simply say "something" that leaves the spectator shaken in unfamiliar ways, to see the world in a different light. Rather, the reparative labor of art is ultimately about *reason*—more specifically, how the aesthetic shelters a form of reason that interrupts the violence of disenchanted thought.[60] In Adorno's own terms, "aesthetic rationality wants to make good on the damage done by nature-dominating rationality."[61]

The argument to follow hinges upon an expansive reading of this claim to reason. The most common interpretation highlights the "reconciliation" character of the artwork, located in the relationship that it stages between content and form. Aesthetic form gives shape to its contents in a way that avoids the violence of disenchanted meaning; it brings its elements into meaningful relation without effacing their tensions (e.g., the role played by dissonance in modernist musical composition).[62] And where the theme of reconciliation plays an important role for Adorno, this critical emphasis has too often neglected a set of potentials that rest in the event that binds audience and work.[63] To develop these resources, it is necessary to approach the problem from a broader angle. It is not simply that the work inaugurates a non-reified form of experience within the spectator who finds him- or herself bound, enthralled, and troubled by its opening. Rather, art has become fundamentally "enigmatic" within modernity.[64] Aesthetic forms have been exiled from the socially recognized sphere of knowledge, and thus, if the artwork's claim to truth is to be recognized, it demands the spectator as a kind of co-participant. As Adorno argues, "the demand of artworks that they be understood, that their content be grasped, is bound to their specific experience; but it can only be fulfilled by way of the theory that reflects this experience."[65] In dialectical terms, the work cannot *work* without the patient intervention of the subject who grapples with its provocation without ever exhausting its claim or grasping it fully. And thus, the unfolding of an aesthetic reason is not delimited "within" the formal structures of the work or in some unilateral impact on the spectator, but rather takes place through a broader set of coordinates, involving author, work, material, recipient, claim, and interpretation.[66]

The foregoing only scratches the surface of Adorno's aesthetic writings. A more comprehensive account would need to address the truth that is meant to be preserved in the artwork; it would need to engage the complex aesthetic autonomy that enables art's critical distance from the "totally administered society"; and it would likewise need to address the historical dynamics through which art has come to shelter these potentials of reason.[67] Even this limited engagement, however, raises possibilities that will be crucial for what is to follow: if an aesthetic mode of reason "seeks to aid the nonidentical," then one of its core features must be a stance of receptivity without which the provocation of the work is stillborn. In Adorno's terms, the "need of artworks for interpretation, the need for the production of their truth content, is the stigma of their constitutive insufficiency."[68] As Richard Leppert glosses this point, the work "*cannot speak on its own.* If it is to be more than sound and fury signifying nothing, the listener must make the conscious decision to do what's necessary to meet the music halfway, so to speak."[69] Such formulations shed important light on the questions raised above. Most importantly, this appeal for interpretive engagement cannot be construed as a practice in which the subject projects meaning upon the work through a series of legislative acts.[70] This is the situation of the bad reader—the one who does not enter the aesthetic event in any meaningful sense. Rather, the subject of aesthetic experience must enact a *willingness to be shaken.* The recipient must be able to suspend her or his perceptual habits to attend to this patch of color, this constellation of lines and planes, this sequence of tones, silences, and rhythms as events that demand perceptual care—

even when they do not fit tidily into extant habits of sense-making.[71] More fundamentally, such a stance requires the viewer to recognize the question posed by the work, which is already to recognize its authority as something that demands response, even if the contours of the claim are not yet clear or the appropriate response uncertain. The subject, in Adorno's terms, "must not project what transpires in himself onto the art work . . . but must, on the contrary, relinquish himself to the artwork, assimilate himself to it, and fulfill the work in its own terms."[72] Without this mode of engagement, the work does not *happen* at all. Instead, the viewer walks past, looks through, reduces it to monetary value, thinks of something else, and emerges from the encounter just as he or she entered.

This receptive mode of sense-making (what Romand Coles has termed a "receptive generosity")[73] will help to detail a more robust political vein in Adorno than is often acknowledged. That said, the course of the argument will take these leads in an unorthodox direction. Rather than address these reparative hints as a sui generis case, limited to the art world (a staple of the resignative reading), the remainder of this chapter will emphasize how these aesthetic threads reflect the normative concerns that run throughout Adorno's thought.[74] And by pursuing these leads, what will come to the forefront is not art in the narrow sense, nor even "aesthetic experience" in broader terms—but rather a mode of sense-making that speaks to the reparative ideals that have haunted this chapter from the outset.

* * *

From the foregoing, some provisional conclusions are available. At the very least, it is difficult to endorse one of the standard charges against Adorno—that he forsakes the normative promise of the rationalist tradition in order to pursue some mysterious Other of reason. And yet there are considerable questions as to how this imperative to "aid the nonidentical" could extend beyond the professionalized sphere of culture.[75] Minimally, such a stance would mean tarrying, slowly and patiently, with the objects of thought, even if the subject finds their provocations difficult to accommodate through conventional canons of meaning and value. To put the point into Adorno's idiosyncratic terms, it would require the subject to acknowledge the "priority of the object" (*Vorrang des Objekts*)—to acknowledge that objects *mean* beyond the concepts and categories that thought brings to bear upon them (without thereby presuming some immediate, nonconceptual contact with their claims).[76] And yet, one of the familiar difficulties of Adorno is the strong discrepancy between his politicized language of object-relations, and the frustratingly few guides for what this could look like as a practice taken up by subjects in their relations with one another.[77]

Though sporadic, Adorno's texts are not without hints in this direction. A particularly fruitful moment, for instance, confronts the legacy of the Holocaust and gestures at some positive guides for thought and practice: "A new categorical imperative has been imposed by Hitler upon unfree mankind: to arrange their thoughts and actions so that Auschwitz will not repeat itself, so that nothing similar will happen. . . . Dealing discursively with it would be an outrage, for the new imperative gives us a bodily sensation of the moral addendum—bodily, because it is now the practical abhorrence of the unbearable physical agony to which individuals are exposed even with individuality about to vanish as a form of mental reflection."[78] When read in a strict sense, the passage offers a set of substantive directives: individuals must refuse complicity with state violence; gratuitous physical suffering is intolerable.[79] And yet a broader engagement reveals a philosophically deeper level to the charge: that the badness of somatic suffering possesses an authority in excess of the discursive claims offered on its behalf—a position that gains force in tension with those deliberative theories that have risen to prominence in the contemporary normative landscape. Although the deliberative school takes many shapes, they typically revolve around a few core commitments: if social coordination is secured through a practice of communication, positions and claims are justified only when they are backed by discursive reasons (themselves exchanged through carefully delimited procedures).[80] It is *through* this collaborative work of justification that positions gain rational authority. And it is by exchanging and responding to reasons that politics takes an appropriately intersubjective form—where individuals, divided by needs, interests, and values, nevertheless forge a consensus over the institutions that structure their shared space.

When set against this discursivist background, the cited imperative speaks more directly to the concerns engaged to this point.[81] Minimally, Adorno suggests that the subject of moral care is not reducible to an abstract rights-bearer or an etiolated legal "person"; rather, both fictions ultimately inhere within flesh that lives, desires, suffers, wants, and hurts. In a more pointed sense, however, the authority of the sensuous is meant to resonate in a manner that troubles any dialogical reduction of the normative.[82] As Adorno puts it: "the smallest trace of senseless suffering in the empirical world belies all the identitarian philosophy that would talk us out of that suffering . . . The physical moment tells our knowledge that suffering ought not to be, that things should be different. 'Woe speaks: 'go.' "[83] To witness flesh recoiling in pain is already to encounter a claim for restitution that "speaks" at the singular, sensuous level: this is something that *must not be*. And, by extension, to rationalize this pain—to construe its authority as a result of discursive deliberation—would be to betray it.[84] What is most significant for current purposes, then, is how this episode stages the provocation of nonidentity. Minimally, the somatic moment (this body before me that bleeds, that cries, that hungers) memorializes a form of authority that is sapped of legibility within a discursivist moral grammar. And the challenge goes beyond debates over moral normativity (its sources, location, etc.) to raise an *imperative* for the onlooker. It is not simply a materialist insistence that the claims of bodies cannot be translated, without remainder, into discourse. Instead, to recognize the authority of suffering is to attend *to* the flesh that turns in upon itself in pain, hunger, or humiliation—even if the words do not come, are ill-formed, unintelligible, or unavailable.

The critical literature dedicated to this "solidarity with tormentable bodies" offers an ambivalent contribution to the concerns of this chapter.[85] Although readers have distilled important resources for a materialist ethics, they often sidestep Adorno's insistence that "the quest for the good life is the quest for the right form of politics, if indeed such a right form of politics lay within the realm of what can be achieved today."[86] To pursue the political implications, it is helpful to read this engagement with nonidentity in light of the aesthetic guideposts detailed in the previous section. To recall: the artwork expands and problematizes the limits of rational meaning, as it makes a truth claim that cannot be conveyed through the framework of disenchanted reason. And yet, such moments cannot *happen* (as events of sense) without a stance of receptivity willing to tarry with their provocations, rather than sticking to coordinates of meaning in which these claims have no intelligible place. In Adorno's terms, an aesthetic practice of encounter "is not aimed at domination but at the expiation of domination, in that the subject places the control of itself and its other in the service of the nonidentical."[87] And where a wing of post-structuralist thought would stress the subject as the site of "control," Adorno persistently calls attention to the broader canons of reason that structure and delimit what *counts* as an authoritative claim. Even the most sovereign subject operates within a social horizon of intelligibility (whether this be a "social imaginary" or Gramsci's "common sense")[88] that extends authority to some forms of claiming and reduces others to gibberish or nonsense. In the terms of *Dialectic of Enlightenment*: it is not an individual preference for scientized or quantified forms of meaning that is at stake; rather, it is the social hegemony of disenchanted reason over truth-discourse, and the attendant dismissal of those knowledges (e.g., folklore, narrative, art, emotion) that cannot be conveyed in symbolically attenuated terms.

From this background, Adorno's effort to link aesthetic and normative concerns offers more robustly political resources than is typically recognized. To hazard a quick formula (to be filled out in the final section): an aesthetically informed reason signals a particular mode of sense-making, through a willed sensitivity to those gestures that cannot be fully redeemed within extant grammars of meaning. In Martin Morris's words, aesthetic rationality would "foster an awareness of that which is beyond capture by the concept."[89] To press beyond the case of suffering at the heart of the "new" categorical imperative, this form of responsiveness would attune itself more broadly to those remnants of sense that clamor for attention, even if the subject cannot fully articulate their authority through prevailing vocabularies for rational validity. It would grapple with those claims that take shape at the moment when official discourses of reason break down—to interrogate why they break down at *these* moments, what is foreclosed thereby, what happens to these contents, and why this suppression matters.[90] It would mean not worshipping one's familiar habits of meaning, but rather inhabiting them as provisional guides, open to expansion as they mutate and falter in relation to the provocations at hand. And to heed the ambivalent case of Odysseus within *Dialectic of Enlightenment* (i.e., his decision to expose himself to the disorienting claims of the Sirens), a stronger stance suggests itself: a *desire* to seek out those claims that throw into question the familiar assurances of the self in question.[91]

The final section will thus pursue these leads to propose that Adorno's thought possesses significant democratic insights, even if these possibilities were never fully pursued by his own texts. As the final section will detail, such care for the nonidentical is not reducible to the material and sensuous element of objects; nor is it limited to subjects who struggle with the claims of cultural products in galleries, concert halls, or seminar rooms removed from the hurly-burly of social life. And neither is it even exhausted in greater moral sensitivity toward the trembling and hurt of material bodies. Rather, it fruitfully informs the arts of sense-making that define the unpredictable conversations of civil society. To explore these possibilities, it is ultimately necessary to press these reparative hints into the messy, agonistic world of democratic practice.

* * *

At this point, it is necessary to return to Adorno's contested legacy. As noted, recent literature has argued for a more strongly political character to his work—signaled, for example, in his insistence that the individual must take a distance from social dynamics of violence so as to minimize complicity with their harmful effects.[92] And yet, even this sympathetic position leaves readers to ask whether distance can deliver meaningful resources for normative repair, or whether it threatens an apolitical, stoic withdrawal from the engagements of citizenship.[93] Given Adorno's notorious reluctance to provide guides for action, answers are elusive in his writings. To engage this problem, then, the remainder of this chapter will bring the resources developed thus far to bear on democratic citizenship—a practice that turns on negotiations with strangers who present demands we may find unclear, incoherent, unsettling, or preposterous. From this vantage point, a more readily politicized "care for the nonidentical" might be thought as a form of *hearing* what is presented amidst the din of democratic life—to engage what might originally be encountered as purposeless noise—and to recognize authority in claims that strain against familiar normative vocabularies.

There are more and less robust ways to theorize hearing as a form of reparative politics. As Didier Fassin has detailed, for instance, political appeals to listening came to characterize a moment in late capitalism when "suffering" offered the framework for normative analysis. Due to the decline of the social state and the pressures associated with financial precarity, increasing numbers came to experience a compromised form of social membership—unable to fulfill the consumerist imperatives for social esteem, or lacking the resources for full social participation.[94] In response to these dynamics, agents of the state sought to mitigate the effects of market exposure by organizing teams of public health professionals to listen sympathetically to those who inhabit this position of suffering. And yet this initiative was indicted from a number of directions—more specifically, for substituting a therapeutics of integration (where the suffering individual is reinserted into the structures of market capitalism) for the concerns of justice (where damaging social conditions would be transformed toward a more equitable world). In a word, such imperatives for empathy and validation too easily substituted for forms of *agency* that would dismantle exploitative regimes of class power. Or, for another instance, one might recall an episode of the neoliberal state—to enact "listening sessions" by which citizens could air their concerns, wants, and needs. This, in the terms proposed by New Labour, construed the work of government as a "Big Conversation" between citizen and administration (a relationship increasingly construed as that between "consumers" and "service provider"). In both cases, listening was invoked as a task of government, to secure responsiveness to its constituents—though, in practice, such initiatives did little more than substitute a therapeutic trope for the transformative work of politics. What such "listening sessions" ultimately represented was a forum in which grievances are expressed, but one where they go nowhere, give rise to no policy outcomes, and ultimately disappear once the temporal parameters of the "listening" exercise have elapsed.[95]

A more politically generative framework can be gained, however, by situating the practice of listening within the work of democratic citizenship—in tension with those deliberative schools engaged briefly above.[96] As detailed, there are many varieties of a deliberative politics, and trying to give any single account of their aims would prove far beyond the scope of this chapter. What is most significant for current purposes is the commitment to a discursive practice of social coordination: a normatively defensible form of politics would be one where subjects exchange arguments over the norms, structures, and institutions that shape access to core benefits and entitlements. This dialogical practice is at the heart of a communicative rationality: positions are presented to an audience of one's peers and justified with reasons designed to solicit their assent, rather than mere authority, force, or power.[97] And by doing so, the deliberative approach does not simply resituate politics within the conversations of civil society, but rather highlights the rational possibilities located within everyday communication—the unforced consensus that takes place in dialogue oriented toward mutual agreement.[98]

There is surely something attractive in basing politics on discursive exchange (rather than force, tradition, wealth, gerontocratic privilege, etc.). And yet, critics have posed compelling questions about this effort to root democratic practice within a model of communication. Most relevant for current purposes is what might be termed the "neutrality" challenge raised by critics such as Iris Young and Lynn Sanders.[99] Where communicative theorists tend to privilege the exchange of reasons in forums of will-formation, they fail to take seriously how hegemonic modes of discourse and argumentation systematically authorize some claims, social positions, and experiences while de-authorizing others. More serious yet, these standards tend to reflect the discursive conventions of groups that already have disproportionate power to set the terms and agenda of social conversations. This is the misleading implication behind deliberative appeals to Wilfrid Sellars's "space of reasons"—the intimation that deliberation is a practice where *arguments* meet, as if these positions (justifications, warrants, reasons, etc.) could be distilled from the languages in which they are (or must be) articulated.[100]

Such critiques intersect productively with the themes considered thus far. They do not simply identify a privilege extended to certain forms of speech; rather, they detail how other forms are trivialized and diminished through hegemonic grammars of political discourse.[101] To return to Adorno's own terms, these are the *nonidentical moments* of democratic life: those speakers whose claims do not "fit" within dominant discourses of justice and are thus sapped of authority. Take, for instance, the subject who appeals for common social goods in neoliberal times and finds her claims dismissed as the mere wants of nonproductive subjects. These agents may speak and offer well-formulated arguments for their interests, yet existing languages of citizenship undermine the purchase their claims may have within a public culture systematically worked over by neoliberal narratives of citizenship, market ideals, and desert.[102] Rather than justified claimants to public goods, these are "takers" or parasites—those diminished in their civic standing, due to ideological closures upon the "proper" citizen (i.e., the self-reliant, entrepreneurial individual).

To give heft to this suggestion, it will be useful to consider two cases, each of which raises importantly different considerations. First, the ongoing difficulties surrounding reparations for the history of slavery in the United States. Compelling arguments have been raised that the harms of slavery cannot be reduced to the abduction of human beings, their reduction to chattel, the brutality of the middle passage, or the dissolution of families for purposes of profit. Rather, a large literature has detailed how the institutional underpinning of slavery has had far-reaching reverberations, saddling generations of blacks with institutional obstacles to their full equality as citizens. Indeed, scholars have identified a formidable array of these strategies—spanning disenfranchisement, residential discrimination, debt peonage, mortgage policy, educational funding, law enforcement, and criminal sentencing regimes (and this is hardly an exhaustive list).[103] The point of this example is not to detail the protracted, ongoing history of institutional racism in the United States. Rather, the question is how claims for reparation have found little traction, due to their tension with dominant vocabularies for construing the things for which polities *could* be held responsible. As Iris Young has argued, the going model operates according to a logic of "liability." Responsibility hinges upon a readily identifiable agent behind a given harm—a disputant who can be held to account for those acts willfully done—and clearly identifiable causal chains, which stretch from the agent in question to the past harm.[104] And if this is the case, then the long-standing political resistance to reparations claims (at least in the context of the United States) can be appreciated along the lines sketched to this point. That is, political indifference or hostility toward these proposals cannot be reduced to racist beliefs (though this is surely not to be discounted); nor need it even be reduced to the neoliberal privatization of merit and blame (where maladaptive social outcomes are symptomatic of individual choices or failures). Rather, one significant way that these arguments fail to find purchase is due to the social grammar of responsibility on the basis of which harms are tracked back to agents and calculations made over which offenses demand remediation. If those who planned, maintained, and profited from the institution of slave labor are now long-dead, then who (on these premises) could meaningfully be held accountable? Within a presentist grammar of justice claims, the legacy of slavery represents a historical lesson, to be memorialized in classrooms and monuments, rather than a political exigency that demands reparative measures.

Alternately, consider the "climate refugee" within a globalized time of industry and commerce. The consumption and production habits of wealthy, industrial nations leave this agent facing rising seas, changed weather patterns, and more violent, more frequent weather episodes. The evisceration of regulatory agencies that could oversee production and enforce controls on pollution generates soil that is toxic and water that cannot be used. The causes or long-ranging effects of global climate change are not the target under consideration, but rather the difficulties that such agents face in bringing their grievances to political attention.[105] One could easily shoehorn an analysis into the terms sketched above (where a series of attenuated contributions cannot be tracked back in any clear, causal fashion to a single set of "responsible" agents). The case of the "climate refugee," however, generates at least one further complication: what is the authority to whom these agents can appeal? As Nancy Fraser has suggested, such agents find themselves within a situation of "abnormal justice"—where conventions are lacking to assign responsibility for these global transformations, and (within a Westphalian model) there exist no agencies to regulate these transnational dynamics or repair the far-reaching effects to which they give rise.[106] And yet, the abnormality of this situation reaches farther than this neologism will reach. For it is not only that climate refugees cannot find judges or organizations to adjudicate their challenges. Rather, it is also that they lack a vocabulary in which their suffering could be understood as claims of *justice*, demanding reparation by institutions with the power to constrain transnational economic agents. Instead, they speak from a position of natural disaster—a situation to be pitied or lamented—one that might be addressed by the goodwill or charity of nongovernmental organizations—but one that cannot hold agents to account and demand remediation.

It is not my intention to interrogate the histories of these complex cases; nor do I wish to elide their significant differences. More significant at present are the dynamics of closure that both positions face within the present shape of justice discourse. Each example highlights how the exchange, formulation, and reception of arguments is constrained by grammars that condition what can be meaningfully regarded from the vantage point of justice, and what, by extension, cannot. If this is the case, then Adorno's gestures toward an aesthetic grammar of repair contain more democratically robust resources than is characteristically recognized. For if democratic citizenship entails speaking and listening to strangers—strangers divided on grounds of need, interest, history, and values—then a less violent practice of citizenship would grapple with the challenge posed by the democratic nonidentical. Such claims "seek to be audible," and yet are diminished by economies of civic discourse that leave some unable to convey their suffering, needs, or humiliations in authoritative terms.[107] When located in the sphere of citizenship, then, the appeal to nonidentity goes beyond a materialist rejoinder to an overreaching, idealist epistemology; rather, it challenges the basic premises behind any uninterrogated faith in dialogue as a form of social inclusion. Even the most facially neutral participatory forms enact dynamics of closure through their civic languages and forms of membership—dynamics that extend authority to some claims while sapping others of their urgency and seriousness. And the point can be given more bite. The democratic nonidentical exposes how the vocabularies of justice are crafted by the winners of history and reinscribe their privilege, while undermining those who would challenge the core terms of the established order. It calls us to recognize that some will not be *heard* in the terms through which their lives and commitments are intelligible, since they must adopt another discourse altogether in order to enter into the language-game of justice.[108] As Renée Heberle elaborates, "the conceptualization of suffering, which is what occurs when we lend it a voice that communicates in the public domain, is never adequate. The object never goes into its concept without remainder. There is always already something not heard, not rendered, in the conceptualization of suffering."[109]

Many of these implications are already contained within Adorno's warnings toward moral self-certainty. Indeed, he persistently enjoins humility regarding the act of moral judgment and concern for whether extant norms or moral categories are adequate for cognizing situations of moral injury.[110] Such hints could be pressed beyond a stance of reflexive caution by the line of reading developed in this chapter. Any effort to salvage the nonidentical requires the subject to attend to those contents that haunt current economies of sense and meaning—and in so doing, to rescue such remainders from practices of meaning in which they find no meaningful place. Where this "care for the nonidentical" was introduced in aesthetic terms, a more clearly politicized rendering would turn upon this same perceptual care for those claims that strain against existing norms and languages for adjudication. This, in terms offered by Kate Lacey, would be a "listening out"—a willed scrutiny, designed to pick out those remnants of meaning that fall outside the familiar patterns of democratic debate.[111]

I want to close, then, by proposing an ambivalent appreciation for the resources of Adorno's thought—particularly how an aesthetically informed reason could contribute to the arts of democratic citizenship. As suggested throughout, it is difficult to endorse the standard reading of Adorno. Sensitive readers have discovered a rich range of normative resources within his texts, revealing a concern toward difference and demanding a critical distance from social dynamics of exploitation and violence. That said, the political legacy of Adorno may be more democratically substantive yet, once these resources are pressed beyond his reluctance to spell out their implications. At the heart of this concern for the aesthetic is an insistence to attend to those remainders that are excluded, silenced, and bracketed from the forms of reason that structure what is (or can be) recognized as authoritative. In more democratically thick terms, the task is to cultivate a sensitivity for those claims that "seek to be audible" and yet find little purchase within the official languages of citizenship. In this sense, Adorno's provocation resonates with those who have challenged a modernist political idiom (e.g., autonomy, insurrection, taking) in order to highlight receptivity as an axis for democratic agency. As Nikolas Kompridis argues, for instance, a politics of receptivity might "spontaneously and accountably make room for the call of an other, rendering intelligible what may have been previously unintelligible. Becoming receptive to such a call means facilitating its voicing, letting it *become* a voice that we did not allow ourselves to hear before, and responding to it in a way that demands something of us that we could not have recognized before."[112]

Even here, it is necessary to be careful. It would be easy to slip into some vague, ethicized effort to "make room" for the "call of an other"—as prepared by a fashionable academic discourse. To situate these resources within the agonistic field of justice claims, however, yields a more substantive complication for the work of citizenship. As the cited cases elaborate, civic exchange cannot be construed as a practice where nonviolent consensus will prevail, according to the "unforced force of the better argument." To presume such a situation is to begin with an unsustainable premise: that civic languages are common to all, and permit all to participate on equal terms. Rather, the norms and languages that organize discursive authority foreclose certain kinds of appeals and undermine the possibility that certain situations can be recognized as those that demand the reparative work of justice. To render this point in a more clearly politicized sense, the "ordinary" situation of justice can be distinguished from its emphatic sense. Where an idealized grammar of social coordination would presume that norms are settled and clear to all parties (and require only more adequate actualization in social practice), a critical framework recognizes that civic norms are operationalized in ways that actualize certain potentials while foreclosing, undermining, and distorting others. For example, a brutely individualist approach to "equal opportunity" represents, for others, a profound inattention to histories of dispossession that erode parity in social participation. It is on this terrain that the concerns of this chapter reveal their fullest dividends. If the "normal" situation of justice is to measure arguments in light of accepted norms, it is a staple of aesthetic reason to be moved by gestures that cannot yet be recognized *as* claims within these languages—and yet that trouble observers, that stay with them even when this content is not currently thinkable within official standards for adjudication. More strongly yet, an aesthetic mode of encounter allows such experiences to expand the familiar coordinates of sense, while remaining attentive to how *all* stances of meaning yield their own violence, exclusion, and closure.

This is not, of course, to maintain that Adorno was faithful to these resources—that he realized their full democratic potential—or that many such reservations toward his thought are not well founded. Indeed, his suspicions toward the leveling features of mass culture and his investment within elite cultural formations represent rather less attractive responses to the destabilizing features of democratic life.[113] More significant for current purposes is an unsatisfying one-sidedness in the resources that Adorno offers for rethinking an emancipatory politics. Where a politics of nonidentity would rest upon attentiveness to these fumbling, inchoate claims, Adorno has frustratingly little to say about how such closures on meaning are contested *by* those who find themselves straining against dominant languages of citizenship to identify or denounce situations of injustice. If this chapter has argued that there is a meaningful politics embedded within the resources of Adorno's philosophy, this constructive approach should not obscure the questions that he persistently avoids. Though such a politics rests upon tarrying with strange, unfamiliar claims, Adorno shows scarce attention to how marginal claimants disrupt, problematize, and expand these hegemonic vocabularies such that their challenges can enter into the conversations of civil society. And to locate the argument within contemporary geographies of power, it likewise fails to ask how this listening subject would engage such claimants within an increasingly segregated social landscape—one in which possibilities for encounter have been diminished through decades of attacks on meaningfully "public" spaces or goods.[114]

It is on this point that the familiar reservations bear fruit. On the one hand, the normative resources of aesthetic reason offer a provocation for democratic citizenship: a demand to attend sensitively to experiences and narratives of suffering that do not fit easily into extant languages of justice claims—and a willingness to allow these remainders to trouble the fixity of those languages. And yet, Adorno's own texts systematically fail to engage how these gestures erupt from positions of social disqualification. It is tempting to conclude, then, that a more politically robust rendering would remain more faithful to the cues embedded within these aesthetic remainders of reason. To take seriously Adorno's own argument, such emphatic forms of experience cannot be separated from those provocations that *demand* a renewed reflection upon those limits and forms of sense one may have previously taken to be transparent or unproblematic. Any such "care" for the nonidentical cannot be thought outside of experiencing how one's categories of sense or meaning break down in response to these provocations that trouble the subject and claim her attention, but cannot be translated (or not fully so) into existing vocabularies of sense. This may be the abiding lesson to this aesthetic politics of nonidentity: that the violence and insensitivity behind accepted categories of sense and meaning will come to light only when the subject actively engages those remainders that claim beyond limits that are familiar, predictable, and comfortable. It is only (to use the terms of *Negative Dialectics*) by conceding the "priority of the object" that the limits, blind spots, and thinness of the subject's categories will be exposed, shaken, and put back into play. And so, if there are substantial democratic cues within this interrogation of an aesthetically informed reason, they would demand not a moralist framework (in which the action is located in the subject's own commitments), but rather a politicized attention to those who speak and act to throw into relief the closures built into the languages misrecognized as accessible to all.

2

Foucault

Arts of the Self, Questions of the Common

There are some easy ways to bring the work of Michel Foucault into dialogue with the concerns of the Frankfurt School. Both offer detailed genealogies of how power insinuates itself into the depths of social life. Both interrogate the connections of reason and power. And both harbor deep suspicions toward the self-assurance of the everyday—a sphere where "nothing is innocuous" (Adorno)[1] and "everything is dangerous" (Foucault).[2] Foucault himself draws this affinity in a late interview, when he suggests that an earlier engagement with the Frankfurt School "would have avoided many of the detours which I made while trying to pursue my own humble path—when, meanwhile, avenues had been opened up by the Frankfurt School."[3] Of course, the task at hand is not simply to draw some loose set of associations between theoretical schools that missed the opportunity for a natural dialogue. For the purposes of this study, it is more fruitful to explore the political and normative stakes of Foucault's late work, where he draws an explicit tie between aesthetics and emancipatory agency. In one of the best-known formulations, Foucault poses the question: "What strikes me is the fact that, in our society, art has become something that is related only to objects and not to individuals or to life. That art is something which is specialized or done by experts who are artists. But couldn't everyone's life become a work of art? Why should the lamp or the house be an art object but not our life?"[4]

These allusive gestures can be read in any number of ways—and it is no small inconvenience that Foucault died before he could fill out their normative possibilities. Minimally, readers have puzzled over what it could mean to construe one's life in aesthetic terms and how questions of style might speak to Foucault's long-standing interests in social power. Indeed, the secondary literature often seems to multiply an ever-expanding menagerie of cases (criminals, dieters, weight lifters, drug users, bodily modifications of all stripes, etc.), rather than answers to the substantive questions regarding power, domination, truth, and discourse. And this indeterminacy quickly gives way to concerns that lead beyond those sketched in the previous chapter (i.e., passivity, quietism, irrationalism, etc.). Perhaps the best-known challenge runs something like the following: are these "arts" of the self compatible with normative commitments, or are they doomed to the kind of noxious aestheticism that characterized the Marquis de Sade—one where even the torment and violation of other bodies could be appreciated as so many paints to be used on the canvas of one's personal masterpiece?[5] These suspicions would only seem confirmed by the privilege Foucault extends to Baudelaire's "dandy" as an exemplar of self-making.[6] Indeed, if one were looking to criticize a political thinker, it would be difficult to choose a term more damning than this stylized, apolitical ironist.

The chapter will evaluate these challenges at a later point. What is ultimately most interesting about them is not their explicit claims—as we will see, they tend to rest upon distortions, misunderstandings, and phrases torn out of context. Rather more fruitful are (a) the anxieties these charges evoke and (b) what these anxieties convey regarding the perceived boundary between the political and the aesthetic. To pose the question in a characteristically Foucaultian vein: what is gained or lost by approaching political life in such terms? What interests are served by drawing the limits of criticism along *these* lines, and bracketing other possibilities? And just as significant: if every framework for analysis opens some possibilities while foreclosing others, what regimes of power or agency do such challenges shield from view?

Before leaping into the fray, it will be useful to sketch the terrain for the chapter. Minimally, the task is to complicate the terms according to which many familiar readings operate. To this end, the chapter will first situate Foucault's aestheticized appeals within his philosophical development. Upon doing so, however, the exposition will take a less familiar path. Indeed, much of the controversy surrounding this "art of the self" stems from Foucault's untimely demise, which left this proposal with a series of unresolved questions. For instance, how is one to read the genitive at the heart of the phrase: the art *of* the self? Are these arts a delimited field of the subject's experience and thought—in which case, they offer a discretionary stance that the subject may (or may not) take toward the world? Here, it is useful to think of the person who seeks to see what is beautiful in all things, and is "mindful" of his or her place in the universe (typically involving some brew of new-age spirituality, ethically sensitive diet, fastidious recycling, and "conscious consumerism"). Or do these arts rebound upon the subject, such that the self is the object of this aesthetic practice? And if this ambiguity can be resolved, how might either direction contribute to the work of world-making that has traditionally occupied the *praxical* imagination? Pressing upon these questions will not only help gain clarity on this evocative formula; rather, it will suggest some ways to reevaluate Foucault's contributions to emancipatory political thought. Ultimately, then, this chapter will pursue two significant claims. First, it will depart from widespread consensus on Foucault's legacy to suggest some more fruitful connections between these "self-arts" and the associational forms that have long occupied the political imagination. And secondly, the chapter will propose that these resources help address a question left unresolved by the first chapter of this study: just how is it possible for the subject to resist dynamics of social shaping in order to approach democratic practice in less violent ways?

* * *

There is a familiar interpretation available: this gesture toward an "art" of the self reflects a long-standing problem in Foucault's thought. Even his most cursory readers will locate his contributions to political thought in an effort to complicate standard assumptions regarding power—more specifically, the stranglehold that a model of "sovereign" power exerts over the political imagination. A brief tour through *Discipline and Punish* will lay some helpful groundwork. Where earlier systems of power operate through spectacles of torture and excess, designed to stage the authority of the sovereign, "disciplinary" strategies take root in the everyday and unexceptional. Perhaps best known, Foucault details an "optics of power" that works through surveillance and spatial configuration—not as a neutral terrain for action, but rather as a stage that elicits (or discourages) specific behaviors, movements, groupings, or divisions.[7] This regime of compulsory visibility is known to the observed subject and thereby intervenes "even before the offences, mistakes or crimes have been committed."[8] And these tactics extend far beyond the official spaces of control. Indeed, the expansion of surveillance technology within the private sector offers a helpful guide to the creation of a perpetual, decentered visibility—one that does not require the state or a single, central watcher behind the proliferation of eyes.

As the reference to civil society conveys, these disciplinary tactics "swarm" beyond the institutions in which they are forged, and "circulate in a free state."[9] A disciplined body is not simply one that has been incarcerated or detained by the state; rather, it is the body that has been made productive through the ordering of its movements and powers.[10] It is the laborer who has practiced a specified task repeatedly, so as to eliminate idiosyncrasies and inefficiencies; it is the soldier, drilled on the training grounds, so that appropriate movements are hard-wired at the level of reflex, no matter what shock, fear, or confusion may arise on the battlefield; it is the pupil whose handwriting has been forged through repetition after repetition (and systematic correction for messiness or aberration). And this regimentation of experience is deepened through a core technology of disciplinary power: the examination. Here, Foucault highlights the forms of knowledge to which disciplined subjects are submitted, no matter their standing vis-à-vis judgments of criminality. From earliest childhood, the agent is subjected to practices of observation, such that behaviors, capabilities, and tendencies are measured against all those who belong to relevant categorial groupings (e.g., the student, the worker, the man, the woman, the healthy sexual subject).[11] Within a normalizing society, these judgments are not simply descriptive, but are invested with a broad set of expectations regarding appropriate forms of desire, effort, expression, embodiment, abilities, and so forth. To run afoul of these expectations is to enter the medicalized sphere of the abnormal, degenerate, pathological, or damaged; accordingly, such types will be subjected to corrective interventions, ranging from the pedagogical to the therapeutic and the punitive.

Disciplinary society accordingly upsets many long-standing beliefs surrounding the operations of power.[12] Rather than construe power as something that is "held" as a possession, it runs throughout the roles, relationships, and forms of knowledge that structure social institutions.[13] Rather than think its effects as solely repressive (i.e., the "anti-power" that only says "no"), "power produces; it produces reality; it produces domains of objects and rituals of truth."[14] And rather than limit the manifestations of power to territory, wars, treaties, laws, or ideology, power takes on a micro-political character. That is, "power relations can get through to the very depths of bodies, materially, without having been relayed by the representation of subjects."[15]

This broad overview is not comprehensive, nor will it surprise anyone familiar with the rudiments of Foucault's work. It does, however, help to render the problem for which this "art" of the subject is typically read as an answer: Foucault's ostensible thesis of closure. Put quickly, if the operations of social power are this far-reaching—if power is not only built into social institutions, but also into economies of knowledge, discourse, and the organization of the body (its reflexes, forces, movements, or rhythms)—then it would seem to foreclose any meaningful possibilities to resist the untoward effects of these technologies. Frank Lentricchia, for instance, has argued that "because he leaves no shaded zone, no free space for real alternatives to take form, Foucault's vision of power, despite its provisions for reversals of direction, courts a monolithic determinism . . . and determinism courts despair."[16] And Richard Wolin contends that this vision "is so totalizing and convincing that there remains no prospect of escape."[17]

Though overwrought, these anxieties gain substance when framed by the concerns of the previous chapter. The members of the Frankfurt School were likewise concerned with power's capacity to insinuate itself into the motivational economies and need-interpretations of subjects within late industrial societies. And yet (the standard reading goes), there remains an essential difference. If their darker moments suggested a near-total mobilization by late capitalism, the theorists of the Frankfurt School nonetheless hint at resources for emancipation. It is in suffering, fantasy, and longing (no matter how buried or minimal) that impulses for an undamaged life yet abide.[18] The ostensibly hopeless character of Foucault's early thought stems from how his work is thought to refuse any such reserve. For critics of this stripe, Foucault's subject is not a being with some biological substrate that is served or repressed by social organizations; by extension, there is no hope of returning to a "human nature" that has been repressed or deformed; rather, even the subject's needs, desires, and reflective capacities are crafted and forged through regimes of power.[19] As Axel Honneth argues, Foucault "regards the psychic properties of subjects, and thus their personality structures, entirely as products of specific types of corporal disciplining. Because of his structuralist beginnings, Foucault, as soon as he gives his theory of power the form of historical investigations, portrays subjects behavioristically, as formless, conditionable creatures."[20] To dig a bit deeper, many such challenges reflect the privilege long accorded to a certain model of political subjectivity. Though rarely articulated so clearly, the intuition tends to run as follows: if resistance is to be possible, then it must presuppose the existence of a critical, autonomous subject—one who can step back from social practices to place them at an evaluative distance. And though the specifics of this autonomy raise significant questions, it minimally demands that the subject possess psychic or motivational resources that exceed the social formation of her wants, needs, desires, and pleasures. It is this premise that Foucault is thought to refuse when he (ostensibly) dissolves the subject into a web of discourses, strategies of power, and institutionalized forms of knowledge.[21]

It would not be difficult to contest these readings at the level of their premises. For example, it scarcely follows that the omnipresence of power means, for Foucault, a lack of critical agency, along the lines of a brute either/or (i.e., where power exists, agency does not).[22] That said, the broad strokes of the story offer one familiar narrative for approaching Foucault's late "art of the self." At one level, his work moves from an "archaeological" approach (one that uncovers the transcendental conditions for social phenomena)—to a "genealogical" period (one that disinters the historical formation of social practices so as to expose their contingency and exclusions)—to a period described as "problematization" (i.e., those practices by which societies render areas of their lives "problematic" and in need of particular vigilance).[23] By shifting from methodological to substantive considerations, however, Foucault's turn to the self is typically read as an answer to a perceived lacuna within his earlier thought: the lack of a meaningful engagement with the subject that most readers privilege within their own habitation of the world. The subject that occupies these late texts is not simply forged by techniques and strategies of power, but rather possesses the capacity to submit social dynamics to criticism and challenge. And yet, the account to follow will diverge from this familiar interpretation. Rather than reduce this aesthetic "turn" to an answer to a problem, this chapter will rather take it up as a starting point that opens a rich range of critical possibilities. The question will not be whether there are resources for agency in Foucault's thought, but rather what kind? How do they help to supplement the gaps of the account considered in the previous chapter? And what might these resources contribute to ongoing strains of critical politics?

* * *

To this point, this chapter has detailed the standard story on Foucault's theoretical development. What was perceived as a tendency to "erase" the subject gives way to a renewed interrogation of its forms, modes, and possibilities. As he renders the aim of these texts, "I have sought to study . . . the way a human being turns him- or herself into a subject."[24] This subject is not the passive imprint of social economies of power and knowledge (themselves manifest in a wide range of institutions), but is actively engaged in giving shape to her life, wants, values, and motivational priorities. In an oft-cited formulation Foucault proposes: "from the idea that the self is not given to us, I think that there is only one practical consequence; we have to create ourselves as a work of art."[25] From such passages, it may seem (to paraphrase a point from Martha Nussbaum) that Foucault's late work has overcorrected and "retreated from" the institutional context that lent such bite to his texts on disciplinary power.[26] Where before all the action was located on the side of institutions, now the pendulum is thought to swing to a different extreme: subjects engaged in a promethean work of self-creation. The discomfort here reflects the charges recently leveled at critical positions organized around a language of "performance"—that they are too thin and unrooted to reflect the material constraints under which actual human subjects live, outside the pages of philosophy books.

There are a number of reasons to resist such conclusions. As Foucault's more sensitive interpreters contend, for instance, this narrative of extremes goes wrong from the outset, since the subject was never fully absent from the earlier texts in the way presumed by an all-or-nothing style of interpretation.[27] Rather than pursue this rejoinder, however, the argument of this chapter will set its sights at a different level: the possibilities and discomfort that attend the specifically aesthetic resonance of this project. To do so, it will be useful to clarify some of the fuzziness that attends its central category. As readers have noted, Foucault's late texts can swing between long meditations on antiquity, while invoking a distinctly modern conception of aesthetic production, and thus obscure just what sense of artistry (a practice that is socially and culturally overdetermined) is at stake.[28] To follow the suggestion of Timothy O'Leary, then, perhaps the clearest point of entry is found within an ancient framework of artistic fashioning. That is, the core of aesthetic making—a *techne* rather than *physis*—rests in the patient crafting of a material into an intelligible shape.[29] It is the intentional act of shaping within a set of constraints imposed by (a) the material at hand and (b) the conventions that condition what can be considered a work of that type. Minimally, then, this aesthetics of the subject is situated within the activity of self-shaping by which one *comes to be* a subject of any sort whatsoever.[30] This emphasis on craft finds support in Foucault's own rendering of his aims: "I am referring to what might be called the 'arts of existence.' What I mean by the phrase are those intentional and voluntary actions by which men not only set themselves rules of conduct, but also seek to transform themselves, to change themselves in their singular being, and to make their life into an *oeuvre* that carries certain aesthetic values and meets certain stylistic criteria."[31]

On a quick reading, this passage may seem to confirm one of the anxieties cited at the outset: that Foucault here departs from moral considerations, such that style overrides all other criteria for conduct. For this subject, other agents would not be autonomous beings whose dignity must be respected, but rather instruments to be used in this subject's self-fashioning.[32] And yet, one way to mitigate this impression is by noting how the framework of self-artistry plays upon a series of distinctions *internal* to moral practice. What is at stake is not simply a distinction between (a) morality as a set of social codes (i.e., the "rules" that can be codified for behavior), and (b) the behavior of subjects in relation to these rules (that one may or may not obey, may do so selectively, etc.).[33] Instead, these "arts" of selfhood are rooted in the transcendentally deeper element of moral experience: how the moral subject comes to define herself in relationship to these norms and the authorities they invoke. As Foucault puts it: "there is another side to the moral prescriptions . . . the kind of relationship you ought to have with yourself, *rapport à soi*, which I call ethics, and which determines how the individual is supposed to constitute himself as a moral subject of his own actions."[34] Put differently, the moral subject is not something independently given, prior to the norms that structure its actions and self-relation; rather, it is a form of self-relation, to be articulated in light of social norms, regimes of truth, and the forms of life these norms solicit. This insight is signaled by a terminological shift noted by Foucault's careful readers. In the genealogical writings, the process of coming-to-subjecthood is characteristically figured as "*assujettissement*," which marks the mechanisms by which social institutions delimit, forge, guide, and correct the individual.[35] In the late texts, by contrast, Foucault increasingly deploys the verb "*subjectivation*," which carries a rather more active set of connotations—the process by which the subject negotiates her own form, in relation to norms, discourses, and authorities that exceed and implicate the self.[36]

Accordingly, there are at least two ways to understand Foucault's appeals to an aesthetic work of self-making. To untangle these registers, it is necessary to begin with an assertion: even those forms of life that might strike the observer as profoundly conservative are also characterized by a series of tests, exercises, and self-evaluations designed to give it shape.[37] This is what might be termed the transcendental reading of the "self as an artwork"—a condition of selfhood that attends all alike. No matter how conventional a life may appear, it nonetheless rests upon an effort to orient the self toward a certain set of norms (rather than others) and a set of exercises designed to augment, resignify, or diminish those motives accordingly deemed fraught. In Nietzschean terms, every moral stance is a practice of self-formation that shapes those who live by them. Social norms do not only offer a horizon against which actions and desires take on practical thickness; nor do they simply privilege certain forms of knowledge; rather, they provide techniques to orient the subject toward a specific ideal of personhood. As Foucault proposes, they furnish "technologies of the self, which permit individuals to effect by their own means, or with the help of others, a certain number of operations on their own bodies and souls, thoughts, conduct, and way of being, so as to transform themselves in order to attain a certain state of happiness, purity, wisdom, perfection, or immortality."[38] This practice of self-articulation defines the medieval Christian, scouring his or her dreams for signs of demonic possession; it characterizes the ancient Pythagorean, intentionally facing temptations in order to test and heighten his self-mastery; and it is likewise the case for the straight subject of sexuality, vigorously rooting out and disavowing any traces of same-sex desire. What distinguishes these subjects, for Foucault, is not the willingness to engage in this shaping, versus those who refuse the project entirely, but rather the code in relation to which they situate their ideals and desires; the source of normativity that will be authoritative for the subject; the ethical substance (i.e., the part of the self that will come to be scrutinized and managed) upon which this reflective shaping seeks to work; and the kind of person this agent is trying to become (i.e., the telos of this shaping).[39]

At this point, the ostensible "turn" in Foucault's thought could be read as a more phenomenologically sound accounting of the subject—where (a) socially available models and discourses of knowledge offer a horizon in light of which the subject negotiates her attachments, ideals, and role-performances, though (b) this will not exhaust the relationships that she may take toward those norms. This subject is neither the impoverished, asocial agent of econometrics (e.g., preference-maximizers, rational choosers, etc.), nor is she dissolved into her social conditions in the way long feared by Foucault's less careful readers.[40] To put the point in terms offered by Judith Butler, subjects work both with and against the terms by which they become socially legible. As they enact these norms, they may restage them in exaggerated, parodic, or innovative ways that reveal new possibilities for what they might mean, where they might apply, and how they could be taken up by others.[41]

Already, this minimalist rendering presses the argument beyond social ontology and into a more strongly *praxical* register. These critical potentials come clear by interrogating the differing aims of self-fashioning within the classical texts. Where Foucault presents the self-governance of the Christian as an obligation generated by the word of a universalist deity, and the Stoic self as mandated by the universal obligations of a rational being, the classical art of the self reflects divergent aims. As he elaborates:

> In antiquity this work on the self with its attendant austerity is not imposed on the individual by means of civil law or religious obligation, but is a choice about existence made by the individual. People decide for themselves whether or not to care for themselves . . . they acted so as to give to their life certain values (reproduce certain examples, leave behind them an exalted reputation, give the maximum possible brilliance to their lives). It was a question of making one's life into an object for a sort of knowledge, for a *tekhne*—for an art.[42]

Such moments help to press these reflexive technologies beyond a more robust phenomenology of selfhood and rather into a labor to individuate the subject. Where a universalist mode of self-governance works to align the subject with universally binding norms or codes (one that would "purify" the subject of idiosyncrasy or self-will), Foucault highlights how these techniques could also be used to generate an exemplary self. As he renders the point, "in this form of morality, the individual did not make himself into an ethical subject by universalizing the principles that informed his action; on the contrary, he did so by means of an attitude and a quest that individualized his action, modulated it, and perhaps even gave him a special brilliance by virtue of the rational and deliberate structure his action manifested."[43] From this lead, there is a quick route to how these projects of self-articulation could furnish the emancipatory resources that are hinted in Foucault's late writings: such practices offer possibilities for the subject to develop pleasures, intensities, abstentions, or connections in the service of a self that would diverge from socially enforced patterns of intelligibility. As Ladelle McWhorter argues, such techniques do not simply permit subjects to model exemplars built into moral codes; rather, they furnish possibilities to become "other than what we have been made to be."[44] And by so doing, these self-arts may mitigate the dynamics that measure and bend subjects back toward a compulsory common—whether this is a dispensation inscribed in all beings by their maker, the teleological aims inscribed within organismic health, or the universal mandates of reason.[45]

To pursue the *praxical* implications, it is useful to return to Foucault's core insights. What defines a society of normalization is the institutionalized practice of knowledge that delimits, ranks, and hierarchizes forms of personhood. Within this social framework, certain forms are privileged as ideal—or, in a scientized vein, as *normal.* To exceed the norm (with regard to desires, wants, needs, beliefs, embodiment, pleasures, morphology, etc.) is not simply to become a statistical outlier or an eccentric—rather, it is to fall into the ranks of the pathological.[46] And because this category is overlaid with medicalized dynamics of health or sickness, those who fail its terms are rendered targets for a broad range of corrective interventions. In contemporary terms, it is useful to think of coercive "conversion" therapies that aim to re-engineer those with same-sex desires back to the "normal" circuits of heterosexual attachment. Alternately, one might think of the shaming and behavior modification exerted upon those whose forms of embodiment do not meet normalized patterns of morphology (now schematized in the spurious Body Mass Index)—one that is extended through a wide variety of marketing tactics, dieting regimens, transit pricing schemes, the exercise-industrial complex, insurance premiums, employment practices, and body fitness fetishism within civil society. These are agents whose appetites are medicalized, managed, and supervised *for their own good.* And there is a further register to these dynamics that must be flagged in passing. Where Foucault is characteristically interested in how an economy of normality authorizes interventions in lives that fail its terms, Judith Butler has proposed that a more robust engagement with psychoanalytic frameworks (something Foucault typically evades) can help account for a related question: the reflexive damages that attend the subject-position of the abnormal. For if the subject's self-relation is mediated through social categories of intelligibility, then significant harms may result when the subject must present as aberrant, perverse, or damaged in order to be legible at all.[47] As Lana Wachowski, for instance, describes the illegibility of the transgendered subject from within a binary grammar of gender: "in the absence of words to defend myself, without examples, without models, I began to believe voices in my head—that I was a freak, that I am broken, that there is something wrong with me, that I will never be lovable."[48]

From an emancipatory perspective, then, there is a quick path to understanding what "fascinates" Foucault regarding these reflexive technologies of selfhood. There is much that could strike the reader as trivial or juvenile in this experimentalist opening—for instance, his often flippant references to drug usage and intoxication.[49] When taken at their word, however, these experiments may permit a more normatively substantive possibility: to carve a space for more variegated lives within social economies of observation, control, and coercive intervention. Where normalized economies of personhood bend subjects toward a delimited range of possibilities (and marshal sanctions against those who resist or "fail" these assignments), such arts might yield ways to live these disqualified positions (of desire, embodiment, attachment, appetite, etc.) as different practices of the human, rather than as degenerate cases to be measured in their distance from a shiny, happy norm. In Foucault's own terms, "maybe the target nowadays is not to discover what we are but to refuse what we are. . . . We have to promote new forms of subjectivity through the refusal of this kind of individuality that has been imposed on us for several centuries."[50] To "refuse what we are" in this sense would be to practice and explore these counter-hegemonic possibilities while resisting the meaning they have been assigned through a coercive social pedagogy. Stronger yet (to introduce a point that will be expanded in the final section below), such experiments may ultimately provide resources for marginal subjects to contest those official knowledges within which their "truth" can only be disease, lack, deviance, or aberration. To propose a radical self-artistry is thus not reducible to some effort (as some of Foucault's readers maintain) to restore a Hellenic elitism within egalitarian times.[51] Rather, it suggests possibilities for inhabiting a life with less shame, self-loathing, hopelessness, and recrimination—a life that is less prone to interiorize categories of pathology as the truth of its social existence and the limit of what it can be.

* * *

From the foregoing, there are a number of ways to read Foucault's "fascination" with "the aesthetics of existence" where "the *bios* [is] a material for an aesthetic piece of art." Broadly, the argument plays upon two threads characteristically elided by the semantic unity of "the" aesthetic. First, the artifactual characteristic of artistic making offers one path to this art of the self—where the subject is neither some asocial *fundamentum,* nor solely the imprint of social dynamics of shaping (to invoke a long-standing caricature of Foucault's thought). Rather, it represents a significant labor *by* the subject, to craft him- or herself in relation to social codes, norms, roles, and expectations of personhood. Secondly, this practice of self-shaping is supplemented by what might be termed the modernist register of aesthetic production. To channel the Nietzschean inspiration of the argument, this crafting is oriented toward a particular end: to gain a self of distinction—one that is irreducible to any universal category or type—one that transcends what has been made of it by social institutions.[52] As Foucault puts this, "extensive work by the self on the self is required for this practice of freedom to take shape in an *ethos* that is good, beautiful, honorable, estimable, memorable, and exemplary."[53]

This constellation of themes permits a more comprehensive access to the promise and controversies surrounding a Foucaultian politics of the subject. Even the quickest scan of the literature reveals a wide range of anxieties toward this stage of Foucault's thought. For purposes of clarity, it will be useful to list some of the major charges in schematic form:

a) By leaning so heavily upon the texts of antiquity, Foucault commits two errors. Not only does he overstep his (philological and historical) training to distort the historical record, but he ultimately betrays his own methodological commitments. From his earliest texts, Foucault has insisted that human thought, norms, and subjectivity are fundamentally rooted within a "historical *a priori*" that conditions the roles and possibilities that one can take up.[54] Only within this historical embeddedness is the subject socially legible—whether this takes the form of the calculating businessman, the melancholic housewife, the madman, the samurai, the courtly lover, or whatever. By placing such weight upon these classical technologies of the self, and emphasizing their emancipatory possibilities for a very different time and place, Foucault commits the same kind of ahistorical error against which he persistently warns.[55]

b) Upon highlighting these "arts of the self," Foucault is driven into an apolitical narcissism. Where his genealogical texts highlight how institutions systematically rest upon relationships of domination or exclusion, the late texts sidestep these questions of power. These subjects of artistry do not protest, strike, revolt, or stage walkouts; instead they turn inward, into an "attitude of narcissistic self-absorption."[56] Or, to render the point in slightly different terms, Terry Eagleton proposes that this "vigorously self-mastering individual remains wholly monadic. Society is just an assemblage of autonomous self-disciplining agents, with no sense that their self-realization might flourish within bonds of mutuality."[57]

c) Perhaps the most bitter denunciations come from those who target the aesthetic basis for this analytic of selfhood. This line of critique stems from the broadly Weberian/Habermasian premise treated in the first chapter of this study: that the constitutive history of modernity is a process in which the categories of experience have been divided into a set of autonomous spheres. From this vantage point, Foucault's effort to render subject-formation as an aesthetic project represents not only an antihistorical effort to muddy these categorial waters. Rather, it commits him to a position where the aesthetic "colonizes" the moral sphere, corroding its forms of reasoning and its authority to orient social practice. As Richard Wolin charges, "Foucault's standpoint favors either an attitude of narcissistic self-absorption or one of outwardly directed, aggressive self-aggrandizement. In neither case is there a discernible trace of human solidarity, mutuality, or fellow-feeling. Instead, the ethical universe of aesthetic decisionism is a Hobbesian state of nature . . . with a flair for style."[58] In these projects of self-fashioning, all becomes material for the subject's project of expression—including other subjects.

d) These indictments give way to a more broadly shared discomfort. Even if the reader does not begin with a strong investment in the categorial divisions of modernity (regarding the ostensible conditions for thought and experience), this aesthetic turn nevertheless yields a troubling normative instability. To put the anxiety in specific terms, this aesthetic framework lacks resources to guide which projects of self-fashioning could be justified on intersubjectively shared grounds and which cannot. Where Foucault persistently valorizes transgressive moments of "becoming," it is uncertain why the subject should engage in such projects or what shapes would be preferable to others. In a word, this line of interpretation continues long-standing concerns about the indeterminacy of Foucault's writings on power and resistance.[59] To employ an ugly turn of phrase, Foucault either lacks normative guidelines altogether (and exhibits an

> anarchist preference for transgression that he never justifies in any meaningful sense) or he is ultimately a "crypto-normativist"—he tacitly relies upon normative foundations that he is unwilling or unable to elaborate and defend.[60]

The list is not exhaustive.[61] And yet some of these concerns can be addressed by turning to Foucault's own responses. For instance, when pressed by an interviewer over whether he simply advocates a return to antiquity, as a counterpoint to a normalizing modernity, Foucault responds "No! . . . you can't find the solution of a problem in the solution of another problem raised at another moment by other people."[62] Or, for those who fear that Foucault has disavowed his standard of methodological care to endorse a self-making subject, unfettered by social institutions, norms, or discourses,[63] he offers a more careful rendering: "if I am now interested in how the subject constitutes itself in an active fashion through practices of the self, these practices are nevertheless not something invented by the individual himself. They are models that he finds in his culture and are proposed, suggested, imposed upon him by his culture, his society, and his social group."[64]

To address the specific points further would swamp this chapter in a sea of details. The remainder will instead channel a number of these anxieties into one core concern: how these reflexive concerns guide, constrain, or deform the modes of agency that characterize an emancipatory politics. The question is particularly urgent, since it did not only trouble Foucault's contemporaries, but has recently been pressed against a neo-Foucaultian literature (e.g., William Connolly, Judith Butler, Stephen White) that likewise targets the micro-political effects of power.[65] The anxiety can be put quickly: if the task is to contest the installations of power "within" the subject, then does this proposal leave space for the collaborations by which citizens forge alternatives to undesirable social conditions?[66] Is there any meaningful connection to others in the way that historically defines the disruptive movements of civil society? There is no shortage of challengers from this vantage point. Lois McNay, for instance, maintains that a Foucaultian politics "runs the risk of lapsing into an atomized politics of introversion."[67] And Ella Myers asserts that "what [this reflexive model] makes very difficult are 'horizontal conjunctions'—collectivities whose members are . . . capable of acting together as co-creators of 'counter-power.' "[68]

Such challenges lend political teeth to the charges raised above. If these reflexive considerations do not necessarily lead to an aestheticized narcissism, they nonetheless erode resources for the struggles, risks, and pleasures of politics. At best, we are told, this Foucaultian approach fails to ask into traditional intersubjective commitments (e.g., solidarity, care, association). At worst, it locks subjects within patterns of self-regard that are both stoked and serviced by consumer markets (plastic surgery, diet regimes, self-help gurus, mindfulness workshops, etc.).[69] These are subjects who learn new languages, hit the gym, engage in polyamory, go to retreats, try out different spiritual practices, and hone their golf swings. They may even change their consumption habits so as to waste fewer resources or avoid corporations that engage in unpalatable labor practices. What these subjects do not do is engage in the risks, exhilaration, or discomfort of an agitational politics. This reading offers a stark diagnosis of Foucault's critical legacy: the subject that takes center stage is not one who engages in collaborative acts of world-making (or remaking), but rather one who withdraws from the worldly engagements of politics. For a broad range of critics, this is the conclusion that must ultimately be drawn regarding Foucault's late thought. Where this self-artistry reflects a long-overdue concern for the subject, it does so by sacrificing the subject's connectedness to others—and thus cannot account for associational forms of counter-power. Or, more simply yet: if Foucault's late texts address an outstanding dilemma within his thought, the solution comes at a prohibitive political cost.

* * *

As the remainder of this chapter will argue, there are grounds for resisting many such conclusions. At a broad level, it would be false to suggest that Foucault was not interested in the assemblies, groupings, and alliances that are required to contest intolerable social arrangements. As Foucault's biographers have captured, his involvements in a wide range of political struggles reflect a significant investment in emancipatory movements. Foucault's participation within the Prison Information Group (GIP), for instance, is well known for its efforts to permit prisoners to speak of the conditions they face within spaces of incarceration.[70] Likewise familiar is his admiration for the uprisings in Iran or Tunisia, where the protesters took on considerable risk to contest the "unbearable quality of certain situations produced by capitalism, colonialism and neocolonialism."[71] More broadly, it could be said that Foucault's investment in these "bottom-up" movements reflects his sympathies toward a radical politics—notwithstanding his stated reservations toward the shape this commitment took within many contemporaries.

This is not to say that Foucault offered a rigorous accounting of political agency. Although he repeatedly invokes the necessity of resistance, his official writings provide a fairly anemic accounting for what kinds of resistance would be desirable in light of contemporary formations of power. Instead, he persistently maintains that the tactics, aims, and objectives of struggle must be decided by those on the ground, facing conditions they take to be intolerable. They must speak of their own wounds, humiliations, and frustrations, in their own language. They must decide what kinds of tactics would best alleviate the conditions they face (e.g., no shows, slowdowns, time-theft, contractual negotiations, walkouts, strikes, pilfering, union organization, information distribution, whistle-blowing, etc.). As he elaborates: "if I don't say what needs to be done, it isn't because I believe there is nothing to be done. On the contrary, I think there are a thousand things that can be done, invented, contrived by those who, recognizing the relations of power in which they are involved, have decided to resist them or escape them."[72] From such openings, it would be possible to think a style of radical politics—not as the conclusion of deeply rooted historical dynamics, and not as some Marcusean "Great Refusal" by which subjects would be reconciled with their true natures[73]—but rather as "the impulse by which a single individual, a group, a minority, or an entire people says, 'I will no longer obey,' and throws the risk of their life in the face of an authority they consider unjust."[74] This would be a resistance that could only be spoken in local terms, that chooses specific tactics, within specific arrangements of power, to secure specific aims and objectives.

And yet, a vague concern for "opposition" would not resolve the problem of this chapter. For if Foucault scatters approving references to acts of insubordination throughout his work, they neither constitute the systematic elaboration desired by his critics, nor do they address whether (or to what degree) such gestures reflect the transformative self-arts interrogated to this point. To address some of these issues, it will be useful to begin with Foucault's concerns for sexual practice as a particularly rich site of control and contestation. There is a well-known moment in the first volume of *History of Sexuality* where he suggests that practices of sexual normalization could be contested neither by a return to some natural set of desires, nor to the suppressed "truth" of sexuality. Both of these answers would fail to recognize the deep historicity of the human subject, the fact that the body itself "is the inscribed surface of events," shaped fundamentally by regimes of history, labor, discipline, and power.[75] Instead, "the rallying point for the counterattack" must be located within an economy of "bodies and pleasures."[76] The vagueness of this "rallying point" offers a characteristic moment of frustration. And yet, to end with this indeterminacy would overlook the more disclosive moments that appear within Foucault's late reflections on an insurrectionary sexual practice. For instance, when asked about the forms of pleasure forged by a gay counterculture (fisting, BDSM, leather men), he responds: "it's the real creation of new possibilities of pleasure, which people had no idea about previously. What all those people are doing is not aggressive; they are inventing new possibilities of pleasure with strange parts of their body—through the eroticization of the body."[77]

What may be most interesting in this statement is not the specific claim regarding embodiment, invention, or strategy—nor even how it illustrates what it means to pursue pleasures upon or within sites of the body that do not easily fit the genital reduction of sexuality. All of this hews to the project that Foucault elsewhere describes as "fabricating other forms of pleasure, relationships, coexistences, attachments, loves, intensities."[78] Rather, I want to emphasize a register that is left unaddressed by those who charge Foucault with a stark individualism: that an essential feature of these experiments is how they were negotiated in commerce with others—how they relied upon the multiplicity of partners, the anonymity of their couplings, the spaces in which these encounters were sheltered, the signs by which desires were communicated, and the social forms created to solicit, develop, and practice these pleasures. In a formulation that merits careful thought, Foucault says: "I think it is politically important that sexuality be able to function the way it functions in the saunas, where, without [having to submit to] the condition of being imprisoned in one's own identity, in one's own past, in one's own face, one can meet people who are to you what one is to them: nothing else but bodies with which combinations, fabrications of pleasure will be possible."[79] What might initially appear to be an offhand reference to an episode in gay counterculture takes on critical heft when read against the "coercive individuation" characteristic of disciplinary power. Where disciplinary knowledge fixes the subject through his or her divergence from an idealized norm—so, too, does the bathhouse work upon this terrain of individuality. Rather than place the subject into a managed, isolated position, however, this space permits a distance (if temporary and provisional) from the forms of individuation that have been used to define the subject as a known social quantity (e.g., name, social coordinates, institutional record, marital status, occupation, class position, professional networks, etc.). And by so doing, this practice of cruising renders possible forms of pleasure, subjectivity, and connectedness that would not be available without these spaces or those who participate. As Tom Roach puts it, the space and culture of the bathhouse render possible "the movement of desubjection to subjectivation: the undoing of socially, historically determined selves and the creation of new ones."[80] Anonymity, in this sense, is not a bare absence of sociality (as suggested by the "monadic" reading)—but is itself a distinct relational form that is cultivated, sustained, and protected by both institutional and interpersonal supports.

The broader significance of this moment requires some patience. From a historical perspective, for instance, Whitney Davis has proposed that Foucault may be guilty of idealizing the bathhouse culture of San Francisco—a culture that generated its own forms of normalization and exclusion.[81] And yet, from a *praxical* vantage point, this engagement yields some unexpected resources: such transformative projects relied upon intersubjective forms (no matter how episodic or anonymous) to take root within a heteronormative sphere structured by norms and policies hostile to their flourishing. This collaborative dimension is central to those moments where Foucault offers that the task of this self-artistry is not to actualize some "authentic" self, nor to return to some undamaged "nature" of the subject; rather, "we need to produce something that doesn't exist yet, without being able to know what it will be . . . it's the destruction of what we are as well as the creation of a completely different thing, a total innovation."[82] For those readers concerned with questions of normative grounding, this proposition contains important ambiguities (e.g., under what conditions would a "destruction of what we are" or "a total innovation" be normatively desirable?).[83] More significant at present, however, is the appeal to the "we" in this negotiation between unmaking and making-otherwise. Although Foucault resists any easy appeal to community or alliance, there are persistent hints in his late thought that counter-hegemonic possibilities rest upon conditions that are inalienably social. As he maintains, for instance, the emancipatory work of a gay politics cannot be reduced to struggles for rights or legal recognition as formalized, institutional aspirations, no matter how important these institutional safeguards have proven for sexual minorities. Rather, it demands "the creation of new forms of life, relationships, friendships in society, art, culture and so on through our sexual, ethical and political choices."[84] In a more prescriptive mode, Foucault insists that "we have to create our *own* culture We have to *create* culture"—which he glosses to mean "culture in the large sense, a culture that invents ways of relating, types of existence, types of values, types of exchanges between individuals which are really new and are neither the same as, nor superimposed on, existing cultural forms."[85]

Such gestures help to problematize the either/or from which many of the standard challenges have been raised. As detailed above, there is a strain of critical literature that presumes Foucault must construe these arts in staunchly individualistic terms. This is the premise that leads Lois McNay to argue that "Foucault cannot produce a satisfactory answer . . . because his theory of the self prioritizes an isolated individuality, rather than demonstrating how the construction of the self is inextricably bound up in various processes of social interaction."[86] And Kennan Ferguson contends that "what is lacking in Foucault's arts of the self (and, indeed, in Nietzsche's more general aesthetic) is a consideration of how a mechanism of self-fashioning can be broadened to include, or even to form, collective kinds of political assemblies, coalitions, or affiliations."[87] Such readings typically root themselves within Foucault's repeated invocations for a care *of* the self, *by* the self—where other agents are ancillary to the subject's own projects of self-elaboration. This interpretation targets an important thread that runs throughout Foucault's writings.[88] And yet, a nuanced engagement with these late texts and interviews reveals closer ties to the social forms that guide, complicate, or support such experiments.[89] For if we heed Foucault's insistence that the practice of subjectivity is negotiated through *necessarily social* resources,[90] then it follows that these transformative projects likewise require social exemplars, guidance, stimulation, complications, or support if they are to be sustainable.

This intuition is supported by two distinct textual trajectories. To begin with the historical path, Foucault persistently interrogates the self-directed observations, exercises, and tests by which the individual conducts this *askesis* in order to attain a different practice of life. As he proposes, the central question of antiquity is largely presented in a personal vein (i.e., are you taking care of yourself?); and the technologies highlighted systematically tend toward self-reflection (diaries, dream writing, self-chosen tests, etc.). That said, this strongly individuated register is tempered by the related (though seldom noted) insistence: that this care of the self frequently *requires* the direction, insight, or provocation of another. In a 1982 lecture, for instance, Foucault concedes that "in the practice of the self, someone else, the other, is an indispensable condition for the form that defines this practice to effectively attain and be filled by its object. . . . The other is indispensable for the practice of the self to arrive at the self at which it aims."[91] In specific terms, this "someone else" might be the philosophical "master" who aids the subject in negotiating his need interpretations, accessing the true wellsprings of desire, or untangling the thickets of moral epistemology; it may be the community of adherents, dropouts, hippies, or penitents who collaborate to sustain an order of life in stark distinction from the world of the everyday (bearing different practices of pleasure, ownership, belief, or hierarchy); it may simply be a friend (i.e., the *parrhesiastes*) who risks discomfort or rejection in order to criticize the choices or habits of the subject in question.[92] In all such cases, the complication remains the same: if the self is the object of this *askesis* (demanding a committed work of self-surveillance, testing, indulging, observing, or abstaining), the work is not conducted in isolation; rather, these transformative practices are indebted to a range of others who elicit, guide, and cultivate these projects in such a way as to loosen the grip of familiar habits and to support their transformation.[93]

While such passages offer historical complications to the standard interpretation, Foucault's reflections upon contemporary sexual practice contribute most directly to current concerns. To recall the challenge that Foucault poses: a gay counter-politics must press beyond a liberal rights-discourse, where sexual minorities come to be protected by rights that had previously been denied or withheld. Instead, a *culture* must be developed to enable the kinds of relationships, encounters, and couplings that would dislodge normalized patterns of attachment and pleasure. For instance, when queried about marriage rights as a rallying cry for gay politics, Foucault responds by displacing the terms of the question: "we live in a relational world that institutions have considerably impoverished. Society and the institutions which form it have limited the possibility of relationships because a rich relational world would be very complex to manage. We should fight against the impoverishment of the relational fabric."[94] In such moments, a more collaborative dimension of these arts of the self comes to the fore: it is not simply an "I" that must experiment upon itself so as to cultivate a new economy of pleasures or loosen the claims of normalizing technologies; rather, a "we" (defined by a shared refusal of normalizing dynamics) must develop the intersubjective forms through which counter-hegemonic attachments, pleasures, meanings, and forms of sociality could be sustained, developed, and made available.[95]

Such proposals gain substance when set against a prominent model of sexual emancipation: a "coming out" against norms that force subjects to lead (or mimic) a life they cannot recognize as their own.[96] From this vantage point, a politics of sexuality rests in refusing normalizing expectations and resisting the coincidence of the self with the categories by which it has been made socially intelligible.[97] And surely, the importance of this moment cannot be overstated. As Foucault himself suggests, "to say no is the minimum form of resistance. But, of course, at times that is very important. You have to say no as a decisive form of resistance."[98] That said, it would hardly suffice to describe this refusal as a movement of unmitigated liberation, enacted by a subject to finally live his or her "truth" (which had, to this point, been buried, constrained, or repressed). The difficulty is not the theoretical question (i.e., whether there exists some suppressed truth of the subject that can be reclaimed or expressed), but rather a practical concern: once enacted, these refusals may generate attendant forms of danger, violence, or social dislocation. As Cressida Heyes argues, such a practice of "challenging norms is likely to render us less intelligible as integrated subjects; by working successfully against normalization we may ourselves (in some contexts, and, we hope, temporarily) become more marginal, less credible or, most probably, be denied the comfort of those forms of recognition on which we have come to rely for our self-certainty."[99] That is, when normality is the overriding social norm, to depart from its limits is to slip out of the expected circuits of desire, attachment, or pleasure. It is to live in a way that is not fully *legible* within the current topography of personhood. And to inhabit this position is ultimately to court a wide range of sanctions, ranging from employment instability to personal violence, housing discrimination, social banishment, incarceration, and death. These sanctions may be enacted by state authorities (tasked with maintaining standards of virtue, propriety, or national/moral "hygiene") or, perhaps more commonly, be levied by the unofficial authorities of civil society.

One way to understand the ties (if admittedly fumbling and inchoate) between these transformative self-arts and associational forms, then, is through the exposure that attends those who refuse this economy of normality. To live against the norm (whether compulsory straight attachment, or whiteness, or appropriate embodiment)—to live in such a way as to throw into relief its exclusions, denials, and foreclosures—is not simply to confound the classifications of social technicians. Rather, it is to enter a space of danger, threat, and instability. It is to risk being refused by those one took to be closest. It is to court rage and violence from those for whom the norm must remain intact for their own lives to be intelligible.[100] Accordingly, these experiments must be linked into broader collaborations that would allow them to be sustained, supported, protected, and practiced in the face of such repercussions. In terms that are current, these linkages reflect the need to create counter-hegemonic *worlds* that would shelter these experiments from the sanctions they otherwise incur.[101] And such "worlds" likewise perform another crucial labor. Where rhetorics of emancipation often presume that the marginal subject needs only a "lifting of constraints" to flourish, this overlooks a persistent lesson from social practice. As Michael Warner argues: "the sexual cultures of gay men and lesbians are, after all, *cultures* in ways that are often forgotten. . . . They recognize themselves as cultures, with their own knowledges, places, practices, languages, and learned modes of feeling. The naive belief that sex is simply an inborn instinct still exerts its power, but most gay men and lesbians know that the sex they have was not innate nor entirely of their own making, but *learned*—learned by participating, in scenes of talk as well as of fucking."[102] In other words, these experiments do not simply reflect a self that throws off convention and embraces its essence (something that it has kept hidden or masked), but rather draw from a shared reservoir of practices, openings, and counter-knowledge that furnish possibilities to live otherwise than is prepared by hegemonic regimes of health, propriety, and normalcy.

Such insights suggest a more politically generative way to approach Foucault's efforts to link these transformative practices of living to a "culture" or "way of life."[103] Here it is necessary to heed the lessons of subaltern movements—how they persistently forge more *livable* lives by crafting economies of meaning in which they are not legible solely through categories of pathology or lack.[104] These forms of life are founded upon alternative sensibilities, different ways of grappling with hurt or refusal, and different imaginations of the future.[105] Stronger yet, these are collaborative practices through which marginal subjects can *learn* to be other than (a) what they have been to this point, and (b) what has been reflected back to them by hegemonic cultures. Participants in these worlds might learn to perform embodiment in different ways, learn new presentations of the self, learn new languages through which to inhabit the world, or learn new pleasures. Such agents might change their morphology, perform different racialized identities, or tap into a reservoir of experience that could not previously be understood as a viable form of life. They might salvage suppressed traditions, develop new bodily postures, or restage forms of culture that have been elided through colonial practices of compulsory forgetting. And these broader renderings expand beyond the cases of sexual minorities that occupy much of Foucault's late thought. Within the context of the United States, for instance, a transformative politics of blackness has long invested in a similar work of "worlding" so as to furnish alternatives to a dominant white culture. Where some movements for racial equality have pursued a "politics of respectability" or assimilation, radical black activism has persistently staked emancipatory energies on a renewed commitment to what blackness can be and mean when practiced external to the organizing logic of white sociality. Such groups do not only forge networks of educational, nutritional, and economic support to counteract their histories of social dispossession; rather, they have developed a wide range of cultural exemplars, languages, and sensibilities through which blackness could be *practiced* in ways unprepared by a hegemonic culture of whiteness.

To bring this section to a close, there are two important features to note. First, such counter-hegemonic cultures cannot be reduced to "counterpublics" in one familiar sense of the term. There is, after all, a vision of the counterpublic as a social form organized around narratives, testimony, and arguments. In the terms of a deliberative politics, they are organized around the discursive resources that structure these sites of experience. As the foregoing reveals, however, the formation of these relational cultures cannot be reduced to such rationalized terms. Certainly, these radical "ways of life" might offer reflective challenges to hegemonic beliefs, values, and commitments—challenges that might be expressed in literature, discourse, and narratives. Beyond this, however, they offer styles of embodiment, dress, speech, pleasure, attachment, commonality, risk, and loss (among other things). They teach different bodily postures, different ways of loving, different ways of moving, different ways of feeling—and ultimately different ways of being-in-common. Secondly, as Warner reminds us, it is essential to avoid shoehorning these alternative publics into the familiar category of community, along with the organicity that this framework typically carries. Although the lure of this term runs deep, these worlds are typically populated by strangers.[106] They solicit the participation of strange persons, from different places and sites and backgrounds, which means that they are, by definition, fragile. To form and open a world is not to guarantee what directions it will take or what its future might be. It is, in a word, an *experiment* for a different habitation of the world—one that is more risk than guarantee.

* * *

It would be unwise to push this reading too far. The point of these reflections is not to say that Foucault's appeals can be seamlessly translated into Hegelian terms of intersubjectivity or demands for recognition. It is not to say (in some Levinasian fashion) that the Other is at the core of Foucault's transformative politics. Nor is it to say that these arts of selfhood can be mapped without remainder, upon the coalitional commitments of a *praxical* Left. All such assertions would correct one distorted reading by swinging so far in the other direction as to generate just as many errors. Rather, the chapter is meant to highlight what might be termed a minority report in Foucault's thought, overlooked by those who read him too neatly to do justice to his tensions and ambiguities. It is assuredly true that Foucault never dedicated adequate time or energy to elaborating the kinds of "resistance" that he located at the heart of a reconceived social power. He scarcely spells out what he describes as the "years, decades, of work and political imagination [that] will be necessary, work at the grass roots, with the people directly affected, restoring their right to speak."[107] And many concerns toward the individualist register of these "experiments" are surely well-founded, as evinced by the sheer volume of appeals to "an exercise of the self on the self by which one attempts to develop and transform oneself."[108] That said, a more patient reading yields some undertheorized connections between these "arts of the self" and the traditional modes of emancipatory politics. Such arts might not only offer possibilities for a less pathologized practice of selfhood, but they reaffirm the significance of collaborative forms for lives that would depart from normalized patterns of social legibility. The rhetoric of the subject that works on itself—that submits itself to a regimen of testing, observation, and transformative exercise—is tempered by a set of allusions toward partners, communities, and spaces through which these experiments find support, guidance, protection, and provocation. And these gestures resound with a characteristic labor of the subaltern: to generate a *world* in which minoritarian discourses, meanings, histories, and experiences furnish a counter-knowledge that could open sustainable paths for living otherwise.

If many questions remain, they are perhaps different than what is typically taken to be the case. Rather than ask whether there is any intersubjective substance to Foucault's late thought, it may be more accurate and productive to ask just what *kinds* of entanglements are at stake in this transformative politics of the subject. Those approaching Foucault from the perspective of social movements will likely remain frustrated, since he characteristically resists the core commitments of a movement politics. If a social movement might offer the collaborative means to challenge or remake institutions—founded upon different discourses, knowledges, and sensibilities—Foucault nevertheless highlights how they threaten new spaces of normalization and new forms of management by elites or party organizations.[109] In Foucault's terms, the gains that social movements make for a *praxical* Left come at a significant cost: they threaten a "confiscation" of these diffuse, minoritarian energies in favor of programs that pursue "the" aims of the movement in question. For this reason, the collaborative work in these arts of transformation is defined by a persistent negativism—one that resists the temptation to mobilize around some single aim (to which all others will be subordinated), or some shared identity as the "truth" that will make these subjects free and whole and undamaged again.[110]

Accordingly, it is useful to close with greater clarity on some key points. In the broadest possible strokes, it is tempting to say that Foucault's emancipatory arts of the self offer precisely the kind of resources absent from the model sketched in the first chapter. Where Adorno persistently hints that a less violent practice of meaning and encounter could be found by salvaging the aesthetic remainders of reason, he offers precious little to account for how subjects shaped by the "false" society could nevertheless come to adopt different modes of meaning, value, and desire toward the objects they encounter. Though such a stance may have attractive normative potentials, it leaves the reader with significant questions as to how the subject would be able to carve out a space for greater responsiveness within social economies of instrumentality and aggression. And, to render the point with a bit more bite: if Adorno persistently enjoins the subject to take on a stance of critical responsibility, it too often remains a bare assertion, unwilling (or unable) to spell out just how the subject could displace the effects of a social practice that form the subject's wants, values, and desires. It tells the reader *what*, but does not possess the analytic resources to spell out *how* these normative resources could be built into a more sensitive practice of citizenship—or how they could come to reorder motivational economies that have been subjected to the formidable social pedagogies of the "totally administered society."

It is in light of this lacuna that Foucault's "arts" of the self bear critical fruit. If power can insinuate itself at this deep a level—to inflect what subjects want, feel, need, and believe—then it is likewise here that forms of resistance might take root. In a word, Foucault's *askesis* represents something of a missing piece to Adorno's emancipatory gestures; it offers a set of openings to disentangle those normalizing technologies that leave the subject with a life she cannot recognize as meaningfully her own. And yet, to avoid some of the widespread concerns in the literature, this transformative art cannot be reduced to some internal project with all the monastic resonances this typically carries. Rather, in Foucault's more politically sensitive moments, these different habitations of the world—these different engagements with strange lives—rest upon fragile, collaborative efforts by strangers to forge a more livable world. They hinge upon subjects and bodies in common, offering new possibilities and provocations toward a life that before was not thinkable, was not livable, was not practicable.

3

A Machine of Vision

Rancière and the Politics of Sensibility

The work of Jacques Rancière offers a significant complication for the themes considered thus far. To this point, the study has considered a set of arguments over power, sensibility, agency, and aesthetics. And these positions are often challenged in at least two significant directions. Minimally, critics have indicted these concerns for sensibility as a politics of the second-best. By this phrase I mean the following: in these disenchanted times, when revolutionary dreams have failed, we can no longer hope for a politics in the grand style. We can no longer hope for corrupt institutions to be swept away in one revolutionary moment. Instead, normative resources have come to abide within the domain of aesthetics—within those practices of interpretation, sensibility, subjectivity, and feeling that are typically pressed aside by a thin institutionalism. And in this case, the argument takes on an apologetic cast: perhaps these resources are minimal, but they are the best hope remaining, given current technologies of power.

Stronger indictments stem from Walter Benjamin's well-known diagnosis of fascist politics. Here, the sights and sounds and rallies carry citizens away, stoking their passions, leading them to support policies that could not be rationally justified. It is common to make this point through Leni Riefenstahl's work for Nazi Germany, memorializing the fascist spectacle of virile bodies, each of which sheds its individuality to join the unity of the people.[1] These are not citizens who submit institutions to scrutiny and evaluation; rather, they leave behind all that separates them so as to recapture some mystical solidarity or actualize a common destiny. In such cases, it is not just that aesthetic tactics attend or enliven the practice of politics. Rather, spectacle is feared to *substitute* for the work of reflection, dialogue, and deliberation that rests at the heart of a democratic politics. These are citizens inflamed by charismatic speakers and taken in by visions of loss, humiliation, vengeance, or glory. To recall a theme from the introduction of this study, the danger that threatens is the *aestheticization of politics.* And from this premise, Benjamin concludes that the normative task must be to manage these spheres (and the resources they contain) in a different direction. Where fascism hollows out the normative core of political life in favor of spectacle and passion, an emancipatory politics must reconfigure how these domains inform one another. As he charges, "Communism responds by politicizing art."[2]

This terse formulation can, of course, be unpacked beyond specifically communist aims. More broadly, it suggests that the work of the aesthetic is fundamentally ambivalent. While aesthetic means have been used to short-circuit a critical practice of citizenship (and thereby justify projects of state violence), they could likewise be used to expose violence, disclose suppressed truths, memorialize historical wrongs, revalorize defamed social groups, or mobilize agents toward more normatively desirable aims. The details of a politicized art are not significant for current purposes. Of greater importance is the conceptual and normative premise that operates in the background: that the aesthetic and political are distinct spheres that can be fruitfully (or disastrously) brought to bear upon social practice. They can be recombined in ways that yield violence and war; or they can be managed in such a way as to serve an emancipated future. Though what is not in question is that they are intrinsically distinct spheres of experience and value.

In response to these well-worn concerns, Jacques Rancière begins with a stark rejoinder: "there has never been any 'aestheticization' of politics in the modern age, because politics is aesthetic in principle."[3] The justification for this claim will be considered as the chapter proceeds. More urgent at present is to ask how these terms have been defined such that they might occupy this position of indeterminacy (what Gabriel Rockhill terms the "consubstantiality thesis").[4] As earlier chapters have detailed, there is a significant tradition that draws a principled line between these domains. Where the political is meant to address topics of common concern, the aesthetic has long been associated with the idiosyncratic, the personal, or the merely arbitrary. Or, an alternate rendering: where the aesthetic is often construed as an arational domain of sensation, spectacle, play, or pleasure, the political signifies the exchange of rational arguments by which citizens negotiate a shared world. And there are many other ways to figure the distinction, which raises the significant question: given these familiar lines of division, what does it mean to say that these domains are *in principle* founded upon a common ground? Is there a way to do so without dissolving politics into the category of the aesthetic or betraying a basic confusion over the categorial spheres of modernity? Most important for current purposes, then, is to ask how this formula turns upon interrogating the terms upon which the standard opposition is founded, so as to destabilize the conclusions that follow.

There are many paths to these questions in Rancière's thought. One route would address his considerable investment in art practice and what art can do to establish unexpected connections between regimes of experience.[5] Given the interests of this study, however, these reflections on art will be left aside in order to engage the broader constellation of aesthetic themes that run throughout his political thought: perception, sense-experience, audibility, and visuality. For instance, one of Rancière's central concepts is what he terms the "partition of the perceptible" (*partage du sensible*) that exists in agonistic tension with politics. And elsewhere, he describes politics as a "machine of vision."[6] Accordingly, this chapter will take its cue from the questions these formulations tend to evoke: what exactly does it mean to say that politics is bound up with economies of vision or sound? In what sense can perception or sensibility constitute a terrain for power or agency? Over the course of this chapter, I will propose that Rancière helps to address at least one of the concerns that has haunted this study: that this aesthetic turn ultimately reflects the fate of politics within a time of devitalization and disillusionment—a situation in which subjects seek to change themselves once they have lost faith in changing the institutions that form (or deform) their lives. As the following will elaborate, Rancière's thought offers a different way to construe an aesthetic register to politics—one that demands a strong investment in worldly action to remake the world in more egalitarian directions. And yet, the chapter will ultimately argue that his vision would benefit from taking these aesthetic resources more seriously if it is to deliver upon the substantive democratic aims at its heart.

* * *

Approaching perception as a vehicle of power has a venerable history within the Left imagination. Indeed, there is a well-known Marxian trope that figures ideology as an inverted form of vision—one that mistakes cause for effect and contingent social formations as natural, immutable features of the world.[7] And such concerns are not limited to this axis of truth and falsity. In the *1844 Manuscripts,* for instance, Marx claims that "the forming of the five senses is a labor of the entire history of the world down to the present."[8] That is, historically and socially specific modes of consumption, labor, and production inflect the subject's sensible habitation of the world. Senses that might be misrecognized as "natural" (i.e., inscribed within some immutable facts of biology) are forged by a wide range of material and cultural practices. And this mutability gives rise to more politically thick anxieties. To recall some themes from the Frankfurt School, this subject might be saddled with "false" needs that lead him to pursue consumer systems of reward rather than his rational interests.[9] Or the modes of consumption characteristic of mass culture might generate the kind of subject required by authoritarian fascism—one who does not participate in the production of social meaning, but is a passive recipient of messages that come from on high.[10]

As familiar as these charges may be, Rancière offers a different approach to this constellation of power, perception, and sensibility. To revisit the passage cited above:

> There is thus an "aesthetics" at the core of politics that has nothing to do with Benjamin's discussion of the "aestheticization of politics" specific to the "age of the masses." If the reader is fond of analogy, aesthetics can be understood in a Kantian sense. . . . It is a delimitation of spaces and times, of the visible and the invisible, of speech and noise, that simultaneously determines the place and the stakes of politics as a form of experience. Politics revolves around what is seen and what can be said about it, around who has the ability to see and the talent to speak, around the properties of spaces and the possibilities of time.[11]

One path to this linkage of politics and perception, then, is through a Kantian lens. At stake is not perception as a brute given, but as an act that constitutes (in negotiation with the contents of sensation) the shape that experiential contents will take. And where this analogy begins on epistemological terrain, Rancière is not ultimately interested in some value-neutral apparatus that articulates the real into cognitive categories (space, time, number, etc.), but rather in "the place and the stakes of politics as a form of experience." This means that the perception in question addresses what can be seen or heard (or, conversely, not-seen or not-heard) in the perceptual economy that structures social space and possibilities. To put this "partition of the sensible"[12] into Rancière's peculiar idiolect: "I call the distribution of the sensible the system of self-evident facts of sense perception that simultaneously discloses the existence of something in common and the delimitations that define the respective parts and positions within it."[13]

As with much of Rancière's writing, this language may seem obscure and socially underdetermined. To arrive at some more concrete insights, then, two implications can be noted. First, it will be useful to press upon a phrase within the passage cited above: "politics revolves around what is seen and what can be said about it." One way to understand this phrase is through a classic liberal device: the public/private distinction. What can be considered meaningfully "public" in this framework is recognized as an object of debate, scrutiny, and solicitude; it is, in Rancière's terms "what can be seen" within this articulation of social space. What is private, on the other hand, is taken off the table of public deliberation. It can neither be the basis for authoritative public claims (in Rawlsian terms), nor can it be subjected to regulation through public norms or authorities. And this partitioning yields more politically substantive questions upon recognizing how it sets into motion consequences that do not weigh upon all alike. Consider, for instance, a familiar challenge from feminist quarters: the systematic harms suffered by female bodies (uncompensated labor, acceptable violence, marital rape) are tied to how domestic life has long been categorized as private and thus blocked from scrutiny or regulation. In this sense, the work of "partitioning" turns upon delimiting what is seen as the "proper" scope of politics and what, conversely, lies beyond its limits.[14] As Rancière proposes, "traditionally, in order to deny the political quality of a category—workers, women and so on—all that was required was to assert that they belonged to a 'domestic' space that was separated from public life, one from which only groans or cries expressing suffering, hunger or anger could emerge, but not actual speech demonstrating shared *aesthesis*."[15]

This strategy of partitioning works at another register, however, that stems from the taxonomy of roles and possibilities it sets out within social space—"the manner in which a relation between a shared common and the distribution of exclusive parts is determined in sensory experience."[16] To mitigate the obscurity of the formulation, it can again be negotiated through precedents within the political tradition—in this case, Rancière's reading of Plato. It would not require great feats of interpretation to propose that Plato's *Republic* offers a hierarchical social order, founded upon a logic of natural types—bodies inscribed with certain capabilities, each of which predisposes them toward certain social roles. In this sense, the "partition of the sensible" reflects those inscriptions of power that divide the polis into natural types (farmers, merchants, philosophers, warriors, etc.), only certain of which possess the natural capacity to lead, and are thus authorized to engage in the work of politics.[17] It is not simply that subjects are equipped with certain talents, but that they *must* play these roles to avoid disrupting the order of justice upon which all depend.[18] Where these reflections might threaten little more than a lesson in the history of philosophy (one that was idiosyncratic even at the moment of its writing), Rancière insists that it symptomatizes one of the abiding features of an everyday "machine of vision"—to regularize a contingent assignment of social roles, naturalize the privileges or burdens they carry, and delimit their social possibilities within the bounds deemed "appropriate" for agents of this type (gender, ethnic grouping, wealth, etc.).[19] To expand this diagnosis beyond the history of philosophy, it is useful to think of how a naturalized instinct for care has long been used to justify women's "place" within the domestic sphere (an assignment that not only diminishes their public standing, but also tasks female bodies with uncompensated and unrecognized forms of social labor).

From these brief observations, there are some preliminary ways to pursue the thesis that opens this chapter: the aesthetic and the political share a common ground that binds them more tightly than is conveyed by the charge of aestheticization. On a quick read of this formula, it would be easy to dismiss Rancière as a thinker unwilling to acknowledge the history of modernity, in which these spheres have come to be distinguished through a "social learning process."[20] The brief reconstruction to this point, however, suggests a line of thought that is more critically rich. To say that "politics is aesthetic in principle" is not to dissolve one category into the other; nor does it bring one to bear upon the other (thus conceding the premise that they are categorically distinct, but might yet inform one another in carefully managed ways). The aim is, instead, to highlight a ground common to these spheres, elided by rationalist efforts to eviscerate politics of its sensible dimension. In brute terms, both rest upon a symbolic constitution of social space and social possibilities—what Rancière terms the "systems of relations between *doing*, *seeing*, *saying* and *sensing*."[21]

The point could be put more precisely yet. These social economies of perception (i.e., partitions of the sensible) are ultimately action-guiding. They do not rest upon sensation in the abstract, but rather delimit, expand, or fix perceptions of who belongs where, what can meaningfully be challenged, who deserves what goods, or what represents an overreach beyond one's proper place. And importantly, these delimitations cannot be reduced to a "thin" model of ideology—beliefs that can be shuttled into the familiar epistemological categories of "true" or "false" (e.g., who really benefits; what is really natural, etc.).[22] Rather, the "aesthetic" dimension of this diagnosis gains its depth from how these judgments settle below the reflective level of belief, into the sensible resources by which the subject *perceives* the world and the order by which each part belongs in its appropriate place (a perceptual economy that is often thought to rest outside of politics). It is to the wide-ranging implications of this diagnosis that the chapter will now turn.

* * *

From the foregoing, there are a number of ways to pursue this aesthetic framework for politics. Minimally, it demands an expansion of political inquiry beyond institutions, laws, or treaties—and instead into the pre-reflective habits (themselves inscribed by a committed social pedagogy) that condition the meaning that bodies, spaces, and practices will have. This is politics *as* an aesthetics, drawing upon the full resources of the ancient term *aisthēsis*. Secondly, the argument takes a strong distance from much that is recognized as political philosophy—those doctrines concerned with who deserves what, when, and how. According to Rancière, this distributive approach reflects not politics, but the aims of "policing": to fix the order and movement of bodies, while legitimating these assignments by means of a symbolic labor.[23] "Policed" social assignments are not described as such because they are managed or enforced by the armed wing of the state. They do not rest upon the dogs, the tanks, the fire hoses, or "the truncheon blows of the forces of law and order" mobilized against subordinate populations. The basis for "police" order lies instead with the perceived nature of the agents or topics in question.[24] Or, as Rancière proposes, "the police is not a social function but a symbolic constitution of the social."[25] A telling example here is the trope that was deployed against civil rights activism within the United States—the rhetorical privilege extended to those who "knew their place" (i.e., those who obeyed and didn't cause trouble for the white supremacist order that reproduced black domination). To "know one's place" in this sense meant to obey the limits allotted for members of that role and commit such limits to one's own horizon of possibilities.

As clear as these gestures may be, they gain normative bite by asking whether there is a meaningful *politics* at stake in these perceptual orders—or whether this "aesthetic" concern for sensibility and power ultimately reduces to a sociological insistence upon the symbolic formation of role-performances within social space. Some answers can be found by interrogating Rancière's insistence that such perceptual economies do not simply assign agents to certain roles; nor do they simply permit some forms of inquiry while blocking others from the conversations of justice. Rather, they commit an important "wrong." And this charge becomes more precise by heeding his insistence that there are significant differences between "police" orders. To say that social orders persistently allot a legible place to their members (along with the relevant limits and expectations) is not to say that all can be evaluated similarly in terms of the normative possibilities they open or foreclose.[26] To understand the "wrong" that agitates politics proper, then, it is necessary to dig more fully into the implications of these sensory economies.

> Before the debts that place people who are of no account in a relationship of dependence on the oligarchs, there is the symbolic distribution of bodies that divides them into two categories: those that one sees

> and those that one does not see, those who have a logos—memorial speech, an account to be kept up—and those who have no logos, those who really speak and those whose voice merely mimics the articulate voice to express pleasure and pain.[27]

In the most basic sense, this passage suggests a brute, phenomenological point. For a perceptual framework to make certain things visible, it must diminish the visibility or richness of other things. In ocular terms, the precision and vibrancy of the primary object are secured while secondary objects blur and fade into the background. Or, to push these perceptual themes into a more richly political register, at least one of the dynamics that Rancière highlights is how regimes of visibility perform a similar labor within the field of social reproduction. Certain groups (typically those that have attained social hegemony) enjoy heightened prominence within the standing economy of social esteem, while others are devalued or diminished, consigned to the dustbin of history or eclipsed by the imperatives of capital.

At this level, the analysis reverberates with a range of theorists who interrogate how power organizes a differential calculus of visibility, even when official normative doctrines maintain an equal worth or dignity for all. It is not, after all, new to claim that subordinate or marginal social groups have been rendered invisible within social space. They are perhaps those systematically elided from the representations of popular media. Or they are prevented from mobilizing through policies that criminalize their assembly. Or again, they may be sequestered in geographic terms due to zoning restrictions, segregationist housing covenants, or the far-reaching effects of income clustering.[28] They do not *show up* in the ways reserved for groups privileged in cultural, racial, or economic terms. And to add a necessary wrinkle, it may be that the core "wrong" is not simply *in*-visibility (as if the question could be put in binary terms). As Wendy Brown has argued, for many marginal groups, increased prominence could well lead to heightened violence, incarceration, or the termination of employment—and thus less visibility might well be preferable.[29] Perhaps a more nuanced way to put the point: within economies of vision structured by the values of hegemonic groups, certain populations come to be hypervisible. They figure disproportionately in social conversations about where "things have gone wrong" or where the seeds of social or moral decay might be located. These agents become visible as dirty, loathsome, dangerous, listless, uncontrollable, backward, lazy, or undisciplined. And such judgments are not based within direct acquaintance or biography, but are read right off the surfaces of these troubled bodies (that is, bodies *made* troubled through social frameworks of vision).[30]

And yet, these arguments do not quite capture Rancière's challenge. The "wrong" he identifies is not a diminished citizenship in the abstract; nor is it simply a dishonored symbolic status, as proposed by neo-Hegelian theorists of recognition.[31] A richer engagement would address the neologism that runs throughout his writings: the part of those who have no part (*la part des sans-part*). In a symptomatic passage, Rancière argues that "it is through the existence of this part of those who have no part, of this nothing that is all, that the community exists as a political community—that is, as divided by a fundamental dispute, by a dispute to do with the counting of the community's parts even more than of their 'rights.'"[32] This attenuated form of social membership expresses a wide set of meanings. At one level, it suggests a concern for social marginality: those who participate within communal life and sustain its ongoing operation, yet are not included (or not fully so) within its core protections or benefits. This status becomes more politically fraught, however, by revisiting the passage cited above, where relationships of visibility are mapped upon a further line of social division: "those who have a logos . . . and those who have no logos, those who really speak and those whose voice merely mimics the articulate voice to express pleasure and pain." This imbrication of vision and voice lends greater democratic heft to the argument. To revisit a theme introduced earlier, one way of curtailing democratic debate is by classifying topics as private, thus shielding them from evaluation or intervention. Not only are these topics taken off the agenda of public conversation, but this withdrawal is likewise meant to be non-contestable. Another closure on democratic speech stems from those dynamics marked in the first chapter of this study: how hegemonic grammars of debate constrain what can (or cannot) be authoritatively claimed within official deliberative forums. For instance, much recent scholarship has tracked the political abjection of "the underclass" to a neoliberal reconstitution of the civic vocabulary—where appeals for the traditional entitlements of the social state persistently cast the speaker in a parasitic light, unable to meet the requirements for full civic standing.[33]

When read in a robust sense, however, Rancière's diagnosis reaches beyond (a) this delimitation of topics or spaces, or (b) those political vocabularies that leave some speakers lacking authoritative warrants for their claims. The deeper concern isolates how such operations result in untoward consequences for those who hope to present their needs and interests within the contested business of civic life. In a word, the difficulty at hand ultimately concerns *speakers*—who can count as such or, conversely, those who cannot inhabit this status within the symbolic economy of citizenship. As Rancière proposes, '"the people' is the name, the form of subjectification, of this immemorial and perennial wrong through which the social order is symbolized by dooming the majority of speaking beings to the night of silence or to the animal noise of voices expressing pleasure or pain."[34] Such moments must be read with care. It is not, after all, uncommon to argue that a democratic harm occurs when certain populations are silenced. Such groups are blocked from the deliberative forums in which policies are crafted or public opinion forged, and in this silencing they lose an essential component of democratic citizenship. A more nuanced reading comes clear, however, when framed by prominent efforts to root democratic politics within a framework of communication—more specifically, the school of deliberative politics associated with Jürgen Habermas. Although this study has periodically fastened upon Habermasian themes, what is most significant at present is the normative premise for a deliberative politics: that emancipatory resources are located within the transcendental conditions that speakers assume when they communicate toward a non-coerced consensus.[35] More specifically, the consent necessary to secure the legitimacy of laws and policies will be rationally defensible if (and only if) it has been generated through the free, unfettered discussion of all members.[36] Only when all parties have equal chances to participate, raise concerns, place new topics on the agenda, or challenge the norms of adjudication, will the outcomes of these conversations meet the bar of democratic legitimacy.

It is against this background that Rancière's linkage of vision, voice, speech, and noise takes on particular bite. Where deliberative models take the status of speaker as a first premise from which democratic conclusions can be deduced, this role must be viewed in more socially thick terms. To be a speaker (in political terms) is not a fact inscribed within some human capacity for language or communication; it is rather a *political status* that may be fostered, damaged, or suppressed by the perceptual conditions of social space.[37] This is what leads Rancière to propose that deliberative theory "presupposes . . . that both the interlocutors and the objects about which they speak are preconstituted; whereas, from my perspective, there can be political exchange only when there isn't such a preestablished agreement—not only, that is, regarding the objects of debate but also *regarding the status of the speakers themselves*."[38] To unpack this formulation, the speech situation is never an unmediated encounter between two subjects; and neither is it a case where positions can be separated from the speakers who present them. The practice of discourse is instead negotiated through perceptual economies that amplify the speech of some and render others trivial, whining, nothing, or nonsense. This lack of "seeing" renders the speech of the non-part not wholly absent, but something that approximates howls or groans or (more broadly put) noise. And it is necessary to make a further qualification. Such closures on the status of "speaker" are rooted more broadly than matters of individual character or beliefs (e.g., a racist who refuses to listen to minority appeals). Rather, they stem from socially manufactured conditions that de-authorize the claims of some, even when they are not barred from the conversations of politics. These agents may produce discourse—and may have access to the appropriate discursive forums—yet their claims do not trouble hegemonic groups or interests, no matter how cogent or well-formulated they may be.[39] Here, one might recognize the arguments of the urban poor, challenging the defunding of social services; the claims of homosexuals during the AIDS crisis, appealing for public investment to combat a disease perceived in moralized terms of sin or sexual (ab)normality; the claims of indigenous populations, contesting the dispossession of their land by globalized, corporate interests; or the claims of black communities, challenging the deployment of an increasingly militarized police force (itself tasked with some "war" against the pathologies thought to reside within communities of color).

This rhetorical ambivalence between vision and voice, then, is meant to highlight the distinctly political status of speech. Because certain agents are not *seen* as political equals (as fully worthy, as full members, as fully rational, as fully deserving, as full contributors, etc.), they are not *heard* as legitimate claimants to core political goods.[40] On this point, it is necessary to be more sensitive than is conveyed by Rancière's own hyperbolic critical language. At stake is not necessarily those who have no speech or no civic standing (e.g., the slave in antiquity; or women, when only males qualify as citizens). More accurately, the *sans-part* renders the marginality of those agents authorized to speak within forums of adjudication, citizenship, or will-formation—but whose questions will not matter, whose reasons will not be counted as such, whose challenges will be translated into terms that hollow them of force, and who will be answered in terms that do nothing to transform the conditions they find objectionable. In terms offered by Sara Ahmed, they may simply be viewed as "willful" subjects—those who do not understand the "proper" circuits of authority or desert.[41] Like children, they do not understand what is best for them; they do not consider the good of the community; nor do they request according to accepted standards of propriety, desert, or authority. Accordingly, their speech can be tuned out, dismissed, or translated into different terms by "those who know better."[42]

From this diagnosis arise significant questions for the concerns of this study: if these tactics of disqualification take strongly aesthetic form, then how could a meaningful politics be situated upon the same sensible terrain? How (to evoke the formulation with which the chapter began) is it possible to say that "politics is aesthetic in principle" when these economies of vision and sensation have been explicitly indicted as counter-political? In the most brutely practical sense, what kind of agency is available to those who stammer, roar, groan, or howl?

* * *

As those familiar with Rancière's work will be aware, there is a short answer available. If the core "wrong" of social orders rests in how they deny equal standing to some, then politics (in the strict sense) is the activity by which the *sans-part* performs an equality that is withheld in material practice. As Rancière puts this point: "politics exists when the natural order of domination is interrupted by the institution of a part of those who have no part."[43] Broadly put, political agency is proleptic; it is what happens when equality is presupposed by this marginal population and performed within an inegalitarian economy of roles and possibilities. It is not a question of extending protections or goods to those who presently lack them (conducted by parties with the authority to dispense these benefits "from above"), but a rearticulation of equality, conducted *by* those who have no social warrant for the status they claim through their acts.[44] And it is useful to make a further distinction. Where liberal theorists endorse equality as the basis for a justified social order, Rancière insists that it is neither a first premise that demands only preservation, nor can it be an accomplished state where human beings finally live in peace and fellowship.[45] The equality at the heart of politics is that which erupts against the delimitations of the police order, and is thus always in process—conducted against specific closures and exclusions. It is evinced by the disenfranchised who show up at the polls when they are not authorized to participate in this ritual of citizenship; likewise, it is staged by the workers who "reclaim" locked factories to demand the wages they are owed or to contest a decision-making structure in which they have had no meaningful say.

Such insurgent moments help to flesh out the insistence that "politics is aesthetic in principle." If not-mattering is produced by conditions under which the speech of some is sapped of authority, then radical political agency must unsettle who counts as a political subject and what can meaningfully be seen as matters of justice: "political activity is whatever shifts a body from the place assigned to it or changes a place's destination. It makes visible what had no business being seen, and makes heard a discourse where once there was only place for noise."[46] At the most familiar level, these appeals evoke a point from the history of democratic politics: radical agency often aims to politicize—to reclassify spaces and activities so that they are *seen* as bound up with compulsory rights and protections.[47] This trajectory is well illustrated by feminist strategies to have nonconsensual sexual forms (no matter the spaces or partners involved) accepted as a kind of violence, and the word "no" a central pivot in the normative economy of violence, gender, and bodily integrity. Before these arguments could be heard as authoritative, there was first required a somatic expansion of personhood—a recognition of how the gendered body (or, increasingly, the transgendered body) suffers heightened risks and vulnerability—and an extension of these questions into spaces previously located beyond the reach of politics: the bedroom, the back seat, or the workplace. Only by transforming this economy of vision could such acts and practices be seen as rightfully within the parameters of justice, capable of mobilizing the reparative sanctions of social institutions.

And the link can be expanded by interrogating the relationship between this ocular language and the privilege accorded to speech within much contemporary political thought. To consider one of Rancière's examples, when Rosa Parks refused to move from her seat, was she making a claim in discursive terms? Or was her embodied presence itself a kind of claim that problematized a set of norms regarding equality, corporeality, authority, and the geography of power?[48] A more expansive way to read Rancière's appeals to vision, then, would highlight the challenge it poses to a thin discursivism in prominent schools of democratic theory. Where deliberative theorists privilege the exchange of reasons within a speech community, this emphasis tends to miss one of the persistent objectives of radical political agency: (a) to problematize these overlooked boundaries between the linguistic and the perceptual, and (b) to interrupt how the latter inflects, opens, or diminishes the former.[49] The category of the *sans-part* helps to give this point more bite. Political claimants are not simply disembodied sources of reasons that meet and clash in some space where the "unforced force of the better argument" will prevail; and no matter the cognitivist leanings of much deliberative theory, the logos cannot be purified of those extra-linguistic contexts that inform, guide, constrain, and provoke the conversations of civil society. Rather, claims emit from bodies that are raced, classed, and marked by economies of social meaning. Speakers may be marked by calloused hands, by counter-normative practices of desire, by clothing deemed inappropriate, by limbs that do not work according to normalized patterns of function, by shades of skin or the kink of hair. And thus the claims of voice are contaminated by the meaning of these bodies within a hierarchically structured system of value.[50] If this is the case, then a more egalitarian economy of speech requires something other than speaking more persuasively or justifying one's demands to one's fellow citizens. It might first require that one's audience be forced to *see* differently—to see the claimant as a bearer of meaningful reasons in the first place—and only then might authority be recognized within what may have previously been whining or growling or purposeless noise.

These considerations help to distinguish Rancière's argument from some superficially similar approaches. For instance, the persistent appeal to visual metaphors might seem to repeat a familiar situationist position: in order to contest systems of social power, the task is to dislocate common forms of reading and viewing and feeling the world.[51] To do so, it is necessary to use extra-discursive means that trouble citizens at levels they cannot file away in the terms of everyday rationality or the regime of perception that such rationality guides.[52] That said, an abstract language of "disruption" does not do justice to how politics acts upon standing economies of speech and noise. Politics in this sense does not simply extend scrutiny to more areas of social reproduction; nor can it be reduced to a situationist effort to suspend the everyday order of rules, expectations, and satisfactions. More broadly, such agency "introduces into the community of speaking beings some who were not hitherto of its number."[53] In this sense, the work of democratic praxis is not to offer a disruption of the sensible field in principle, as if any such intervention were equivalent in value. Rather, democratic agency aims to introduce a new kind of political *subject*—one who attains the position of full speech (if provisional and fragile) that could not be imagined within the current topography of social roles.[54]

This point takes on greater heft in light of the previous chapter—more specifically, Foucault's effort to negotiate emancipatory politics through similar terms.[55] Where both theorists privilege *the subject* as an axis of political agency, Rancière sidesteps both the reflexive path (i.e., how subjects negotiate their relationship to social norms) and the familiar gambit of identity politics (i.e., that groups should be respected or valued on the basis of the identity categories they happen to inhabit). His appeal to subjectification (*subjectivation*) instead targets how political agency destabilizes the standing regime of social assignments, and thus generates possibilities that were previously unavailable within that order of roles, powers, and entitlements. As he proposes, a radical politics "disrupts the way in which bodies fit their functions and destinations. What it produces is not rhetorical persuasion about what must be done. Nor is it the framing of a collective body. It is a multiplication of connections and disconnections that reframe the relation between bodies, the world they live in and the way in which they are 'equipped' to adapt to it."[56] On this point, it is useful to recall a persistent example in Rancière's thought: the politics of labor. A textbook account would emphasize how the conditions of labor (wages, hours, structures of supervision, technologies of work, and so forth) have come to be accepted as political matters and therefore as subject to collective regulation and remediation, rather than merely private agreements between employer and worker. While such gains are significant, the history of labor politics likewise acts upon a different register entirely: to have the worker perceived *as* a political subject who can speak of labor in terms of compulsory, shared norms—an authoritative site of discourse that was not prepared by previous economies of mattering.[57] To tweak a formulation by Samuel Chambers, this irruption of the worker into the space of politics is prepared by a *desubjectivation* that unsettles the social meaning allotted for labor and the bodies that bear its forces.[58]

In the broadest sense, then, politics does not speak in the name of preexistent groups (whether this carries the name of "women" or "laborers"), nor does it simply inject marginal voices, already coherent in their meaning and interests, into social conversations (according to the familiar terms of interest-group pluralism).[59] Rather, in transforming a given social topography, so too does political agency transform the meaning of these insurgent agents. As glossed by Todd May, "to engage in democratic agency is not to discover a subject of politics; it is to create one."[60] That is, agents become "subjects" in this technical sense by acting in noisy excess of the possibilities allotted for them, thus performing a social position unprepared by the current articulation of political space.[61]

To elaborate this moment of excess, it will be helpful to consider a recent episode from emancipatory practice. In 2013, the state of California witnessed a collective action that spread throughout the California penal system. The inmates housed at Pelican Bay State Penitentiary (one of the "supermax" prisons, designed to warehouse those deemed most hardened or dangerous) managed to organize a hunger strike from within the confines of the Isolation Unit—a strike that then spread to over 30,000 prisoners across the state. The protests ranged from the use of long-term solitary confinement to the quality of prison food to the procedures and criteria on the basis of which prisoners are assigned to the segregation unit. The strike itself raised many questions. For instance, the problem of association: how the coordinators (many classified as heads or members of rival prison gangs) set aside their tensions over race, territory, and power in order to manage a broad-scale insurrection. Or the pragmatic question: how these agents were able to collaborate within the spatial conditions of "short corridor"—where inmates are held in isolation for twenty-three hours of the day, and permitted out of their cells to exercise under similar conditions of isolation.[62] For present purposes, however, it is necessary to ask how this episode resonates with the questions raised by Rancière. From the hints raised above, a quick conclusion is possible: this hunger strike reveals how political claiming can be performed through non-discursive forms—in this case, the intentional withering of the body in a space far removed from the agora or the plaza. Alternately, Lisa Guenther has read the action along Arendtian lines: as an effort to restage the conditions for a meaningfully human life (i.e., a world of shared speech and action) when the use of isolation policies has stripped away these intersubjective supports.[63] The concerns of this chapter, however, call attention to a different framework for analysis: the perceptual economy by which the incarceration state conditions who may be a claimant at all.

The walls of the prison can, of course, be reduced to brutely physical terms. These walls denote the dividing line between two different spaces: the space of liberty and the space of confinement. Within this space, animality is contained and punishment is enacted for liberty that has ostensibly been misused. And yet, the symbolic function of the prison is rather more involved: this institution warehouses the people who *do not matter.* They are dissolute, defective, or broken. They cannot master their appetites. They have broken the social compact that the good and proper observe. They are not to be pitied, for they have disqualified themselves from the benefits of civic life. And thus, the walls of the prison perform an important communicative function: these are the people who have forfeited their right to speak in the binding idiom of citizenship. They cannot *make* claims regarding the conditions under which they live. Their possessions, resources, movements, and privileges are granted, withheld, or removed by authorities that admit of no appeal or negotiation. Within the United States, this symbolic function is redoubled by a policy regime that actively strips citizen rights (voting, housing, social insurance, educational funding, etc.) long after the sentence has been fulfilled and the debt paid for their transgressions.[64] From this vantage point, there is a different way to read the act of refusal that emerged from Pelican Bay. This large-scale mobilization did something more than raise a specific set of claims regarding the conditions of incarceration; and it did something more than identify isolation practices as a concern from the vantage point of human rights or constitutional protections. More than this, the hunger strike aimed to disrupt the sensible topography of citizenship, according to which "we" (the good, the law-abiding, the upstanding) know who matters and who does not—who can speak on which topics in which forums—and who offers nothing that can be recognized as a claim at all. The action ultimately generated a site of speech that did not previously exist within deliberations over how these bodies should be managed, disciplined, and regulated. For Rancière's account of politics, this moment is crucial. At stake is not simply the need to permit these prisoners channels through which they can speak of their situations in their own words (as pursued in Foucault's prison activism); rather, the task is to disrupt the symbological framework through which they could be subjects *in the first place*, making authoritative claims to rights, entitlements, and citizenship under conditions in which they have been stripped of this standing.

From this interlude, some more robust conclusions are possible regarding the linkage of aesthetics and politics. Such a politics cannot be reduced to specific claims or requests; and its claims do not simply take distributional form—to have more of the goods that have been enjoyed by other groups or agents. Deeper yet, political agency lodges an intervention within the social economy of roles, assignments, and limits that govern the authoritative production of speech. In terms proposed by Bonnie Honig, such cases evince "illegitimate demands made by people with no standing to make them, a story of people so far outside the circle of who 'counts' that they cannot make claims within the existing frames of claim making."[65] Where this formulation might seem to founder upon an insuperable contradiction, the paradox isolates an essential register of democratic agency. Such efforts to disrupt invidious dynamics of speech and noise do something more than raise new or different topics for public conversations; ultimately, they perform a reflexive intervention within the scene of politics. These agents *do* what was not previously a social possibility; they insert themselves into an economy of speech that had no place for them. And by unsettling the established order of bodies, spaces, norms, practices, and words these subjects ultimately take on a meaning they could not have possessed in advance.[66]

* * *

Though quick and brutal, the foregoing captures the heart of Rancière's insistence that there is a fundamentally aesthetic dimension to politics. These disruptions of seeing mean a disordering of democratic space—what can be seen, who can be heard, and what can be expected within the everyday economy of social roles.[67] In his own terms, politics "invent[s] the scene upon which spoken words may be audible, in which objects may be visible, and individuals themselves may be recognized."[68] And yet the phenomenological richness of this approach should not obscure the critical questions that it leaves unresolved.

For instance, if the foregoing captures the sole kind of activity that counts as politics, then it is easy to understand why Rancière concedes that it "happens very little or rarely."[69] And, by extension, one can readily appreciate the reservations as to whether he has unduly constrained what counts as political in this strong sense, or what the stakes of this narrowing might be. As Peter Hallward has argued, for instance, this "fugitive" politics may lack resources to theorize the slow, patient work (e.g., tabling, petitions, door-to-door conversations, mobilization, strategy sessions, phone trees, meetings, alliance-formation, photocopying, raising bail money, and so forth) necessary to keep such gains and inscribe them in a more egalitarian institutional sphere.[70] To fill out this reservation, it is useful to return to an example introduced earlier: the oft-cited (though typically undertheorized) case of Rosa Parks. Where Parks's action has been drafted into the pantheon of radical political moments, critical discussions persistently tear it from its historical context and instead treat it as a heroic act of individual refusal. As Holloway Sparks reminds us, Parks's action was not some singular moment, unprepared by social networks of resistance, and neither was she the only (or first) individual to perform this act of refusal; rather, it was the culmination of an extended campaign with regard to the Montgomery bus system—one that entailed a committed grassroots organization, media campaigns, and legal assistance.[71] And it is this unglamorous work of preparation, education, and organization that too often tends to disappear within Rancière's tendency to privilege the "headline" cases of political agency—those rare moments of upheaval, insubordination, or refusal that seem to transcend context, setting, or history.

Critics such as Lois McNay and Ella Myers press this concern in a slightly different direction—that Rancière may fail to acknowledge another significant lesson of a Left history: what is to be done once the dust settles from these spectacular, headline moments. More specifically, how can these provisional gains be built into the institutions that structure the day-to-day exercise and management of power?[72] Here the charge identifies an overbid that saps Rancière's thought of important resources. Even if institutional power generates its own forms of regulation, de-democratization, and disempowerment, it might nevertheless serve emancipatory aims: to build these fragile gains into a more equal, less violent *reality* for subjects who require protection from elite parties, the expansionist imperatives of capital, or everyday violence against the different. In McNay's terms, Rancière ultimately stumbles upon a "quasi-mystical notion of the political [that] has no sense of the importance of working from within the system to create conditions for greater equality, nor of how to sustain counter-hegemonic political challenge beyond the initial moment of demand."[73]

There are many moments in Rancière's texts that complicate this "evental" reading.[74] In the space that remains, however, I hope to press a different set of concerns: not the material-institutional features left out by his definition of politics, but rather some unresolved difficulties regarding what he borrows from the aesthetic—and significantly, what he leaves behind. More specifically, if Rancière maintains that the task of political agency is to establish "an obligation to hear" (*une obligation d'entendre*) what was previously dismissed as noise, then generating such an obligation encounters significant difficulties when measured against the full range of conditions that structure the sensible arena of politics.[75] At the very least, it is necessary to ask where such an obligation comes from and what grounds its compulsory power. As the critical reception demonstrates, Rancière's model of praxis resonates strongly within debates over agency and emancipation—from immigration movements (Honig), to the *sans-papiers* (Schaap), to European chocolatiers (Panagia), to the recent "plaza movements" of democratization (Prentoulis, Thomassen), to queer activism, demanding recognition of counter-normative forms of attachment (Chambers).[76] And yet, this widespread interest persistently leaves unasked how such interventions are taken up, engaged, or refused within these agonistic reconfigurations of democratic life. Or, in terms offered by Aletta Norval, what goes uninterrogated is how these openings can be "inscribed" more broadly through social space by those who witness and undergo their provocations while "occupying privileged position within the extant order."[77]

This rejoinder can be pushed in a more focused direction by taking seriously Rancière's own rendering: "Political argumentation is . . . addressed by a subject qualified to argue, over an identified object, to an addressee [*à un destinaire*] who is required to see the object and to hear the argument that he 'normally' has no reason either to see or to hear."[78] From this rough constellation of themes follow some important difficulties. Does the requirement to see and hear anew proceed solely from the insurrectionary activity of the non-part or is a contribution to be made by those who have thus far failed to see these agents or hear their demands? Is this "addressee" to be construed as a (potential) participant in these transformative moments or must it be read in the passive case, interpellated (in some quasi-automatic fashion) into this role through acts of contestation? In more pointed terms, is there a *politics* of reception that might assist to reconfigure the space of communication, or alternately, that might refuse these disruptive moments, divert them from their intended course, or re-actualize them in unanticipated ways?[79]

To focus on the core point, it is necessary to take seriously how these interventions enter into the sensible field of citizenship. Such challenges might expand what is visible to the lens of justice. They might reconfigure the evaluative economy that conditions whether acts are perceived as injustice, accident, abuse of power, the just deserts of the wicked, or brute necessity. They might problematize those histories or accomplishments that once filled a community with pride. They might expose uncomfortable valences of privilege or unsettle long-standing narratives about "who we are" as a polity (or likewise, who counts as part of the "we" in question). And yet, to revisit a point developed in the first chapter of this study, a staple of aesthetic theory is that this action is never one-sided. Only the crudest phenomenology would speak of an artwork's claim, without reference to the spectator who engages the claim and permits it to trouble her habits of seeing, hearing, reading, and feeling. In theoretical shorthand, the aesthetic moment is fundamentally dialectical. It hinges on a provocation—which is then elaborated, interpreted, taken up, troubled over, fumbled with, mocked (or whatever) by the recipient who tarries with this opening rather than ignoring it or simply moving on to other things.

To put the difficulty in left-Hegelian terms, Rancière's thought contains a surplus in excess of his own accounting. For, where the questions have thus far been pitched in exegetical terms, they highlight a dimension of democratic practice that is routinely neglected by critics who privilege a grammar of insurgency or disruption. What typically remains unthought in such formulations is how these irruptive claims are *received* within a framework of meaning in which they previously had no intelligible place. The difficulty reflects one of the core features of democratic agency: action takes place in a sphere of meaning that is not wholly managed by either the subjects of communicative acts or their recipients, but rather in the negotiation between these unruly voices, these habits of hearing (or not-hearing), and the norms that such challenges restage in unfamiliar, transgressive ways. Or the point could be put in Arendtian terms, suggested by readers such as Patchen Markell and Cristina Beltrán.[80] To act in the world is not some unilateral moment of disruption, nor is it simply to restage accepted norms with greater scope or flexibility. Such interventions enter a world *constitutively* shared, and thus demand a multivalent approach to what they will come to mean—whether one's fellow citizens will respond to the opening, take it up, pervert its original intention, press it farther, crush it by force, or simply let it die on the vine. And from this insight, it is necessary to ask whether practices of reception *also* work to reconfigure the space of citizenship, or alternately refuse these disruptive moments, divert them from their intended course, or re-actualize them in unanticipated ways.

One way to think these challenges is by returning to the first chapter of this study. As previously considered, Adorno confronts a similar set of questions and gestures toward an aesthetically informed practice of engagement—more specifically, an active receptivity by which the subject strains to register challenges, experiences, humiliations, and damages that are elided by dominant normative vocabularies. It would be tempting to conclude that Rancière lacks precisely those resources that rest within Adorno's thought: a practice of receptivity oriented toward (a) claims that have no legible place within existing vocabularies of justice, or (b) those claimants that have been de-authorized by an invidious grammar of meaning.[81] To invoke a formulation from Danielle Allen: perhaps the unresolved question is not simply learning how to talk to strangers, but learning to *hear* strangers whose experiences, hopes, desires, or needs might unsettle our sense of who "we" are and what "we" need.[82] And yet such a rendering possesses its own liabilities. Where the rejoinder reflects the plurality of democratic life, it seeks to maintain the polity in a spirit of greater inclusion, rather than press for a transformative remaking of practices and institutions. The point of this intervention, then, is not to claim that reception is superordinate to the disruptive strategies privileged by Rancière. To go too far in that direction would risk a patrimonial anti-politics that (a) relies upon the generosity or goodwill of hegemonic groups, and (b) domesticates radical claims within what hegemonic forms of hearing permit to matter (while their privilege to make such determinations remains unchallenged).[83] Instead, a *praxically* stronger rendering is required. To channel a suggestion by Davide Panagia, a more democratically generative politics of reception would demand "a relinquishing of our self that creates an ethical relationship with that from which we turn and with that toward which we turn; it is, in short, an ethical practice of *attending to* the world of appearances."[84] To avoid losing the political thread in the language of appearance, this "turning toward" would be a practice of attending to those *persons* abjected by the civic space of appearance—and, more radically, to render such an engagement possible by a willingness to risk the familiar distribution of roles and possibilities.

On this point, it is necessary to be more careful than the foregoing has allowed. For it is not the case that such themes are wholly absent from Rancière's thought. In addressing theatrical spectatorship, for instance, he offers a line of argument that places the recipient in a rather more "active" role.

> Emancipation begins when we challenge the opposition between viewing and acting; when we understand that the self-evident facts that structure the relations between saying, seeing and doing themselves belong to the structure of domination and subjection. It begins when we understand that viewing is also an action that confirms or transforms this distribution of positions. The spectator also acts, like the pupil or scholar. She observes, selects, compares, interprets.[85]

And yet, these hints regarding the activity of spectatorship are too often absent from Rancière's reflections on *political* agency, which leaves readers to wonder how these interventions "from below" find purchase within civic conversations. For instance, how might citizens listen in more generous, inventive ways when exclusionary dynamics of mattering diminish their capacity to attend to the claims of certain agents?[86] How might these noisy moments of refusal or insubordination be heard as the claims of citizenship that demand response or reparation? How might this work of the spectator also be thought as a nodal point within these reconfigurations of social space? There is no shortage of examples to give life to these questions. How does the white citizen hear claims from racialized subjects that (uncomfortably) expose the social and institutional privilege of whiteness? How might subjects morally opposed to same-sex attachments learn to hear queer claims for civic equality, when the subjects' deepest intuitions tell them that such forms of desire are aberrant or sinful? How might the neoliberal citizen, navigating the individuation of risk and responsibility through an entrepreneurial practice, thoughtfully grapple with those who speak in terms of civic guarantees or entitlements?

To boil these instances down, the core difficulty rests in how the citizen could maximize his or her responsiveness toward marginal claimants, such that their rage, noise, and despair could be received *as* authoritative speech, bearing claim to compulsory, shared norms. Such a position would not take the path of advocacy, in which the privileged stand in for the marginal, and press the latter's interests into elite forums and channels; rather, it would represent a moment in which the subject is implicated by these moments of rage or heartbreak or accusation, and yet abides in this discomfort so as to serve the substantive commitment to equality that mobilizes the democratic imagination. More broadly, the challenge calls attention to a standing torsion of democratic practice. Actions that open a more bearable life for some might be received as a threatening loss for others. Such interventions might suggest the loss of a world in which social roles make sense, a shared history is legible, or the direction of community is known. It is here that political conservatism has long found its axiological roots—in the experience of undoing, discomfort, and disorientation that follows from social disruption. And when these anxieties are taken seriously, they highlight the difficulties that attend an agonistic politics. To undergo such provocations is not simply to act as a witness of events from which one is separated, in the well-known mode of Kant's moral spectator.[87] It is rather to experience an unsettling of the social ground on which one's commitments made sense; it is to be forced to confront the violence in which one has been complicit; and it is to face a horizon against which one's investments might no longer lead to a legible future. The political task, then, is to cultivate a practice of citizenship that could abide this experience of undoing and court what Alexander Hirsch has termed the risk of "exposing [oneself] to shattering self-loss."[88] To practice a politics of equality would, in less hyperbolic terms, require a kind of civic courage—a readiness to pursue egalitarian commitments over the comforts and certainties that have thus far defined one's position in social space.

This oversight permits a final rendering of the difficulty. Where Rancière offers resources to cognize the irruptive possibilities of agitation "from below," too often his texts court what might be called a political realism—a tendency to presume that these disruptive openings *must* give way to transformed practices of seeing these insubordinate subjects and hearing their unsettling claims. As Jay Bernstein suggests in a different context, this stance is symptomatic of just how deep realist desires run within a thinking of transformative social practice: "with these terms, we are back to the language of 'ought' as existing above and independently of our activities."[89] Confessions *ought* to be met by forgiveness—great artworks *will* generate their own audience—and these political challenges *must* give way to a transformed economy of social vision (and the participatory potentials that would follow).[90] As the foregoing elaborates, however, no such conclusions can be presumed. The history of radical politics demonstrates that these irruptive openings persistently meet with significant tendencies in the other direction: a willed desire to refuse such claims, to hold onto standing dynamics of privilege, to prefer an order based on violence and dispossession rather than a world in which familiar moorings are undone.

To close, then, it is necessary to revisit the programmatic statement that opened this chapter. To say that politics is "aesthetic in principle" has yielded a rich set of connections involving the sensible resonance of power—and how public economies of sensibility offer a terrain for emancipatory politics that typically goes unrecognized within thinly rationalist approaches. And yet, what Rancière fails to take seriously is the full resonance of the aesthetic resources from which he borrows. For if politics works to disrupt public economies of seeing and hearing, then a sufficiently robust engagement with the aesthetic tradition would acknowledge the broader constellation at work in these shifts. Such a position would account for how these perceptual interruptions do not simply introduce new coordinates and possibilities of meaning, but are also taken up, refused, radicalized, misread, subverted, or pursued in unforeseen directions by those who undergo these provocations. In slightly different terms, it is only for the most one-sided approach that these claims would explode into social space and guarantee their effects, immune to the indeterminacy that attends all claims for meaning: that every utterance is subject to the conditions under which it is received, the new contexts into which it might be displaced, or the practices of seeing, hearing, and reading that are co-constitutive for its meaning.[91] Or, to close on the point most salient for construing political agency, a more robust analysis would need to engage more vigorously with the dimension of reception by which acts might come to outlast the exemplary moment of their articulation. If this insight is less filled with the pathos of the avant-garde (with its characteristic effort to privilege the spectacular moment over the long work of preparation and follow-up), it is nevertheless more true to the work of politics in a world where one is never fully the master of one's actions, speech, and deeds.

4

Bringing the Threads Together

Toward an Aesthetics of Democratic Agency

The preceding chapters have covered substantial ground, stretching over a variety of approaches to critical theory. The concerns have ranged from the institutional practice of art (and the social resonance of these productions), to the self as an object of transformative practice, to interventions within social economies of speech and vision. Indeed, it is useful to note the important distinctions between these approaches, lest this study compress them into a single, undifferentiated category of "the aesthetic" that would elide the differences in their aims, resources, and objectives. In terms that Hegel pressed against Schelling, such an approach would yield the infamous "night in which all cows are black."[1] And yet, to lean too heavily upon these differences may generate a liability of its own: uncertainty as to how this range of themes can speak to any common set of concerns. Although each chapter addresses the contested intersection of the political and aesthetic, it may seem that they symptomatize what is often lamented as the fracturing of the contemporary Left. From such a vantage point, the theorists treated above offer a set of aims and objectives that range so broadly across the critical landscape that they cannot be synthesized into any single, coherent strategy. To poach a phrase from Pirandello, it may appear that we have gained little more than three theorists in search of a narrative.

To take a step back from the thicket of details, there are some helpful ways of drawing out some common threads. At the broadest level, the arguments at the heart of this study help to complicate a thin rationalism that has increasingly oriented political theory in the latter half of the twentieth century. And in this sense, each intervention can be read in tension with the deliberative school that has presented itself as the sober redemption of political theory after the "irrationalism" or "neo-romanticism" of the postmodern moment. Although deliberative premises have popped up periodically throughout this study, one theme remains constant: when such theorists stress discursive exchange, this emphasis can too easily elide the sensible dimension of political practice. More specifically, the deliberative focus upon a rationalized exchange of arguments (over norms, institutions, policies, etc.) threatens to efface how the contested negotiations of political life also take place through the sights, sounds, smells, and feelings that bind subjects, move them toward common aims, open worlds as objects of hope and struggle, or close off potentials with the weight of resignation. Democratic practice is populated by agents that do more than hold beliefs and offer justifications; rather, they want, fear, lust, rage, love, envy, and suffer heartbreak. And, to follow the lead of Sharon Krause, even the minimalist agent of deliberative theory demands considerably more attention to questions of sensibility.[2] To grapple with injustice is not simply to identify a practice at odds with official normative commitments (as if evaluation were reducible to the cognitive activity of measuring a practice against accepted standards of legitimacy); rather, it is to *feel* it as an intolerable violation, something that should and must be rectified. To confront a normative injury is to be troubled or unsettled in ways that do not reduce to whether universal entitlements have been extended in substantively universal fashion. To put the point in the terms that swirl around Kantian approaches, practical judgment does not stem from some nonsensuous activity of "pure" reason that is cleansed of feeling; rather, such evaluations are shot through with sensible considerations that condition what will be *perceived* as necessary sacrifice, gratuitous humiliation, intolerable injustice, or the simple way of the world. In a different philosophical idiom, the moral sentiments are ultimately *constitutive* of having something recognizable as a moral world at all.[3]

Accordingly, it is necessary to account for a more richly sensuous practice of democratic politics than is typically the case. The discursivist approach highlights the exchange of discourse, backed with reasons, conveyed through speech—itself rooted within an Aristotelian problematic of logos. To engage in rationally defensible politics is to raise questions or positions that can be conveyed within the forums of civil society and understood in cognitive terms (e.g., the minimum wage should be increased; gerrymandering undermines democratic ideals; campaign financing must be reformed, etc.). As this study has suggested throughout, however, such an approach is too thin to do justice to the unruly work of politics. For more descriptively sensitive approaches, politics is likewise situated within chants, masses, gatherings, and occupations that transform the spaces of the city. Citizens act not only by speaking in public, but by disturbing what is *seen* as public, and troubling the ways in which possible publics can be felt or imagined. From this vantage point, at least one way to explain the contemporary return to the nexus of aesthetics and politics would be a desire for a more adequate phenomenology of political agency. As Meg McLagan and Yates McKee write: "politics revolves around what can be seen, felt, sensed . . . These forms have force, shaping people as subjects and constituting the contours of what is perceptible, sensible, legible."[4] That is, politics is not simply conducted as a discursive affair of debate, petition, and justification. Rather, the effects (and contestation) of power take place on a considerably more expansive field of sensibility—one that opens certain possibilities of agency, imagination, desire, and connection while blocking or foreclosing others.[5]

To elaborate the full implications of this thesis, it will be useful to engage one familiar effort to link political agency to aesthetic resources—that politics is fundamentally concerned with visibility. Earlier chapters detailed a Foucaultian precedent for thinking the imbrication of politics and vision: the deployment of space and technology in order to render agents perpetually visible to the eye of "panoptic" power. This surveillance now extends beyond the built environment, so as to track words, purchases, and inquiries in the virtual spaces where agents spend much of their lives. A more productive *politics* of visuality, however, stems from a thinker who has haunted the course of this study: Hannah Arendt. Arendt's work is something of a staple for those working on the contested terrain of the aesthetic and the political. As she argues, the practice of politics is not reducible to institutions or laws or treaties, but rather offers an art of appearance to one's fellow citizens, within a sphere that all work to sustain. Further yet, political action rests in a capacity for "natality"—that is, the ability to introduce new beginnings into the space of citizenship through one's words and deeds. In her own terms, the polity "is the space of appearance in the widest sense of the word, namely, the space where I appear to others as others appear to me, where men exist not merely like other living or inanimate things but make their appearance explicitly."[6] To avoid getting lost in the rich details of Arendt's thought, one theme bears particular attention: what distinguishes the political from other forms of social reproduction is that it is fundamentally a practice of *appearance*. The political is what can be made public for consideration by fellow citizens, so as to rearticulate the institutions, values, and traditions that they share. The private, on the other hand, is deprived of publicity; it is what remains in darkness, of import only to those individuals it directly concerns.[7] And if appearance is the condition for politics, this means that citizens bear a responsibility to sustain the space within which they mutually appear to one another. More specifically, it requires citizens to safeguard the plurality of this space, where things appear differently according to where one is situated (no matter how "common" they might be). For Arendt, this deep plurality demands an art of judgment akin to aesthetic judgment, in which binding, determinate answers are not available, and claims to validity must therefore accommodate the varied perspectives of others.[8]

It is for this reason that commentators have persistently classified Arendt's political writings as "dramaturgical."[9] This is not to say that she submerges the distinctive concerns of the political into categorially different terms, objects, and criteria—but rather to say that there is an essentially aesthetic component to the practice of politics.[10] Politics hinges upon the possibility of introducing novelty into the space of citizenship, such that things once thought settled appear differently, that accepted values can mean new things, that unrecognized possibilities of tradition can be actualized, or that established communal narratives can be destabilized and seen anew. And this push to novelty extends beyond institutions or norms. More broadly, democratic agency persistently seeks to introduce new claimants upon the stage of politics—those who previously did not rate as full members of the community in question and thus were not full members of "the public."[11]

From this vantage point, it is possible to isolate a less obvious thread that runs throughout the arguments treated in the course of this study. At least one of the questions that recurs in these chapters is what *can* be seen or heard in the space of the polity. Or, in democratically thick terms, *who* can be seen as an agent who can claim the full protections and benefits of membership? How do the operations and techniques of power heighten the visibility or audibility of some groups while others are left in obscurity? This move to invisibility is a familiar metaphor for understanding political marginality.[12] To consider the well-known opening lines of Ralph Ellison's *Invisible Man*, the black protagonist elaborates: "I am invisible, understand, simply because people refuse to see me. . . . That invisibility to which I refer occurs because of a peculiar disposition of the eyes of those with whom I come in contact. A matter of the construction of their inner eyes, those eyes with which they look through their physical eyes upon reality."[13] Where this reference to an "inner eye" might be read in an individualized, liberal sense (where the refusal is based within private beliefs or commitments), these forms of invisibility are inalienably social. Such invisible agents may be blocked from the participatory domains in which public opinion or policy is crafted. They might not enter the representations of popular media—or do so only as villains, whores, scoundrels, schemers, prostitutes, criminals, or shapes in the background.[14] Their contributions are absent from official narratives over who "we" are and where "we" are going. Their histories of humiliation or dispossession are discounted, unrecognized, or refused. Finally, they may be the disabled or the elderly—those whose bodies do not generate value in the ways recognized by neoliberal market frameworks and thus fail to meet the bar for full citizenship. From this diagnosis, it is necessary to push beyond the terms detailed thus far. That is, appearance is not simply the condition for politics, but a political good—one that can itself be the object of contestation or an aim to be secured. If the invidious operations of power work through rendering certain things visible, and removing others from public consideration, then at least one valence for emancipatory politics will be to *make seen*. Such a politics introduces new topics, themes, and claimants into the discourses of justice. It must bring visibility to what (or who) has existed in the shadows, whether these be hidden crimes, histories of oppression, relationships of exploitation, unrecognized contributions to a given community, or lives forced into the margins.

This imperative has been avowed by a range of emancipatory movements, and it will accordingly be useful to engage their specifics in order to complicate some standard terms of analysis. For instance, a language of visibility has long been invoked by a politics of sexual "pride"—one that seeks publicity for those who have historically been forced to hide their attachments and desires.[15] To be visible in this sense would be to "come out"—to live without the shame or fear imposed by a heteronormative public culture. Likewise, visibility has become a watchword within struggles over rights and protections for domestic labor. This is the work that renders all other work possible, the labor that permits others to enter the public space of visibility, but itself rests in invisibility. And this initiative takes a particularly complex shape within the contemporary movements of undocumented immigrants—those who have strong incentives *not* to be publicly recognized due to legal regimes that criminalize their presence within the space of the nation. For such agents, to demand visibility is to take on substantial risk, since it may just as well make one visible to the deportation state that dedicates itself to incarcerating and removing those deemed "illegal."[16] In light of the potential sanctions, it may ultimately be preferable to remain in the shadows of unregulated, predatory labor arrangements.[17]

Such allusions to visibility are thus not only a staple of theoretical work, but are reflected by the demands of radical groups as they insert themselves into democratic conversations. The Zapatistas, for instance, describe their iconic aesthetic of masking in the following terms: it is only through the mask (the traditional guise of anonymity) that they (the laboring, the poor, the indigenous) become visible, against those dynamics of global capital that routinely render them invisible and unheard in everyday life. In their own terms, "we cover our faces in order to be seen."[18] And yet, to rest with this politicized appeal to visibility (as a thing that is withheld, gained, or lost) would not do justice to the ambivalences and complexities that attend these movements. Perhaps most obviously, it is inadequate to map visibility and invisibility upon the axis of the public and the private (a staple of Arendt's work). Where this framework assigns invisibility to the private (i.e., those things that do not appear as objects of common solicitude), one of the complications raised by recent literature is that *invisibility is itself a kind of public appearance.*[19] This is the mode, for instance, of Rancière's *sans-part.* They appear *as* those whose words can be ignored and whose needs do not matter in deliberations over social goods or the allotment of risk and protection. To be socially invisible (in the familiar phrase) is to be *socially* invisible—to occupy an attenuated role within social economies of membership, rather than to exist abstractly "external" to the public, along a binary axis of presence/absence.[20] Ultimately, then, democratic struggles over the economy of appearance are not always an effort to "break into the sphere of appearance"—or at least are not reducible to these terms.[21] Rather, as the masks of the Zapatistas make clear, the marginal likewise endeavor to *make visible the invisibility* that has stunted their social possibilities and attenuated their citizenship. Only by staging their everyday anonymity, now rendered strange and uncanny, do such groups expose the violence that structures the perceptual economy into which they insert themselves.

And there is another reason to question "thin" appeals to visibility: if a core axis of politics is appearance, it cannot simply be construed as something that is granted or withheld (a point that will be revisited and thickened below). Rather, it is crucial to ask how these economies of vision map onto broader circuits of meaning and experience—and what the practical implications of this mapping might be. One point of entry to this question is through Judith Butler's claim that a "racist organization and disposition of the visible" has persistently legitimized state violence against black bodies.[22] Minimally, this linkage of vision and violence suggests that a politicized concern for sensibility must go beyond whether certain groups do or do not appear in socially meaningful ways. Rather, the meanings that attach to these agents prefigure a range of appropriate treatments and responses. This broad point gains substance and bite through ongoing debates over race as a principle of social (and police) vision. Within the scopic regime of whiteness, the black body shows up as a source of menace, of impulse unfettered by reason, of lusts and appetites that drive it beyond the limits of law. When such bodies appear where they "do not belong"—when they pass through white spaces—they portend danger and criminality. As such, heightened police violence is demanded to maintain order (itself the order of whiteness).[23] It is a violence that is not *seen* as violence at all.

In recent texts, Butler has expanded this insight to highlight how sensory dynamics of disqualification implicate a wider range of social positions. Where a liberal standpoint avows dignity as a human good, this universalist moral commitment is regularly falsified by social practice. Some lives are supported in their needs and protected in their vulnerability, while others are hunted in desert crossings, exposed to indiscriminate drone strikes, subjected to state violence, or abandoned to social exposure. Where we might expect such violations to be met with outrage, they are routinely buried in the back pages of newspapers or shrugged off as the unfortunate order of things. These are just the things that happen to *those people.* Ultimately, Butler roots this disparity in responsiveness within the normative structures that organize social perception. As she queries: "How do our cultural frames for thinking the human set limits on the kinds of losses we can avow as loss?"[24] From this lead, the status of humanity is not some brute fact that impinges immediately upon the spectator, as authoritative over his or her deliberations. Rather, the category of the human is awarded, narrowed, and diminished according to exclusionary norms of personhood. Some lives are *seen* as meaningfully belonging to the human (and, in loss, will be met with grieving, protest, and outrage), while others fall beyond its limits.[25] They are instead monsters, irrational, subhuman, aberrant, perverse, barbaric, or animal; their losses will be unnamed, unmourned, or actively embraced. In formulaic terms, there is a linkage between (a) the *way* that bodies or groups appear within the public space of appearance, (b) the value or meaning these agents will have, and (c) how they will figure within the motivational economy that conditions deliberations over protection, support, risk, and loss.[26]

This expanded field of power and sensibility complicates any effort to reduce a political aesthetics to the singular question of visuality (itself construed in binary terms of presence/absence). Sensible inscriptions of power do not simply rest at the symbolic level, as if the question were the cognitivist issue of associating predicates to material bodies. It is not simply that certain groups are problematized and assigned a negative social capital through public economies of discourse (lazy, promiscuous, perverse, untrustworthy, dangerous, etc.). Rather, these dynamics of meaning settle into the affectual registers that frame deliberation, mobilize (or foreclose) engagement, and lend to experience normative heft.[27] To appear in social space is to appear *as* something—and the affectual and cognitive resonances associated with such appearance condition appropriate treatment. To see these fraught bodies is to receive them as sources of unpredictability or undoing; it is to sense their potential danger; it is to know, from their very surfaces, that they demand avoidance or mastery.[28] And so too does this sensible economy structure existence from within marginal categories of personhood. To live this subject-position is to be "epidermalized."[29] It is to exist as a feared, loathed thing, to have one's pathology reflected back within everyday comportments, aversions, glances, and gestures. As George Yancy describes the experience of moving through white spaces, seen by white eyes: "the corporeal integrity of my Black body undergoes an onslaught as the white imaginary . . . ruminates over my dark flesh and vomits me out in a form not in accordance with how I see myself. From the context of my lived experience, I feel 'external,' as it were, to my body, delivered and sealed in white lies."[30] In terms borrowed from the left-Hegelian tradition, social visibility cannot be taken as a brute fact or status (something that either happens or does not); rather, it is mediated through forms of social meaning, narratives of worth, embodied habits of relationship, affectual frameworks of danger or safety, and technologies of circulation.

This linkage of meaning, sensation, and deliberation offers important resources to theorize how power works both to qualify and to disqualify certain lives, bodies, and agents within the space of citizenship. That said, it is necessary to press the questions of agency that have thus far remained in the background. If politics (in the robust sense) is an art, space, or practice of appearance, then it is necessary to attend not only to the mechanisms by which these sensible economies are made, enforced, and reproduced—but rather to the strategies by which they could be unmade or made differently. To do otherwise would concede too much to these powers of disqualification and overlook the ways that agents persistently restage, disorder, and complicate these mechanisms. Put differently, it would mistake as settled what is ultimately a terrain of contestation. By pursuing the implications for agency, this chapter will move beyond a phenomenological framework to ask some more readily politicized questions. What sorts of interventions might disrupt or destabilize these economies of sensibility, and how might these strategies inform broader reflections on democratic agency? To shift out of the speculative register: what contributions are made by the unsettling spectacles that characterize the contemporary scene of politics? Where the preceding has emphasized a more adequate phenomenology of power, the remainder of this chapter will turn its attention to the *politics* of sensibility and the broader implications for an aesthetics of democratic practice.

* * *

Up to this point, this account has highlighted how the sensible subject is at the heart of political practice—not simply as a body that can be fed or starved, broken or protected, incarcerated or left to practice its freedom—but rather a subject who perceives, feels, sees, and hears. This sensory register is not some passive apparatus that simply registers what is placed before it, nor is it immune to dynamics of shaping, as if it were some brute, biological given. Rather, the sensible basis of citizenship is *worked upon* so as to organize its perception of the claims, bodies, appeals, and lives that it encounters. What is seen and how it is seen reflect a sustained formation through discourses of knowledge, norms of personhood, myths of nationhood, and the role-performances that structure social space (a list that is obviously partial and incomplete). In quicker terms, the subject of politics is shaped by a rich social pedagogy that not only conditions the meaning of the values to which it commits itself, but how it makes sense to respond to the strangers of democratic life—what they are owed, where they belong, and what they can "reasonably" demand.[31] It is for this reason that a politics of the senses must press beyond some imperative to see what was previously hidden or to hear what was previously inaudible. No matter the popularity of such phrases, they are too imprecise to capture the broader field of a sensible politics.

Such complications multiply significantly once perception is approached from a different vantage point: as a site of contestation. If sensibility is not the terminal receptacle of power, capable only of being shaped from without, then what sort of agency might it admit? Given the emphasis this chapter has placed on the theme (and political good) of visibility, it is necessary to focus more rigorously on the question of how citizens see, what is foreclosed from the field of civic vision, and how these economies of seeing might be destructured and structured differently. Admittedly, this line of analysis might raise critical hackles due to the long-standing association of viewing with a depoliticized abdication of engagement. The Situationist International, for instance, indicted how the spectacle of late capitalism reduced the individual to a passive spectator of processes that move beyond the reach of human control or intervention.[32] This is the spectator as mere looker, the one who *does* nothing. And more contemporary theorists have raised the specter of the "spectator-citizen"—the one who cynically disengages from politics, under the presumption that nothing he or she does will matter anyway.[33] All that is left is to pursue one's private aims while watching the play of elites or the professional talking heads on the screens that populate social space.

And yet, recent debates have raised more productive questions as to how the visual regime of citizenship could function as a site for a potential politics—that is, a sphere where citizens could act, rather than passively absorb contents from without. Such accounts reflect a different critical literature on spectatorship, where the "gaze" possesses a capacity to *do* something more than reflect actions from elsewhere.[34] Perhaps most relevant at present are those who interrogate the figure of the global spectator—the one who is confronted with images of distant suffering and must choose how to respond. Indeed, the "humanitarian imaginary" would hardly be thinkable without a visual culture that brings suffering bodies to screens across the globe and frames them as victims in need of aid (from famine, state violence, natural disaster, etc.).[35] From this vantage point, the spectator who learns to see in ways unprepared by existing circuits of value might perform an important agency in the face of distant violence or abandonment. The humanitarian gaze would not simply skim past images of bodies in distress or shrug over things that happen to *those people* (in parts unknown, for reasons unknown), but rather folds these instances within an expanded sphere of moral care and assistance.[36]

When measured against the moral refusals detailed in the previous section, there is much to recommend such a proposal. Where invidious closures on "the human" reduce the range of lives that matter, a broadened practice of moral vision would expand the parameters of protection, care, and support. To *see differently* in this way would open up possibilities for solidarity shut down by resurgent currents of xenophobia or neoliberal indifference. And yet critics have raised reservations from a number of directions. Perhaps most significant at present is what might be termed the "directionality" of this agency. Where the argument enjoins the viewing subject to extend compassion, pity, or empathy toward those who appear in images of suffering, this imperative is too often abstracted from those agents who press the viewer, unsettle her certainties, and undo her familiar habits of meaning.[37] At bottom, the humanitarian gaze provides an agency founded *within* the viewer's moral commitments or choices. For critics, what this vision lacks is a moment when the subject finds her sovereignty troubled by the dispossessed, such that she is called to answer or respond. What is missing, in other words, is a more democratically rich approach to the contested politics of vision, where the viewing subject's meanings, commitments, and values may be undone by the provocations *pressed upon her.*[38]

Though the rejoinder has been addressed in theoretical terms, it becomes more nuanced upon considering an episode from the not-so-distant history of emancipatory practice: the spectacular means by which the ACT-UP movement sought to dislocate perception of the AIDS crisis. Indeed, these activists offered a rich visual vocabulary in order to disrupt the form of public deliberation upon the disease, the population in question, and the role of the state in times of epidemiological crisis. The movement defined itself through the iconic pink triangle, the coffins paraded through the streets, the replica headstones, the red handprint, and the urns filled with the ashes of the deceased.[39] And on a quick reading, it would be tempting to lump these symbolic moments into the story that has been told thus far. What was at stake in all such gestures was an effort to make the queer counterpublic visible. That is, these were subjects who could not be seen through heteronormative economies of vision; these were lives that had to dissemble, cover, and closet in order to avoid a wide range of sanctions from a hostile straight public. In a more fraught sense, these were subjects whose death was viewed as the just desert of their "depraved" appetites and "unnatural" couplings. From this perspective, such interventions aimed to intervene within a social imaginary that rendered queer lives expendable and forgettable. They aimed to contest closures on who counts as a valued human life, such that the queer body could be seen as a body to be sheltered and protected through public investment, research imperatives, and access to experimental pharmaceutical regimens.

Although this reading gets at some important efforts of the ACT-UP movement, it would not do justice to what they aimed to accomplish. After all, it has hardly been the case that the queer was banished from social visibility in any easy sense. There is a long history of the flamboyant queer within a culture of straightness. This is the body that is simultaneously fetishized for its fashion or its sass or its style, and yet reviled for its desires, pleasures, and penetrations. To evoke a familiar Foucaultian point, the queer agent is hardly invisible to the eye of power, but rather a target of heightened vigilance, anxiously policed so as to maintain the "proper" performance, attachments, and morphology of gender. This complex form of visibility came to the fore in an action designed to contest any brute "visibility politics." In 1988, the Museum of Modern Art (MOMA) in New York held an exhibition organized around the photography of Nicholas Nixon—some of which represented those dying from AIDS. The intentions spoke to a familiar intuition about the AIDS crisis: the indifference of the straight sector was, in part, due to the anonymity of those lost. The numbers and statistics trotted out could hardly grab or trouble the straight public; they were simply too large and abstract. Accordingly, the task was to "put a face" to these deaths, so that the lived experience of the disease could not be passed over in favor of statistics regarding infection, antiretrovirals, or death rates. And yet, when the exhibit opened at MOMA, activists from ACT-UP passed out flyers that challenged the exhibit and closed with the following injunction: "The PWA [i.e., Person With AIDS] is a human being whose health has deteriorated not simply due to a virus, but due to government inaction, the inaccessibility of affordable health care, and institutionalized neglect in the form of heterosexism, racism, and sexism. We demand the visibility of PWAs who are vibrant, angry, loving, sexy, beautiful, acting up and fighting back. STOP LOOKING AT US; START LISTENING TO US."[40] For present purposes, I do not want to dwell on the specific charges regarding institutional neglect or malign intentions. It would not, after all, be difficult to track the inaction of public health agencies to an invidious moralization of the AIDS virus. More significant is the paradoxical injunction offered to the reader—to *stop* looking and start listening, instead. Indeed, from the perspective of an abstract visibility politics, it is difficult to make sense of any effort to diminish the visibility of a subaltern population, particularly if the aim is to enter the conversations of civil society.

To return to the reservations considered earlier, some more productive readings become legible. Previously, this chapter offered a theoretical caution: while visibility is often construed as an important political good, the meanings and practice of visibility are more nuanced than a binary equation (i.e., visibility vs. invisibility) can accommodate. As a wide range of scholars has demonstrated, however, the difficulties can be pursued further into the practical register—such that heightened visibility can just as well carry negative sanctions for vulnerable populations. For instance, radical activists have found that greater prominence on the public stage can easily attract surveillance and oversight from the security apparatus of the state.[41] Likewise, within the neoliberal state, welfare assistance demands what John Gilliom terms a situation of "compulsory visibility"; the recipient must open her life to a range of surveillance mechanisms covering drug testing, sexual activity, personal hygiene, spending habits, kinship arrangements, and practices of child-rearing.[42] To step beyond the state, increased social visibility can render one open to reprisal from the unofficial authorities of civil society (e.g., professional, personal, medical, etc.). And even when visibility is secured without such consequences, it may nevertheless fail to secure the autonomy, recognition, or dignity that are persistently associated with this ideal. For instance, marginal groups persistently indict the offer of "token" visibility, where they are assimilated into public culture without meaningfully changing its exclusionary norms or securing essential rights. As Dean Spade, speaking from a transgendered position, challenges mainstream visibility politics: "cultural 'common sense' tells us to struggle for nothing more than incorporation into the existing social order . . . the inclusion and recognition offered by these invitations is not only disappointingly solely symbolic, but actually legitimizes and expands harmful conditions."[43] In this sense, struggles for visibility may secure only symbolic parity within a social order, while leaving intact those structures that leave counter-hegemonic lives in situations of material violence or exposure.

To return to the ACT-UP action at MOMA, what was at stake was not visibility as a self-evident good, so as to insert the queer into the public imagination in ways that can no longer be ignored. Rather, this intervention aimed to transform the optical field surrounding the PWA—who had the right to define its meaning, and what this constellation of meanings might mean for the politics surrounding the AIDS crisis. Where the PWA had achieved public prominence in photos of abject, withered bodies, this sort of visibility (a "looking at") was challenged as disempowering and reifying. It is a de-realizing vision, through which the PWA is an object of management, deliberation, or care. This object may serve as a site of knowledge or edification for the viewer; it may even become the object of pity or compassion; but it does not unsettle the dynamics of power on the basis of which the viewer makes of these images what they might. What is demanded is a different kind of seeing, implicated by the agency and vitality of the PWA. These bodies are not simply "faces" to be attached to an abstract epidemic, such that the straight public can find some wellspring of commonality or empathy in the face of suffering (thereby leaving untroubled the privilege of the onlooker). Rather, they are sources of narratives, challenges, and needs that destabilize the easy coordinates of (a) hegemonic viewers (who view, deliberate, decide, and act), and (b) objects to be viewed, managed, and treated. Or, to put the point in terms that speak to the broad concerns of this study, what this injunction seeks is to dislocate *how* the PWA appears within competing discourses of normality, sin, public investment, intimacy, and sex. By destabilizing these optics, different possibilities open in the deliberative resources for negotiating the politics of the AIDS crisis. Is the PWA simply the site of a disease that strikes with all the implacability of fate? Is this body a text that displays the just deserts for sin or depravity? Is this a body to be ministered out of pity or charity? Or is it an agent that speaks out of rage and indicts the world from which the viewer looks—one that shelters some, while abandoning others? In more brute form yet, is the PWA a victim to be saved, or rather a *citizen* who might place demands upon the viewer and, by extension, upon those institutions that have abandoned the PWA and the queer public?

Similar questions arise with the contemporary Black Lives Matter movement. The rallies and demonstrations associated with that name operate with a rich sensible vocabulary. There are the die-ins that replicate the effects of state violence upon black bodies—there are the hands raised in the air, to stage the institutionalized posture of submission before the police—there are the chants that repeat the words of those who die through state violence ("we can't breathe")—there are the bodies that mass on public roadways so as to block the passage of commuters and the routine movements of capital.[44] And where it would be tempting to interrogate each of these interventions at the local level, the foregoing suggests a broader theme that runs throughout: the demand *to be seen* in a way that has been systematically denied within a public culture of whiteness. Where the black body has long been subjected to an analytic of strength, vitality, and use-value (whether in the plantations or the factories), it now stages the negative relief of "the good citizen" within a racialized optic of nationhood.[45] At times, these are figured as listless bodies, unwilling to work. When framed by securitarian anxieties, they are the bodies of danger, signaled by pants that sag and hats that tilt and hoods that cover their faces. And from a biopolitical perspective, these are bodies of promiscuity and fecundity, those possessed by an unmanageable sexuality. This is hardly an exhaustive list of the meanings that have overdetermined the meaning of the black body within a culture of whiteness. What is most significant to note is how these interventions cannot be classified as a brute demand for visibility or even the quantitative demand for "more" visibility. Indeed, as Arendt recognized, the hypervisibility of blacks in the American context "is unalterable and permanent."[46] These bodies have long staged the bad conscience of a white nation—that which cannot be avowed, cannot be valued, cannot be acknowledged within racialized understandings of the civic "we." Accordingly, these activists demand that black subjects be seen *differently*. These are subjects who demand the same protections extended to the hegemonic white subject—to be seen as legitimate sources of rage over a systematic history of institutional predation or abandonment—and, more fundamentally yet, to be heard as discursive equals whose words demand response and justification.

At this point, it will be useful to reflect upon what these insurgent strategies contribute (if provisionally) to the broader question at the heart of this chapter: an aesthetics of democratic agency. There are at least two things to note. Minimally, these cases complicate the openings considered above by displacing the "directionality" of the agency at stake. When one considers the unruly nature of the interventions detailed here, at least one lesson is that they stem *from* those who resist the roles and meanings assigned by hegemonic grammars of social reproduction. These transformations of vision do not represent a moral turn, on the part of the privileged, but the effects of an agonistic politics of challenge. Such insubordinate agents use the narratives, images, and norms of a given community, but restage them in such a way as to reveal the gap between what they promise and what they deliver. One impetus of these gestures, then, is to intervene within a symbolic economy in which these agents could find no place, could not live, and could not recognize themselves. Such actors throw into relief the violence that subsists within everyday forms of "inclusion" and the ongoing complicity of observers in these systems of violence. Or, to put the aims of this agency in formulaic terms, the task is not simply to appear within a regime of visibility from which one has been absent, but rather to intercede in such a way that its fundamental norms and terms of intelligibility must be reconfigured.[47]

And a second feature of these interventions must likewise be noted. To this point, the account has grappled with the "directionality" of these insubordinate gestures. In order to grasp their full contributions, however, it is necessary to attend more carefully to how these claims are presented and lodged in civil society. As the foregoing demonstrates, such agents do not limit themselves to the traditional modes of petition that have long occupied the theoretical imagination, but rather operate with a wider repertoire for meaning. They lay their bodies before state security forces; they chain themselves together to block roads or runways; they place themselves in cages to replicate the conditions of animals in captivity. These groups do not just appear in public, but do so in ways that are noisy, unsettling, and inconvenient. To cite an action that is taking place as I write (at the July 2017 Hamburg meeting of the G20 leaders), they gather by the hundreds, cover their skin with clay, and assume the postures of the undead—lurching through city streets and staging an eerie, zombie silence as a metaphor for perceived political indifference. Rather than catalog these spectacles (a task that would require a different book entirely),[48] it is necessary to ask how such sensible initiatives enrich or complicate prominent understandings of democratic agency. As the literature demonstrates, it is tempting to fold these acts into familiar, rationalized models of political communication. For instance, Amy Gutmann and Dennis Thompson propose that the utility of these gestures is to call attention to controversial social issues and place them on the agenda of public deliberation (which is where the rational core of politics rests).[49] On their reading, such spectacles are ultimately a kind of amplification device; they should be viewed as "non-deliberative" moments whose real value is to "lead for future occasions for deliberative criticism"—thus leaving in place the characteristic deliberative privilege of the discursive over the somatic, the affectual, or the visual.[50]

When these interventions are taken seriously, however, they expose a dimension of democratic agency more sensuously thick than is captured by this discursivist reduction. To raise a claim is not reducible to the production of discourse (itself translatable into propositions, appeals, requests, or demands).[51] And it is not even limited, as some deliberative theorists concede, to speech that uses emotion to claim the hearts of listeners (emotion that must, itself, be subjected to rational evaluation).[52] Rather, claims are likewise raised by symbols, sounds, movements, and images that displace the standard vocabularies for justice. For instance, claims may be presented by murals on walls that build alternative memories, grievances, crimes, and narratives into the material spaces of the city (all the while contesting ownership of these walls and streets). Claims are made by those who sit at counters where they are not legally permitted; by those who choose to undergo violence at the hands of state agents; or by those who choose the slow withering of hunger, so as to render manifest the violence to which they are already subjected.[53] And in a particularly evocative case, claims are pressed by those asylum seekers, trapped in both legal and geographic limbo, who conspicuously *refuse* speech (and their compromised status as speakers) by sewing together their lips.[54] These are mouths that "speak" in their muteness—now staged, visceral, and unsettling.

A second way to understand an aesthetics of democratic agency, then, rests in *how* these interventions perform their work. Sensibility is not simply the object of power or manipulation, as in the more apocalyptic renderings of the Frankfurt School. Rather, sensible resources furnish rich possibilities to enter and unsettle the democratic imaginary. Elsewhere, I have argued that bodily spectacle defined the work of the recent "occupation" movement, who used their encampments to claim a "right to the city" as a meaningfully public space.[55] There is, however, a more familiar example of bodies "out of place" within the political history of the United States—those civil rights activists who placed themselves in the segregated spaces of whiteness to inaugurate a crisis for the racial state. As Martin Luther King Jr. famously described the rationale for putting bodies in the path of violence (and in the path of cameras that would transmit this violence to a wide variety of onlookers), "we had no alternative except that of preparing for direct action, whereby *we would present our very bodies as a means of laying our case* before the conscience of the local and national community."[56] As the reference to the "national community" reveals, it was not by accident that these images were captured and distributed to distant viewers. Rather, such interventions were crafted around the intuition I have been suggesting here: that *appearances can themselves offer a claim* in a sphere where words have met with limited efficacy.[57] Or, in a different philosophical idiom: appearances can *perform* a kind of claim that exceeds discursive reduction. As King elsewhere detailed the theatrical character of nonviolent resistance, "its heroic and often perilous acts uttered their *wordless but convincing rebuttal* in Montgomery, in the sit-ins, on the freedom rides, and finally in Birmingham."[58] In a familiar rendering of the work performed by civil rights photography, the spectacle of the black citizen undergoing violence testified to the violence that public institutions exert (typically in anonymous, unseen, unheard ways) upon vulnerable minorities.[59] Such images revealed how space that is "public" for the hegemonic white subject is a site of danger and humiliation for others. They attested (against the conflation of blackness with animality) to discipline and dignity when confronted with white rage.[60] And ultimately they staged one of the violent truths of the nation: that the forcible exclusion of the black body is not an aberration (with regard to its universalist ideals) but is rather constitutive of the republic.[61]

To step back from the specifics of this movement, such interventions suggest something more than a mechanism to secure attention to conventional acts of political petition. What they reveal is a *sensible* idiom for claims-making forged by those who do not have full access to the "official" languages of citizenship. To return to a point from an earlier chapter, it is tempting to presume that political languages are neutral mediums for articulating the claims of citizenship. Such languages presume well-defined norms that permit parties to note the discrepancies, inequalities, and shortcomings of social practice—how it embodies these norms in partial form, or inequitably distributes burdens or benefits. Such norms (at least within a liberal moral universe) are meant to cover and protect citizens, without exception or preference. They are discursive resources from which all can draw to justify their claims, challenge institutions, and hold others to account. And yet, such a position is unsustainable. As even the most cursory engagement demonstrates, official political languages reflect the commitments of hegemonic social groups—they authorize certain appeals to "common" norms while foreclosing others—and they systematically leave marginal subjects without resources to demand repair for the violence they suffer. These are subjects for whom the standard avenues of redress block the possibility that experiences of deprivation or humiliation can be recognized as instances that call for political repair. Instead, these groups suffer in ways that are understood as bad luck, the simple way of the world, or harms that are imagined, rather than real. Accordingly, to inhabit this position is to face a double imperative. Before such agents can enter their claims into civil society, they must forge a language in which the violence they suffer can be articulated as such. It is only through this counter-hegemonic idiom that their challenges might speak to established, compulsory norms, all the while destabilizing what these norms might yet come to mean and who they might come to cover.

There are, then, both weak and strong ways to understand what these aesthetic threads contribute to theorizing democratic agency. Minimally, these interventions throw into relief the limitations of a thinly rationalist approach to democratic contestation. For where rationalist models of democratic agency have emphasized the linguistic act of communication, the provocations treated thus far demonstrate how political claims are persistently raised through means that cannot be reduced to logocentric terms. Instead, the claims of citizenship are also asserted by symbols, sounds, bodies, masses, and motions. To situate this reading more firmly within the field of agency, however, a stronger set of conclusions suggests itself. It is not simply that these sensible strategies represent an "excess" of democratic action, unaccounted by a discursivist reduction upon political thought; rather, they represent an idiom of particular utility for those who are ill served by the official languages and forms of citizenship. It is on this terrain that counterpublics might force their way into a democratic imaginary that has been indifferent or hostile to their claims. To close with the words of Abbas Amini, who sewed shut his mouth and refused food in order to protest the conditions of asylum seekers in the United Kingdom (2003): "I sewed my eyes so that others could see, I sewed my ears so that others could hear, I sewed my mouth to give others a voice."[62]

* * *

Such considerations allow for a return to the core questions of this study. The reason for choosing this trajectory of theorists (rather than any number of others) rests in how they contribute to thinking a sensible politics with emancipatory aims. It is not new, after all, to propose that technologies of power might work through sensory means. The Frankfurt School placed significant weight on the integrative labor of mass culture—an industry that guides tastes, manipulates needs, and positions the viewer as a passive consumer of messages that come from on high. This theme of passivity is likewise pressed by the Situationist International—where citizens are mesmerized by the spectacle of capital, and oriented toward consumer rewards, rather than spontaneous expressions of desire and value.[63] And similar considerations have been raised more recently by Jonathan Crary, for whom the interactive technologies of the internet standardize the user's forms of engagement and patterns of cognition.[64] What binds the arguments treated over the course of this study, however, is a stark rejoinder: this sensory regime is not simply a site or target upon which power works to mobilize the subject toward elite purposes; rather, sensibility is a contested site, where an insurgent politics could likewise take root. Just as integrative technologies direct libidinal attachments to certain objects and forms of satisfaction, so too has a traditional strategy of radical politics been to cultivate new needs, new desires, new hopes, and new pleasures.[65] Just as elite agents mobilize fear and loathing toward certain groups, so too might an insurgent counter-politics cultivate different connections with these fraught agents, so as to permit different alliances and different solidarities.

This ambivalence helps to destabilize some of the pessimistic conclusions that result from a broadened analytic of power. For if power is revealed to work in sub-institutional ways—to mobilize thought, reflection, feeling, and evaluation—then it is often feared that this chokes off any possibilities for a meaningful resistance. If power is rooted *this deep* (we often hear), then it would seem that the battle has already been lost: power forges precisely those subjects it needs to ensure its own continuance. It is against this pessimism that the conversations treated in this study work—each of which suggests, in its own way, the degree to which these economies of seeing and hearing and feeling could become the object of a potential agency. And ultimately a politics that takes sensibility seriously has the potential to connect subjects in new ways, in unforeseen connections and alliances, toward a different habitation of the common or what the common might mean.

This is not to say that each chapter addresses these possibilities in the same way or that each offers resources that will appeal to all readers. There is nothing, after all, to be gained by positing some false unity so as to wrap up this study with an overly neat, tidy bow. Some of the authors treated have emphasized the possibility of seeing differently (or of *making* seen differently); others have targeted economies of feeling and desire; others yet have addressed strategies to hear appeals occluded by dominant discourses of justice or rationality. And when the questions shift to the issue of efficacy, additional questions arise. Some of these strategies may seem inadequate. Others may seem misguided. Others may seem too navel-gazing to contest how these formidable powers of dispossession are built into the material structures of a violent world. As the skeptic might challenge, why address sensibility when multinational corporations work to dismantle structures of democratic regulation, revivals of nativism mobilize against the immigrant "threat," nation-states routinely violate the rule of law, and environmental protections are systematically degraded in the service of capital? And yet, each chapter helps to cognize a form of agency that would not take a politics of sensibility as a one-way street, terminal in its effects. Such a diagnosis, it has long been argued, would hardly do justice to the way that subjects inhabit these frameworks of meaning with an inventiveness that permits them to carve out different, unplanned possibilities. In this sense, sensible valences of power are not terminal in their effects, but resources to be used and refashioned. They are not brute excretions of power, but opening points for contestation and repurposing.

If this is the case, then emancipatory theory cannot limit itself to asking *whether* this sensible terrain offers the possibility for transformative political agency. After all, empirically minded social science has long shown that subjects persistently manipulate their symbolic systems in order to generate subversive contents from the very means designed to serve social integration. Rather, the task might be to ask *how* these sensory regimes are ruptured or destabilized—toward which specific forms of union or alliance—or against which forms of violence. To identify a sensible politics is not to turn one's back on a traditional Left politics that targets material violence, institutions, and economic domination. Nor, to allay some persistent concerns, is it to choose momentary acts of "disruption" over the hard, patient work of institutional change. It is, instead, to identify *another* crucial register through which these mechanisms of violence and dispossession are persistently contested and undone. To return to the Arendtian themes that open this chapter, it would be tempting to say that this aesthetic framework reveals just how much agency remains, even in the darkest of political times. In a time when the neoliberal state, political elites, multinational corporations, and think tanks attempt to shrink the bounds of democratic participation and contestation, these are tactics available to those who hope to hold open the space of politics. And yet, even this formulation would not do justice to the possibilities treated over the course of this study. To acknowledge their full weight, this sensible field of politics represents what might be termed the unthought of the rationalist reduction engaged throughout. It is in this domain that the habits of citizenship are forged or reforged; it is in this domain that new idioms displace, problematize, and reorient civic values; it is in this domain that new possibilities for solidarity might be opened; and it is in this domain that groups find resources to act when all official avenues might seem blocked.

Notes

Introduction

1. This phrase appears in Benjamin, "The Work of Art in the Age of Mechanical Reproduction," in *Illuminations: Essays and Reflections*, ed. Hannah Arendt (New York: Schocken Books, 1968), 217–52.

2. See, for instance, Ash Amin and Nigel Thrift, *Arts of the Political: New Openings for the Left* (Durham, N.C.: Duke University Press, 2013); Frank Ankersmit, *Aesthetic Politics: Political Philosophy beyond Fact and Value* (Stanford, Calif.: Stanford University Press, 1997); Ronald Bleiker, *Aesthetics and World Politics* (New York: Palgrave Macmillan, 2009); Russ Castronovo, *Beautiful Democracy: Aesthetics and Anarchy in a Global Age* (Chicago: University of Chicago Press, 2007); Beth Hinderliter, William Kaizen, Vered Maimon, Jaleh Mansoor, and Seth McCormick, eds., *Communities of Sense: Rethinking Aesthetics and Politics* (Durham, N.C.: Duke University Press, 2009); Nikolas Kompridis, ed., *The Aesthetic Turn in Political Thought* (New York: Bloomsbury, 2014); and Ewa Ziarek, *Feminist Aesthetics and the Politics of Modernism* (New York: Columbia University Press, 2012).

3. Claire Bishop, *Artificial Hells: Participatory Art and the Politics of Spectatorship* (New York: Verso, 2012), 28. For similar arguments from the art world, see Shannon Jackson, *Social Works: Performing Art, Supporting Publics* (New York: Routledge, 2011); Chantal Mouffe, *Agonistics: Thinking the World Politically* (New York: Verso, 2013), chap. 5; Susan Platt, *Art and Politics Now* (New York: Midmarch, 2010); T. V. Reed, *The Art of Protest: Culture and Activism from the Civil Rights Movement to the Streets of Seattle* (Minneapolis: University of Minnesota Press, 2005); and Nato Thompson, ed., *Living as Form: Socially Engaged Art from 1991–2011* (Cambridge, Mass.: MIT Press, 2012).

4. See, for instance, Tara Forrest, "Mobilizing the Public Sphere: Schlingensief's Reality Theatre," *Contemporary Theatre Review* 18 (2008): 90–98; Denise Varney, "'Right Now Austria Looks Ridiculous': Please Love Austria!—Reforging the Connection between Art and Politics," in *Christoph Schlingensief: Art Without Borders*, ed. Tara Forrest and Anna Scheer (Chicago: Intellect, 2010), 105–22.

5. See Tom Finkelpearl, *What We Made: Conversations on Art and Social Cooperation* (Durham, N.C.: Duke University Press, 2013). From a critical perspective, Claire Bishop has raised important questions as to whether this appeal to aesthetic participation might ultimately be complicit with a neoliberal anti-politics. See Bishop, *Artificial Hells*, 11–40.

6. This passage appears in Hegel's early essay (1802–3) on natural right. See G. W. F. Hegel, *Hegel: Political Writings*, ed. Laurence Dickey and H. B. Nisbet (New York: Cambridge University Press, 1999), 179.

7. Friedrich Schiller, *Letters on the Aesthetic Education of Man*, trans. Elizabeth Wilkinson and L. A. Willoughby (New York: Oxford University Press, 1967), 9.

8. A productive reading of this performance appears in Elisabeth Anker, *Orgies of Feeling: Melodrama and the Politics of Freedom* (Durham, N.C.: Duke University Press, 2014), 244–50.

9. This political pageantry is helpfully explored by Crispin Sartwell, *Political Aesthetics* (Ithaca, N.Y.: Cornell University Press, 2010). There is always the possibility, of course, that this visual rhetoric can be co-opted and transformed so as to subvert the messages it is meant to serve. The contemporary practice of "ad-busting," for instance, represents one such effort to use the symbolic mythology of brands against the industry or corporation in question. See Naomi Klein, *No Logo* (New York: Picador 2000), chap. 12.

10. Michel Foucault, *Discipline and Punish: The Birth of the Prison*, trans. Alan Sheridan (New York: Vintage, 1979), 32–65.

11. See, for instance, Saidiya Hartman, *Scenes of Subjection: Terror, Slavery and Self-Making in Nineteenth-Century America* (New York: Oxford University Press, 1997).

12. Helpful accounts appear in Amy Wood, *Lynching and Spectacle: Witnessing Racial Violence in America, 1890–1940* (Chapel Hill: University of North Carolina Press, 2011), 1–13; Michael Hatt, "Race, Ritual and Responsibility: Performativity and the Southern Lynching," in *Performing the Body/Performing the Text*, ed. Amelia Jones and Andrew Stephenson (New York: Routledge, 1999), 76–88.

13. To return to the spectacle of "mission accomplished," Elizabeth Anker has suggested a different set of reflexive aims: the image of the warrior-sovereign compensates for the devitalization of politics in neoliberal times. Perhaps the fiction of national sovereignty has been pierced by the irruption of terrorist violence within "the homeland." Still, the spectacle of the warrior conveys strength and autonomy; an agent that strikes at enemies, no matter where they might flee or hide. And if the citizen does not *do* these things, he or she can nonetheless identify with the sovereign and share in the agency it embodies. This argument is elaborated throughout Anker, *Orgies of Feeling*, particularly chap. 5.

14. For an interesting overview, see Giorgio Agamben, *The Kingdom and the Glory*, trans. Lorenzo Chiesa (Stanford, Calif.: Stanford University Press, 2011), chap. 7.

15. On this point, see Rainer Stollmann and Ronald Smith, "Fascist Politics as a Total Work of Art: Tendencies of the Aestheticization of Political Life in National Socialism," *New German Critique*, no. 14 (1978): 42–46. Wendy Brown likewise addresses the material structures by which the state performs its sovereignty in *Walled States, Waning Sovereignty* (New York: Zone Books, 2010), chap. 1.

16. The phrase, of course, stems from Benedict Anderson, *Imagined Communities: Reflections on the Origin and Spread of Nationalism* (New York: Verso, 2006).

17. Peter Maass, "The Toppling," *The New Yorker*, January 10, 2011, http://www.newyorker.com/magazine/2011/01/10/the-toppling. For broader reflections on viewing war as a form of distant spectacle, see Robert Hariman and John

Lucaites, *The Public Image: Photography and Civic Spectatorship* (Chicago: University of Chicago Press, 2016), chap. 6; Jan Mieskowski, *Watching War* (Stanford, Calif.: Stanford University Press, 2012); Nicholas Mirzoeff, *Watching Babylon: The War in Iraq and Global Visual Culture* (New York: Routledge, 2005).

18. This ambivalence has also been noted by Allan Megill. Megill's study, however, tends to endorse the position I contest throughout this study: that "aestheticization" represents an intrinsically dangerous stance that must be carefully rooted out and domesticated. See Megill, *Prophets of Extremity: Nietzsche, Heidegger, Foucault, Derrida* (Berkeley: University of California Press, 1987), 2.

19. This reading reflects the central argument of Clement Greenberg, *Art and Culture: Critical Essays* (Boston: Beacon, 1965).

20. Max Weber, "Religious Rejections of the World and Their Directions," in *From Max Weber: Essays in Sociology*, ed. H. H. Gerth and C. Wright Mills (New York: Oxford University Press, 1946), 342.

21. In symptomatic terms, George Kateb writes: "The preponderant tendency, however, in those who want a self to be like a work of art or a life to be like a well-made story, is not merely nonmoral and not merely intent on seeing that the idea of innocent becoming and activity retain a place in the conceptual landscape and in life itself. There is rather an eagerness to see indifference to or disregard of morality as aesthetically indispensable." This passage appears in "Aestheticism and Morality: Their Cooperation and Hostility," *Political Theory* 28, no. 1 (2000): 29–30.

22. Perhaps the clearest example rests in Nietzsche's notorious reference to the "blonde beasts" who forge a state out of a "shapeless and shifting" mass: "Such beings cannot be reckoned with, they come like fate, without cause, reason, consideration or pretext, they appear just like lightning appears, too terrible, sudden, convincing and 'other' even to be hated. What they do is to create and imprint forms instinctively, they are the most involuntary, unconscious artists there are—where they appear, soon something new arises, a structure of domination that *lives*, in which parts and functions are differentiated and related to one another. . . . They do not know what guilt, responsibility, consideration are, these born organizers; they are ruled by that terrible inner artist's egoism which has a brazen countenance and sees itself justified to all eternity by the 'work,' like the mother in her child." This passage appears in *On the Genealogy of Morality*, trans. Carol Diethe (New York: Cambridge University Press, 2006), 58–59. Likewise, Martin Heidegger places the work of the statesman in analogy with the work of poets and thinkers: those "founders" who use their creative powers to open a shared space of meaning in which community first becomes a possibility. For the clearest instance, see Heidegger, "Origin of the Work of Art," in *Basic Writings*, ed. David Krell (New York: Harper Collins, 1977), 139–212.

23. Cited in Stollmann and Smith, "Fascist Politics as a Total Work of Art," 47. Crispin Sartwell offers a helpful discussion of the aesthetic resonance of fascist politics in *Political Aesthetics*, 15–47. For the specifically Italian case of fascist aestheticism, see Simonetta Falasca-Zamponi, *Fascist Spectacle: The Aesthetics of Power in Mussolini's Italy* (Berkeley: University of California Press, 1997).

24. On this point, see Martin Jay, "'The Aesthetic Ideology' as Ideology:

or What Does It Mean to Aestheticize Politics?" in *Force Fields: Between Intellectual History and Cultural Critique* (New York: Routledge, 1993), 74.

25. As the Retort Collective maintains, "the horrors of September 11 were designed above all to be visible." See *Afflicted Powers: Capital and Spectacle in a New Age of War* (New York: Verso, 2005), 25–26. See also Henry Giroux, "Beyond the Spectacle of Terrorism: Rethinking Politics in the Society of the Image," *Situations: Project of the Radical Imagination*, 2, no. 1 (2007): 17–52; Diego von Vacano, *The Art of Power: Machiavelli, Nietzsche, and the Making of Aesthetic Political Theory* (Lanham, Md.: Lexington, 2007), 190–92.

26. Although many dismiss these productions as flatly "barbaric," they reflect a clear aesthetic strategy. It is not simply the care in framing or scripting or costume that is evident in these videos—but rather the post-production work, where cuts are overlaid with musical cues, and set into sequences with scriptural passages and the symbology of militant organizations (itself carefully crafted through a committed branding effort). This point is detailed by David Carr, "With Videos of Killings, ISIS Sends Medieval Message by Modern Method," *New York Times*, September 7, 2014, http://www.nytimes.com/2014/09/08/business/media/with-videos-of-killings-isis-hones-social-media-as-a-weapon.html. See also Roxanne Euben, "Spectacles of Sovereignty in Digital Time: ISIS Executions, Visual Rhetoric and Sovereign Power," *Perspectives of Politics* 15, no. 4 (2017): 1007–1033; Brad Evans and Henry Giroux, *Disposable Futures: The Seduction of Violence in the Age of Spectacle* (San Francisco: City Lights Books, 2015), 221–40.

27. Nancy Rosenblum, *Another Liberalism: Romanticism and the Reconstruction of Liberal Thought* (Cambridge, Mass.: Harvard University Press, 1987), 98. Richard Wolin puts the "radical aestheticist" move in similar terms: "when one refuses to rest content with the aesthetic realm as merely *one* of life's value-spheres (along with science and morality), but treats it instead as the sovereign and exclusive sphere of value and meaning in life." This passage appears in Wolin, "Foucault's Aesthetic Decisionism," *Telos* 67 (1986): 78.

28. Oscar Wilde, *The Picture of Dorian Gray and Three Stories* (New York: Signet Classics, 2007), 101.

29. In late antiquity, for instance, Augustine indicted how gladiatorial displays rebound upon the spectators, enter in through their eyes, and corrupt their character. See *Confessions*, trans. Henry Chadwick (New York: Oxford University Press, 1991), 100–101.

30. This passage appears in Benjamin, "The Work of Art in the Age of Mechanical Reproduction," 241. A more nuanced rendering of Marinetti's gambit can be found in Andrew Hewitt, *Fascist Modernism: Aesthetics, Politics, and the Avant-Garde* (Stanford, Calif.: Stanford University Press, 1993), particularly chapters 5 and 6.

31. In this connection, Martin Jay offers that the act of aestheticization "repels not merely because of the grotesque impropriety of applying criteria of beauty to the deaths of human beings, but also because of the chilling way in which non-aesthetic criteria are deliberately and provocatively excluded from consideration." See Jay, "'The Aesthetic Ideology' as Ideology," 73.

32. Zygmunt Bauman, for instance, raises concerns about how ready access to images of atrocity may yield to "viewer fatigue," normalizing what was once con-

sidered unthinkable. See Bauman, *Life in Fragments: Essays in Postmodern Morality* (Malden, Mass.: Blackwell, 1995), 149–50. See also Evans and Giroux, *Disposable Futures*, 70–74.

33. Susan Sontag, *On Photography* (New York: Picador, 1973), 20.

34. Sontag, *On Photography*, 110.

35. Such a rejoinder is offered by Ariella Azoulay, *The Civil Contract of Photography* (Cambridge, Mass.: MIT Press, 2012); Mark Reinhardt, "Painful Photographs: From the Ethics of Spectatorship to Visual Politics," in *Ethics and Images of Pain*, ed. Asbjorn Gronstad and Henrik Gustaffson (New York: Routledge, 2012), 33–55; and Mark Reinhardt, "Picturing Violence: Aesthetics and the Anxiety of Critique," in *Beautiful Suffering: Photography and the Traffic in Pain*, ed. Mark Reinhardt and Holly Edwards (Chicago: University of Chicago Press, 2007), 13–36.

36. This turn is particularly evident in Susan Sontag, *Regarding the Suffering of Others* (New York: Picador, 2004). A helpful account of Sontag's shift on this question appears in Michael Kelly, *A Hunger for Aesthetics: Enacting the Demands of Art* (New York: Columbia University Press, 2012), 56–83. See also Hariman and Lucaites, *The Public Image*, 7–11.

37. Judith Butler offers similar reflections on the circulation of the Abu Ghraib photographs. See Butler, *Frames of War* (New York: Verso, 2009), 10–11, 63–100. For broader reflections on the circulation of images and democratic citizenship, see Robert Hariman and John Lucaites, *No Caption Needed: Iconic Photographs, Public Culture, and Liberal Democracy* (Chicago: University of Chicago Press, 2007), 287–305.

38. For particularly clear examples of this approach, see Kateb, "Aestheticism and Morality." Although Kateb eventually arrives at a more nuanced position, described as "democratic aestheticism," the essay persistently turns upon intuitive distinctions between the aesthetic and moral spheres that never interrogate their historical fashioning, changing meanings, or shifts in their relationship.

39. Reinhardt, "Picturing Violence," 21–22.

40. Jürgen Habermas, *The Theory of Communicative Action*, vol. 1, trans. Thomas McCarthy (Boston: Beacon, 1984), 176–77.

41. As Habermas puts it: "The *unmediated* transposition of specialized knowledge into the private and public spheres of the everyday world can endanger the autonomy and independent logics of the knowledge systems, on the one hand, and it can violate the integrity of lifeworld contexts, on the other. A knowledge specialized in only one validity claim, which, without sticking to its specific context, bounces across the whole spectrum of validity, unsettles the equilibrium of the lifeworld's communicative infrastructure. Insufficiently complex incursions of this sort lead to the aestheticizing, or the scientizing, or the moralizing of particular domains of life and give rise to effects for which expressivist countercultures, technocratically carried out reforms, or fundamentalist movements can serve as drastic examples." This passage is found in *The Philosophical Discourses of Modernity: Twelve Lectures*, trans. Frederick Lawrence (Cambridge, Mass.: MIT Press, 1987), 340.

42. Lutz Koepnick, "Aesthetic Politics Today: Walter Benjamin and Post-Fordist Culture," in *Critical Theory: Current State and Future Prospects*, ed. Peter Uwe Hohendahl and Jaimey Fisher (New York: Berghahn Books, 2002), 95.

43. Michel Foucault, "Critical Theory/Intellectual History," in *Critique and Power: Recasting the Foucault/Habermas Debate*, ed. Michael Kelly (Cambridge, Mass.: MIT Press, 1994), 118.

44. Anthony Cascardi articulates these concerns well: "Rather than accept Kant's (or any other) systematic division of the rational faculties as self-contained or self-justifying, as something that can be verified as categorically valid or *a priori* true, I would call attention to the legislative force that must divide reason into these separate domains. . . . The discourse of aesthetics and the problem of reflective judgment could only come to light in an environment that embeds these differentiations socially and materially." These passages are found in Cascardi, *Consequences of Enlightenment* (New York: Cambridge University Press, 1999), 13, 15.

45. Seyla Benhabib, *Situating the Self: Gender, Community, and Postmodernism in Contemporary Ethics* (New York: Routledge, 1992), 41–42.

46. The literature on this theme is far too robust to be adequately engaged here. For some stimulating examples, see Claire Bishop, *Artificial Hells*; Diana Boros, *Creative Rebellion for the Twenty-First Century: The Importance of Public and Interactive Art to Political Life in America* (New York: Palgrave Macmillan, 2012); Paul Clements, *The Creative Underground: Art, Politics, and Everyday Life* (New York: Routledge, 2017); Murray Edelman, *From Art to Politics: How Artistic Creations Shape Political Conceptions* (Chicago: University of Chicago Press, 1996); Boris Groys, *Art Power* (Cambridge, Mass.: MIT Press, 2013); Maggie Nelson, *The Art of Cruelty: A Reckoning* (New York: W. W. Norton, 2011); and Nato Thompson, *Living as Form: Socially Engaged Art from 1991–2011* (Cambridge, Mass.: MIT Press, 2012).

47. Herbert Marcuse, *The Aesthetic Dimension: Toward a Critique of Marxist Aesthetics* (Boston: Beacon, 1978).

48. Theodor Adorno, *Minima Moralia: Reflections on Damaged Life*, trans. E. F. N. Jephcott (New York: Verso, 1974), 76.

49. Elaine Scarry, *On Beauty and Being Just* (Princeton, N.J.: Princeton University Press, 1999), 80.

50. Diego von Vacano has also pressed Scarry's argument with some useful critical questions. See von Vacano, *The Art of Power*, 180–82.

51. Such questions rest at the heart of Pierre Bourdieu, *Distinction: A Social Critique of the Judgment of Taste*, trans. Richard Nice (Cambridge, Mass.: Harvard University Press, 1984).

52. Gabriel Rockhill, *Radical History & the Politics of Art* (New York: Columbia University Press, 2014), 6, 173, 219–24.

53. This effort to interrogate the difficulties of critical theory in "dark" times is the core question of Wendy Brown, *Edgework: Critical Essays on Knowledge and Politics* (Princeton, N.J.: Princeton University Press, 2005), particularly chapter 1.

Chapter 1

1. Max Horkheimer, *Critical Theory: Selected Essays*, trans. Matthew J. O'Connell (New York: Continuum, 1972), 215.

2. Adorno, *Minima Moralia,* 25.

3. Adorno, *Minima Moralia,* 27–28.

4. Jürgen Habermas, *Philosophical-Political Profiles,* trans. Frederick G. Lawrence (Cambridge, Mass.: MIT Press, 1985), 142.

5. Theodor Adorno, *Aesthetic Theory,* trans. Robert Hullot-Kentor (Minneapolis: University of Minnesota Press, 1997), 130.

6. This excellent phrase was suggested to me in conversation by Mark Reinhardt.

7. This is the basis for Gyorgy Lukács's famous indictment: "A considerable part of the German intelligentsia, including Adorno, have taken up residence in 'the Grand Hotel Abyss' . . . a beautiful hotel, equipped with every comfort, on the edge of an abyss, of nothingness, of absurdity. And the daily contemplation of the abyss between excellent meals or artistic entertainments, can only heighten the enjoyment of the subtle comforts offered." Lukács, *The Theory of the Novel,* trans. Anna Bostock (Cambridge, Mass.: MIT Press, 1971), 22.

8. Axel Honneth, for instance, proposes that the work of art offers "a sort of aesthetic compensation for the lost confidence in the revolutionary potential of the oppressed class." See Honneth, *The Critique of Power: Reflective Stages in a Critical Social Theory,* trans. Kenneth Baynes (Cambridge, Mass.: MIT Press, 1993), 65.

9. Axel Honneth, "Communication and Reconciliation: Habermas' Critique of Adorno," in *The Frankfurt School: Critical Assessments,* vol. 6, ed. J. M. Bernstein (New York: Routledge, 1994), 48.

10. Douglas Kellner, "Critical Theory and the Culture Industries: A Reassessment," *Telos,* vol. 62 (1984–85): 197.

11. Habermas, of course, charges that Adorno's indictment of modernity commits a "performative contradiction." Adorno both indicts reason as intrinsically dominating *and yet* employs reason in his own model of a normatively desirable society. As Habermas puts this difficulty: "the description of the self-destruction of the critical capacity is paradoxical because in the moment of description it still has to make use of critique that has been declared dead. It denounces the Enlightenment's becoming totalitarian with its own tools." Habermas, *Philosophical Discourses of Modernity,* 199. This challenge is echoed by Axel Honneth, *The Critique of Power,* 32–56.

12. See, for instance, Albrecht Wellmer, "Reason, Utopia and the *Dialectic of Enlightenment,*" in *Habermas and Modernity,* ed. Richard Bernstein (Cambridge, Mass.: MIT Press, 1985), 35–66.

13. In Habermas's terms, this starting point can no longer address situations of consensus between rational beings; rather, it would be a "condition of reconciliation" in which "we talk with animals, plants and rocks." Habermas, *Philosophical-Political Profiles,* 107.

14. The full passage from David Roberts reads as follows: "Adorno's utopia of reconciliation in turn may be seen as the rational veneer for a profoundly arational mysticism of redemptive mimesis beyond and behind all civilization." This passage appears in Roberts, *Art and Enlightenment: Aesthetic Theory after Adorno* (Lincoln: University of Nebraska Press, 1991), 70.

15. In this sense, the chapter will continue a literature that contests this familiar Habermasian story through a more faithful engagement with Adorno's thought. For other examples, see Romand Coles, "Identity and Difference in the Ethical Positions of Adorno and Habermas," in *The Cambridge Companion to Habermas,* ed. Stephen White (New York: Cambridge University Press), 19–45; Martin Morris, *Rethinking the Communicative Turn: Adorno, Habermas, and the Problem of Communicative Freedom* (Albany: SUNY Press, 2001); and Joel Whitebook, *Perversion and Utopia: A Study in Psychoanalysis and Critical Theory* (Cambridge, Mass.: MIT Press, 1996).

16. Albrecht Wellmer puts this point well: "Once the cognitive structures of a disenchanted consciousness are institutionalized as secularized systems of cultural discourse and social interaction, a process of rationalization—now in the specifically Weberian sense—is set into motion which tends to undermine the social basis for the existence of autonomous and rational individuals. . . . Humanity's becoming rational—i.e., reason's coming of age—by an internal logic triggers historical processes which tend to depersonalize social relationships, to desiccate symbolic communication, and to subject human life to the impersonal logic of rationalized, anonymous administrative systems—historical processes, in short, which tend to make human life mechanized, unfree, and meaningless." This passage is found in Wellmer, "Reason, Utopia, and the *Dialectic of Enlightenment,*" 43.

17. Theodor Adorno and Max Horkheimer, *Dialectic of Enlightenment,* trans. John Cummings (New York: Continuum, 1972), 3.

18. Friedrich Nietzsche, "Truth and Lie in an Extra-Moral Sense," in *The Portable Nietzsche,* ed. Walter Kaufman (New York: Penguin Books, 1959), 46. This parallel to Nietzsche's argument is also noted by Peter Dews, "Adorno, Poststructuralism and the Critique of Identity" in *The Limits of Disenchantment* (New York: Verso, 1995), 19–38.

19. Adorno and Horkheimer, *Dialectic of Enlightenment,* 13.

20. As Morton Schoolman proposes: "reason reduces nature and the world of differences in all their diversity to mere resistance to abstract thought. Knowing is overcoming resistance, substituting thought of the universal features of an object for the object itself, placing the unique difference belonging to an object of thought into servitude to terms alien to what is essentially different about it, servitude as domination." See Schoolman, *Reason and Horror: Critical Theory, Democracy and Aesthetic Individuality* (New York: Routledge, 2001), 33.

21. Theodor Adorno, *History and Freedom: Lectures 1964–65,* trans. Rodney Livingstone (Malden, Mass.: Polity, 2006), 13.

22. This connection has been correctly noted by Adorno's more materialist commentators. See, for instance, Jay Bernstein, "Negative Dialectics as Fate: Adorno and Hegel," in *The Cambridge Companion to Adorno,* ed. Tom Huhn (New York: Cambridge University Press, 2004), 19–50; Simon Jarvis, "The 'Unhappy Consciousness' and Conscious Unhappiness: On Adorno's Critique of Hegel and the Idea of an Hegelian Critique of Adorno," in *Hegel's Phenomenology of Spirit: A Re-Appraisal,* ed. Gary Browning (London: Kluwer Academic, 1997), 57–72. See also Brian O'Connor, *Adorno's Negative Dialectic* (Cambridge, Mass.: MIT Press, 2004).

23. This self-grounding model of experience has been most avidly pursued by Robert Pippin, *Idealism as Modernism* (New York: Cambridge University Press, 1997). See also Terry Pinkard, "Historicism, Social Practice, and Sustainability: Some Themes in Hegelian Ethical Theory," in *Neue Hefte für Philosophie* 35 (1995): 56–94. A helpful discussion of this ambivalence, which takes its point of departure from Adorno's lectures on practical philosophy, can be found in Christoph Menke, "Virtue and Reflection: The 'Antinomies of Moral Philosophy,'" trans. James Ingram, *Constellations* 12, no. 1 (2005): 36–49. I have previously treated this connection in Feola, "Difference without Fear: Adorno *contra* Liberalism," *European Journal of Political Theory* 13, no. 1 (2014): 41–60; and Feola, "'Redemption of the Many in the One': Damaged Life and Aesthetic Reparation," *Soundings* 92 (2009): 213–38.

24. Disenchanted knowledge thus takes on the character of a tautology in which "it recognizes nothing new, since it always merely recalls what reason has always deposited in the object." Adorno and Horkheimer, *Dialectic of Enlightenment*, 26. Or, in slightly different terms, "to prevail as a system, the *ratio* eliminated virtually all qualitative definitions it referred to, thus coming into an irreconcilable conflict with the objectivity it violated by pretending to grasp it." Theodor Adorno, *Negative Dialectics*, trans. E. B. Ashton (New York: Continuum, 1973), 21.

25. As Simon Jarvis expresses the point, disenchanted thought therefore "lives off" contents that it cannot avow in its own terms. See Jarvis, "The 'Unhappy Consciousness,'" 66.

26. Jay Bernstein puts this point well: "The canons of rational belief emerged out of progressive demythologization. . . . these canons themselves recognize no outside, no standards but their own formal ones: consistency, coherence, unity, universality, non-arbitrariness, and so on. Thus their reiterative application ends up voiding all objects—including other humans as ends in themselves—as worthy of devotion." Bernstein, *Adorno: Disenchantment and Ethics* (New York: Cambridge University Press, 2001), 100. My account of this process of rationalization (and its stakes) has benefited greatly from Bernstein's text, particularly chapter 2.

27. Adorno, *Negative Dialectics*, 5

28. This is the argument of J. G. Finlayson, "Adorno on the Ethical and the Ineffable," *European Journal of Philosophy* 10, no. 1 (2002): 1–25. The claim is also made by Robert Pippin, "Negative Ethics: Adorno on the Falseness of Bourgeois Life," in *The Persistence of Subjectivity: On the Kantian Aftermath* (New York: Cambridge University Press, 2005), 98–120.

29. Adorno, *Negative Dialectics*, 161

30. Joseph Winters, "Theodor Adorno and the Unhopeless Work of the Negative," *Journal for Cultural and Religious Theory* 14, no. 1 (2014): 192.

31. As Adorno puts it: "non-identity is the secret *telos* of identification. It is the part that can be salvaged." Adorno, *Negative Dialectics*, 149.

32. Seyla Benhabib, for instance, has challenged these charges of domination as largely metaphorical—based more within rhetoric than rigorous social analysis. As she argues, "the concept of 'domination' must first be specified in the context of interpersonal relations. To reverse the order of explanation, as Adorno and Horkheimer do, only confuses the matter, since a term which originates

in the sphere of interpersonal relationships is then projected onto our relation to nature in order to explain subsequently social relations." Benhabib, *Critique, Norm, Utopia: A Study of the Foundations of Critical Theory* (New York: Columbia University Press, 1986), 219. Similar charges are raised by Honneth, *The Critique of Power*, 50–54.

33. J. L. Austin, *Sense and Sensibilia* (New York: Oxford University Press), 8.

34. See Martin Jay, *Marxism and Totality: The Adventures of a Concept from Lukács to Habermas* (Berkeley: University of California Press, 1986).

35. Adorno and Horkheimer, *Dialectic of Enlightenment*, 28. Or, to put the point in sharper terms: "brutality toward things is potentially brutality toward people." Adorno, *Aesthetic Theory*, 232.

36. As Adorno and Horkheimer charge, "instead of making the object experiential, the purified word treats it as an abstract instance, and everything else . . . fades away in reality. A left-half at football, a black-shirt, a member of the Hitler Youth, and so on, are no more than names." Adorno and Horkheimer, *Dialectic of Enlightenment*, 164.

37. Jean-Joseph Goux offers a productive account of the symbolic economy of capitalism. See *Symbolic Economies: After Marx and Freud* (Ithaca, N.Y.: Cornell University Press, 1990).

38. Karl Marx and Friedrich Engels, "Manifesto of the Communist Party," in *The Marx-Engels Reader*, ed. Robert Tucker (New York: Norton, 1978), 476.

39. Adorno and Horkheimer, *Dialectic of Enlightenment*, 12.

40. This indictment rests at the heart of Adorno's infamous assertion that "no right life is possible within the false [*es gibt kein richtiges leben im falsen*]." Although there is a significant literature on this peculiar phrase, helpful discussions can be found in Jay Bernstein, *Adorno: Disenchantment and Ethics*, 40–74; Fabian Freyenhagen, *Adorno's Practical Philosophy: Living Less Wrongly* (New York: Cambridge University Press, 2013), 26–74; Bert van den Brink, "Damaged Life: Power and Recognition in Adorno's Ethics," in *Recognition and Power: Axel Honneth and the Tradition of Critical Social Theory*, ed. Bert van den Brink and David Owen (New York: Cambridge University Press, 2007), 79–99; and Rahel Jaeggi, "No Individual Can Resist: *Minima Moralia* as Critique of Forms of Life," *Constellations* 12, no. 1 (2005): 65–82.

41. In stark terms "the culture industry has sardonically realized man's species being. Everyone amounts only to those qualities by which he or she can replace everyone else: all are fungible, mere specimens." Adorno and Horkheimer, *Dialectic of Enlightenment*, 116–17.

42. Adorno, *Negative Dialectics*, 309.

43. Christoph Menke has productively elaborated Adorno's normative concerns for this abstract division between universal and particular. See "Genealogy, Deconstruction, Critique: Three Forms of the Questioning of Morality," in *Reflections of Equality*, trans. H. Rouse and A. Denejkine (Stanford, Calif.: Stanford University Press, 2005), 49–85. This account of "abstract" equality draws on my earlier discussion in Feola, "Difference without Fear: Adorno *contra* Liberalism."

44. Jay Bernstein, *Adorno: Disenchantment and Ethics*, particularly chap. 4.

45. On this point, see Jaeggi, "No Individual Can Resist," 68–71.

46. A helpful corrective, which places due emphasis upon the rhetorical *performance* of Adorno's writing, can be found in Axel Honneth, "The Possibility of a Disclosing Critique of Society: The *Dialectic of Enlightenment* in Light of Current Debates in Social Criticism," in *Disrespect: The Normative Foundations of Critical Theory*, trans. John Farrell and Siobhan Kattago (Malden, Mass.: Polity, 2007), 49–62. See also Robert Hullot-Kentor, "Back to Adorno," *Telos* 81 (1989): 5–29.

47. As Susan Buck-Morss puts it: Adorno's "philosophy never included a theory of political action. . . . Although he continued to insist on the necessity for revolutionary social change, such statements remained abstract insofar as Adorno's theory contained no concept of a collective revolutionary subject which might accomplish that change." Buck-Morss, *Origin of Negative Dialectics: Adorno, Benjamin and the Frankfurt Institute* (New York: Free, 1977), 24. See also Gillian Rose, *The Melancholy Science: An Introduction to the Thought of Theodor W. Adorno* (New York: Columbia University Press, 1978), 138–48. A particularly strident account in this direction is offered by Robert Lanning, *In the Hotel Abyss: An Hegelian-Marxist Critique of Adorno* (Boston: Leiden, 2014).

48. Adorno and Horkheimer, *Dialectic of Enlightenment*, 18.

49. Adorno, *Aesthetic Theory*, 135.

50. Adorno, *Aesthetic Theory*, 177.

51. Adorno, *Aesthetic Theory*, 232. An extended version of the argument appears in Adorno, "Extorted Reconciliation: On Georg Lukács' *Wider den missverstandenen Realismus*," in *Notes to Literature, Volume One*, ed. Rolf Tiedemann (New York: Columbia University Press, 1991), 216–40.

52. It is on this point that much of Adorno's polemics with Brecht and Sartre rest. See "Commitment," in *Aesthetics and Politics*, trans. Francis McDonagh (New York: Verso, 1977), 177–95.

53. Terry Eagleton, *Ideology of the Aesthetic* (Malden, Mass.: Blackwell, 1990), 360.

54. I have previously treated this theme in Feola, "'Redemption of the Many in the One': Damaged Life and Aesthetic Reparation." The current discussion explores different possibilities of Adorno's thought and departs considerably from the conclusions of this earlier essay.

55. Adorno, *Aesthetic Theory*, 135. Adorno, of course, does not wish to say that artworks are somehow immune to commodity markets. For reflections on the peculiar commodity status of the work, see *Aesthetic Theory*, 13–22.

56. This character of Adorno's argument is helpfully discussed by Jay Bernstein, "The Dead Speaking of Stones and Stars: Adorno's Aesthetic Theory," in *The Cambridge Companion to Critical Theory*, ed. Fred Rush (New York: Cambridge University Press, 2005), 151–55.

57. Jay Bernstein, *Against Voluptuous Bodies: Late Modernism and the Meaning of Painting* (Stanford, Calif.: Stanford University Press, 2006), 152.

58. For a helpful discussion of the "shudder," see Jay Bernstein, *The Fate of Art: Aesthetic Alienation from Kant to Derrida and Adorno* (University Park: Pennsylvania State University Press, 1992), 220–24. See also Karyn Ball, "Shudder," in *German Aesthetics: Basic Concepts*, ed. J. D. Mininger and Jason Peck (New York: Bloomsbury, 2016), 227–35.

59. Such a reading might seem to be confirmed by those moments, for instance, when Adorno argues that "artworks exercise a practical effect, if they do so at all . . . by the scarcely apprehensible transformation of consciousness." This passage appears in *Aesthetic Theory*, 243. For a reading that stresses this "shock" character of aesthetic experience, see James Hellings, *Adorno and Art: Aesthetic Theory contra Critical Theory* (New York: Palgrave Macmillan, 2014), 102–10. My account of this avant-garde position owes much to Boris Groys, *Art Power*, 111–14.

60. See Bernstein, "The Dead Speaking of Stones and Stars," 140–47.

61. Adorno, *Aesthetic Theory*, 289.

62. In Adorno's terms, "aesthetic unity gains its dignity through the multiplicitous itself. It does justice to the heterogeneous." *Aesthetic Theory*, 191. For a reading that highlights this concern for difference, see Morton Schoolman, "The Reconciliation Image in Art," *Theory & Event* 16, no. 3 (2013).

63. This oversight characterizes readers such as Albrecht Wellmer and Hans Robert Jauss, for whom Adorno's aesthetic theory is meant to overbid on the work (i.e., the internal dialectic of content/form), and fails to grapple with aesthetic experience—the communicative potentials of art that overspill the art world and stimulate broader social conversations. See Jauss, *Aesthetic Experience and Literary Hermeneutics*, trans. Michael Shaw (Minneapolis: University of Minnesota Press, 1982), 13–22; Wellmer, "Truth, Semblance, Reconciliation: Adorno's Aesthetic Redemption of Modernity," in *The Persistence of Modernity: Essays on Aesthetic, Ethics, and Postmodernism*, trans. David Midgley (Cambridge, Mass.: MIT Press, 1991), 1–35. A helpful challenge to Wellmer's reading (as well as its Habermasian basis) is offered by Donald Burke, "Adorno's Aesthetics of Reconciliation: Negative Presentation of Utopia or Post-Metaphysical Pipe Dream?" in *Adorno and the Need in Thinking*, ed. Donald Burke, Colin Campbell, Kathy Kiloh, Michael Palamarek, and Jonathan Short (Toronto: University of Toronto Press, 2007), 233–60. See also the critical rejoinder of Simon Jarvis, *Adorno: A Critical Introduction* (New York: Routledge, 1998), 110–14.

64. In a symptomatic rendering, "Art's enigmatic image is the configuration of mimesis and rationality. This enigmaticalness emerged out of a historical process. Art is what remains after the loss of what was supposed to exercise a magical, and later a cultic, function. Art's why-and-wherefore—its archaic rationality, to put it paradoxically—was forfeited and transformed into an element of its being-in-itself." Adorno, *Aesthetic Theory*, 127.

65. Adorno, *Aesthetic Theory*, 122.

66. A productive account of this engagement between thought and work appears in Lambert Zuidervaart, *Adorno's Aesthetic Theory: The Redemption of Illusion* (Cambridge, Mass.: MIT Press, 1991), 140–44.

67. As this qualifier suggests, it is not the aesthetic, in principle, that is in question. To speak in such terms would commit the "talismanic" error noted earlier in the study: that the aesthetic sphere (typically spoken in ahistorical, singular terms) is somehow superior to the other categorial spheres of modernity, and has access to some "higher" truths (located within a privileged access to Being or Nature or whatever). For Adorno, what art preserves (if anything at all) must be read as the outcome of a history of exclusions and losses, and thus

is only meaningful within this history. Helpful efforts to complicate an "essentialist" or "sovereign" framework for aesthetic capacities are found in Jay Bernstein, *The Fate of Art*, 4–6, 232–40; and Christoph Menke, *The Sovereignty of Art: Aesthetic Negativity in Adorno and Derrida,* trans. Neil Solomon (Cambridge, Mass.: MIT Press, 1998), 3–25.

68. Adorno, *Aesthetic Theory*, 128.

69. Richard Leppert, "Music 'Pushed to the Edge of Existence' (Adorno, Listening, and the Question of Hope)," *Cultural Critique* 60 (Spring 2005): 118.

70. This "active" receptivity is well described by Yvonne Sherratt, *Adorno's Positive Dialectic* (New York: Cambridge University Press, 2004), 163–68.

71. This active sense of interpretive care makes it difficult to follow James Hellings's suggestion that the spectator engages the work by "relinquishing one's subjective agency, choice, and decision-making." See Hellings, *Adorno and Art*, 109.

72. Adorno, *Aesthetic Theory*, 275.

73. See Romand Coles, *Rethinking Generosity: Critical Theory and the Politics of Caritas* (Ithaca, N.Y.: Cornell University Press, 1997), chap. 2. This theme of receptivity is also highlighted by Schoolman's provocative account of aesthetic rationality in *Reason and Horror.*

74. This strategy is also pursued by Lambert Zuidervaart, who likewise offers that a care for the nonidentical is not "restricted" to art in Adorno's thought, even if art is a privileged site for such care within disenchanted modernity. See Zuidervaart, *Social Philosophy after Adorno* (New York: Cambridge University Press, 2007), 70–71.

75. The full quote runs as follows: "Aesthetic identity seeks to aid the nonidentical, which in reality is repressed by reality's compulsion to identity." Adorno, *Aesthetic Theory*, 4.

76. On this refusal of immediacy, see Jarvis, *Adorno: A Critical Introduction*, 181–84. See also Jay Bernstein, *Adorno: Disenchantment and Ethics*, 350–60.

77. Susan Buck-Morss puts the difficulty in stark terms: "Adorno's talk of the mediation between intellectual praxis and political praxis remained abstract and vague, with no explication of the social medium which might serve as a conduit for this medium, once the role of the Party was rejected." Buck-Morss, *Origin of Negative Dialectics*, 42.

78. Adorno, *Negative Dialectics*, 365.

79. This imperative has received considerable critical attention. See Jay Bernstein, *Adorno: Disenchantment and Ethics*, 384–414; Freyenhagen, *Adorno's Practical Philosophy*, chap. 5; Patrice Haynes, "To Rescue Means to Love Things: Adorno and the Re-Enchantment of Bodies," *Critical Quarterly* 47, no. 3 (2005): 64–78.

80. Though Habermas is the touchstone for the deliberative school, this strongly discursive approach is shared by a wide variety of contemporary theorists (far too wide to be treated here). For a representative list, see James Bohman, *Public Deliberation* (Cambridge, Mass.: MIT Press, 2000); John Dryzek, *Deliberative Democracy and Beyond* (New York: Oxford University Press, 2002); John Elster, ed., *Deliberative Democracy* (New York: Cambridge University Press, 1998); James Fishkin, *Democracy and Deliberation* (New Haven, Conn.: Yale University Press, 1991);

Habermas, *The Theory of Communicative Action*; and Amy Gutmann and James Thompson, *Democracy and Disagreement* (Cambridge, Mass.: Harvard University Press, 1996).

81. See Freyenhagen, *Adorno's Practical Philosophy*, 187–208.

82. As Matt Waggoner explains: "morality would have to emerge as the remainder of reason within the moral subject in the form of a somatic impulse reacting spontaneously to what it knows to be bad." Waggoner, "Adorno and the Remainders of Reason," *Constellations* 17, no. 1 (2010): 115. Or, in terms offered by Fabian Freyenhagen, morality has "non-discursive and non-deducible elements to have content and to be efficacious." Freyenhagen, *Adorno's Practical Philosophy*, 193.

83. Adorno, *Negative Dialectics*, 203.

84. As Bernstein puts it: "The thought that the awfulness of suffering *depends* on the vindicability and acceptance of a principle of reason is, he avers, a denial of suffering, its awfulness. Even if that awfulness requires acknowledgement in order to orient significant action, it does not follow that the awfulness has the meaning it does because it is acknowledged by us: offering meaning to suffering is more a way of denying it, its insistence." Jay Bernstein, "The Dead Speaking of Stones and Stars," 155.

85. Adorno, *Negative Dialectics*, 286

86. Theodor Adorno, *Problems of Moral Philosophy*, trans. Rodney Livingston (Malden, Mass.: Polity, 2000), 176. Such gestures are confirmed by his insistence that the responsibility of every agent is to prevent the conditions that led to the Holocaust—a point elaborated in Adorno, "Education after Auschwitz," in *Critical Models: Interventions and Catchwords*, ed. H. Pickford (New York: Columbia University Press, 1998), 191–204. For a more complex rendering of Adorno's political engagements, see Russell Berman, "Adorno's Politics," in *Adorno: A Critical Reader*, ed. Nigel Gibson and Andrew Rubin (Malden, Mass.: Blackwell, 2002), 110–31; Espen Hammer, *Adorno and the Political* (New York: Routledge, 2005), 18–25; and Stefan Müller-Doohm, *Adorno: A Biography*, trans. Rodney Livingstone (Malden, Mass.: Polity, 2005), 325–447.

87. Adorno, *Aesthetic Theory*, 289.

88. For the "social imaginary," see Charles Taylor, *Modern Social Imaginaries* (Durham, N.C.: Duke University Press, 2004). The canonical discussion of "common sense" appears in Antonio Gramsci, *Selections from the Prison Notebooks*, trans. Quintin Hoare and Geoffrey Nowell Smith (New York: International, 1971).

89. Morris, *Rethinking the Communicative Turn*, 170. See also Matt Waggoner's helpful account in "Adorno and the Remainders of Reason."

90. On this point, see Roger Foster, *Adorno: The Recovery of Experience* (Albany: SUNY Press, 2007), 86–87.

91. Here I follow the insight of Morton Schoolman—that Odysseus's gesture is both suggestive and ambivalent. On the one hand, he exposes himself to the lure of sensuality; on the other hand, he chooses to preserve his self-mastery through the technology of the rational man: the rope, the wax, the mast. And the ambivalence is surely instructive: that every engagement with difference threatens its own forms of closure and refusal. See Schoolman, *Reason and Horror*, 61–68. For an account of Odysseus that helpfully stresses the moments of sound and

femininity, see Nancy Love, "Why Do the Sirens Sing? Figuring the Feminine in *Dialectic of Enlightenment*," *Theory & Event* 3, no. 1 (1999).

92. See, for instance, Freyenhagen, *Adorno's Practical Philosophy*, 162–86. Other useful efforts to detail Adorno's practical involvements include Paul Apostolidis, *Stations of the Cross: Adorno and Christian Right Radio* (Durham, N.C.: Duke University Press, 2000); David Jenemann, *Adorno in America* (Minneapolis: University of Minnesota Press, 2007); and Shannon Mariotti, "Adorno on the Radio: Democratic Leadership as Democratic Pedagogy," *Political Theory* 42, no. 4 (2014): 415–42.

93. Lambert Zuidervaart, for instance, argues that such readings that privilege "enlightened individual resistance" ultimately end up with an "apolitical ethics," rather than a meaningful, Adornian politics. See *Social Philosophy after Adorno*, 157–63.

94. Didier Fassin, *Humanitarian Reason: A Moral History of the Present*, trans. Rachel Gomme (Berkeley: University of California Press, 2012), 21–43.

95. On this point, see Jodi Dean, *Democracy and Other Neoliberal Fantasies* (Durham, N.C.: Duke University Press, 2009). For a helpful account that links the practice of "listening" to the consumer-citizen of New Labour, see Elizabeth Vidler and John Clarke, "Creating Citizen-Consumers: New Labour and the Remaking of Public Services," *Public Policy and Administration*, 20, no. 2 (2005): 19–37.

96. By doing so, I follow the lead of Paul Apostolidis and Shane Phelan. See Apostolidis, "Negative Dialectics and Inclusive Communication," in *Feminist Interpretations of Theodor Adorno*, ed. Renée Heberle (University Park: Pennsylvania State University Press, 2006), 233–56; Phelan, "Interpretation and Domination: Adorno and the Habermas-Lyotard Debate," *Polity* 25, no. 4 (1993): 597–616. This chapter's engagement with deliberative thought has benefited considerably from Morris, *Rethinking the Communicative Turn*, 168–88.

97. This is particularly the case for the Rawlsian variant of a deliberative politics. See John Rawls, *Political Liberalism* (New York: Columbia University Press, 1993).

98. Moreover, these are the possibilities (ostensibly) overlooked by the Frankfurt School when they reduce reason to the instrumental mastery wielded by the subject against the world he seeks to control and manipulate. This position is best conveyed in Habermas, *The Theory of Communicative Action*, 366–99. See also Benhabib, *Critique, Norm and Utopia*, 147–85; Albrecht Wellmer, "Reason, Utopia and the *Dialectic of Enlightenment*."

99. Lynn Sanders, "Against Deliberation," *Political Theory* 25, no. 3 (1997): 347–76; Iris Young, "Communication and the Other: Beyond Deliberative Democracy," in *Democracy and Difference*, ed. Seyla Benhabib (Princeton: Princeton University Press, 1996), 120–35. Helpful challenges are also raised by Margaret Kohn, "Language, Power, and Persuasion: Toward a Critique of Deliberative Democracy," *Constellations* 7, no. 3 (2000): 408–29.

100. Wilfrid Sellars, *In the Space of Reasons: Selected Essays of Wilfrid Sellars*, ed. Robert Brandom and Kevin Scharp (Cambridge, Mass.: Harvard University Press, 2007).

101. As Young maintains, for instance, the deliberative emphasis upon "rational" argument might unduly limit the kind of discursive moves that can be recognized as authoritative, demanding attention and respect. Where the deliberative approach advertises participatory equality—permitting all members to speak, raise questions, and challenge policies or institutions—the rationalist reduction on what counts as argumentative discourse (cool, dispassionate, offered in measured tones) forecloses the possibility that other modes of discourse will be taken seriously (e.g., greeting, narrative, jokes, folklore, prayer, history, scripture, mythology—or speech that is suffused with emotion). See Iris Young, *Inclusion and Democracy* (New York: Oxford University Press, 2000), 39–49. This common ground between Young and Adorno has likewise been explored by Apostolidis, "Negative Dialectics and Inclusive Communication."

102. On this point, see Margaret Somers, *Genealogies of Citizenship: Markets, Statelessness and the Right to Have Rights* (New York: Cambridge University Press, 2008).

103. See, for instance, Ta-Nehisi Coates, "The Case for Reparations," *The Atlantic* 313 (2014): 54–71; Thomas McCarthy, "Coming to Terms with Our Past, Part II: On the Morality and Politics of Reparations for Slavery," *Political Theory* 32, no. 6 (December 2004): 750–72.

104. Iris Young, *Responsibility for Justice* (New York: Oxford University Press, 2013), 95–122.

105. Some helpful accounts are collected in Collectif Argos, *Climate Refugees* (Cambridge, Mass.: MIT Press, 2010).

106. Nancy Fraser, *Scales of Justice: Reimagining Political Space in a Globalizing World* (New York: Columbia University Press, 2009), 48–75.

107. Adorno, *Negative Dialectics*, 163.

108. On this point, see Jill Stauffer, *Ethical Loneliness: The Injustice of Not Being Heard* (New York: Columbia University Press, 2015), particularly chapters 1 and 3.

109. Renée Heberle, "Living with Negative Dialectics: Feminism and the Politics of Suffering," in *Feminist Interpretations of Theodor Adorno*, 220. Romand Coles likewise highlights the persistence of violence and closure, even within a politics of dialogical generosity in Coles, *Rethinking Generosity*, 90–95, 127–31.

110. In a 1965 lecture Adorno details: "it follows that there is no such thing as moral certainty or a self-evident morality, or direct moral self-certainty. We might almost say that to suggest that we could ever know beyond doubt and unproblematically what is good, would be the beginning of all evil." Adorno, *History and Freedom*, 262. For this reason, Finlayson identifies humility as one of the core virtues of Adorno's moral theory—where the subject is tasked with a fallibilist stance toward his own moral categories, leaving them open to revision in the face of their aporias and blind spots. Finlayson, "Adorno on the Ethical and the Ineffable," 6–7. Shane Phelan also offers a helpful rendering: "the fallacy in question is the belief that our concepts adequately describe and, even more, construct the world in which we live. Such a belief keeps us blind to the actual forms of domination around and within us." This passage appears in Phelan, "Interpretation and Domination," 600.

111. Kate Lacey, *Listening Publics: The Politics and Experience of Listening in the Media Age* (Malden, Mass.: Polity, 2013), chapters 1 and 7.

112. Nikolas Kompridis, "Receptivity, Possibility and Democratic Politics," *Ethics & Global Politics* 4 (2011): 264.

113. The literature on Adorno's ostensible elitism is considerable. The staple charge is that Adorno disparages popular expressions of culture (as largely complicit with the operations of ideology) and endorses an elitist form of high culture. See, for instance, Bruce Baugh, "Left-Wing Elitism: Adorno on Popular Culture," *Philosophy and Literature* 14, no. 1 (1990): 65–78; Douglas Kellner, *Critical Theory, Marxism, and Modernity* (Baltimore: Johns Hopkins University Press, 1989); see also John Weaver and Toby Daspit, "Promises to Keep Finally? Academic Culture and the Dismissal of Popular Culture," in *Promises to Keep: Cultural Studies, Democratic Education and Public Life*, ed. Greg Dimitriadis and Dennis Carlson (New York: Routledge, 2003), 137–54. A more balanced, sensitive account can be found in Andreas Huyssen, *After the Great Divide: Modernism, Mass Culture, Postmodernism* (Bloomington: Indiana University Press, 1986), chap. 2.

114. For the democratic challenges that attend an increasingly "gated" world, see Romand Coles, *Beyond Gated Politics: Reflections for the Possibility of Democracy* (Minneapolis: University of Minnesota Press, 2005). See also Young, *Inclusion and Democracy*, chap. 6.

Chapter 2

1. Adorno, *Minima Moralia*, 25.

2. Michel Foucault, "On the Genealogy of Ethics," in *Michel Foucault: Ethics, Subjectivity and Truth*, ed. Paul Rabinow (New York: New, 1997), 256.

3. Michel Foucault, "Critical Theory/Intellectual History," in *Critique and Power: Recasting the Foucault/Habermas Debate*, ed. Michael Kelly (Cambridge, Mass.: MIT Press, 1994), 117.

4. Foucault, "On the Genealogy of Ethics," 261.

5. A particularly bitter denunciation is raised by Richard Wolin, who charges that if Foucault's aesthetic vision is "followed to its conclusion, *carte blanche* is accorded to forms of life that are manipulative and predatory *vis-à-vis* other persons." Wolin, "Foucault's Aesthetic Decisionism," *Telos* 67 (1986): 84.

6. Michel Foucault, "What Is Enlightenment?" in *Michel Foucault: Ethics, Subjectivity and Truth*, 303–19.

7. As Foucault puts it: "a whole problematic then develops: that of an architecture that is no longer built simply to be seen (as with the ostentation of palaces), or to observe the external space . . . but to permit an internal, articulated and detailed control—to render visible those who are inside it; in more general terms, an architecture that would operate to transform individuals: to act on those it shelters, to provide a hold on their conduct to carry the effects of power right to them, to make it possible to know them, to alter them." *Discipline and Punish*, 172.

8. Foucault, *Discipline and Punish*, 206.

9. Foucault, *Discipline and Punish*, 211.

10. Foucault, *Discipline and Punish*, 135–69.

11. Foucault, *Discipline and Punish*, 184–92.

12. This is not, of course, to say that disciplinary power comes to replace the exercise of sovereign power, in some sequential, either/or movement of power regimes. Rather, such regimes may overlap, inform, and reinforce one another. On this point, see Wendy Brown, *Regulating Aversion: Tolerance in the Age of Identity and Empire* (Princeton, N.J.: Princeton University Press, 2006), 78–82.

13. In a well-known formulation, Foucault states: "Power must be analyzed as something which circulates, or rather as something which only functions in the form of a chain. It is never localized here or there, never in anybody's hands, never appropriated as a commodity or piece of wealth. . . . And not only do individuals circulate between its threads; they are always in the position of simultaneously undergoing and exercising this power." See Michel Foucault, "Two Lectures," in *Power/Knowledge: Selected Interviews and Other Writings*, ed. Colin Gordon (New York: Pantheon Books, 1977), 98.

14. Foucault, *Discipline and Punish*, 194.

15. Michel Foucault, *Foucault Live: Collected Interviews, 1961–1984*, ed. Sylvere Lotringer (New York: Semiotext(e)), 209. This formulation permits another critical engagement to be noted in passing. Although the reconstruction has thus far emphasized Foucault's challenge to a liberal-contractual model of power, so too does he distance himself from prominent Left appeals to ideology. Rather than situate power within false or distorted beliefs about the world, Foucault insists that disciplinary power installs itself at the most fundamental level of materiality—the body in its movements, rhythms, reflexes, and forces.

16. Cited in David Halperin, *Saint Foucault: Towards a Gay Hagiography* (New York: Oxford University Press, 1995), 22.

17. Wolin, "Foucault's Aesthetic Decisionism," 86. Likewise, Charles Taylor concludes that Foucault's argument is not only pessimistic, but ultimately incoherent, since there is no place for the freedom in light of which these reflections on constraint or domination would gain conceptual and normative content. See Taylor, "Foucault on Freedom and Truth," *Political Theory* 12, no. 2 (1984): 152–83.

18. This reserve is most evident in the writings of Herbert Marcuse—particularly his insistence upon a "biological foundation" for solidarity that rests in the erotic sensibilities of human beings. See Marcuse, *Essay on Liberation* (Boston: Beacon, 1969).

19. Paul Patton offers an important rejoinder to the assumptions that structure this reading. See Patton, "Foucault's Subject of Power," *Political Theory Newsletter* 6 (1994): 60–71.

20. Axel Honneth, "Foucault's Theory of Society: A Systems-Theoretic Dissolution of the *Dialectic of Enlightenment*," in *Critique and Power: Recasting the Foucault/Habermas Debate*, 199.

21. In a well-known passage, E. B. Thompson charges that "Foucault . . . gives us history as a subject-less structure, and one in which men and women are obliterated by ideologies." See Thompson, *The Poverty of Theory: or An Orrery of Errors* (London: Merlin, 1978), 263. Nancy Hartsock proposes that Foucault offers a world where "things move, rather than people, a world in which subjects become obliterated or, rather, recreated as passive objects, a world in which passivity or refusal represent the only possible choices." This passage appears in "Foucault on

Power: A Theory for Women?" in *Feminism/Postmodernism*, ed. Linda Nicholson (New York: Routledge, 1990), 167.

22. In a late essay, Foucault proposes that "most important is the relationship between power relations and confrontation strategies. For, if it is true that at the heart of power relations and as a permanent condition of their existence there is an insubordination and a certain essential obstinacy on the part of the principles of freedom, then there is no relationship of power without the means of escape or possible flight." See Foucault, "The Subject and Power," in *Michel Foucault: Power*, ed. James Faubion (New York: New, 2000), 346. And this point is expanded in interview form: "It should also be noted that power relations are possible only insofar as the subjects are free. . . . This means that in power relations there is necessarily the possibility of resistance because if there were no possibility of resistance (of violent resistance, flight, deception, strategies capable of reversing the situation), there would be no power relations at all. This being the general form, I refuse to reply to the question I am sometimes asked: 'But if power is everywhere, there is no freedom.' I answer that if there are relations of power in every social field, this is because there is freedom everywhere. . . . The claim that 'you see power everywhere, thus there is no room for freedom' seems to me absolutely inadequate. The idea that power is a system of domination that controls everything and leaves no room for freedom cannot be attributed to me." See Foucault, "The Ethics of the Concern for the Self as a Practice of Freedom," in *Michel Foucault: Ethics, Subjectivity, and Truth*, 292–93.

23. This is not, of course, to say that this sequential story is uncontroversial. Colin Koopman, for instance, argues that the approach of "problematization" fruitfully informs the full range of Foucault's thought (rather than representing a late-breaking "turn" or departure). See Koopman, *Genealogy as Critique: Foucault and the Problems of Modernity* (Bloomington: Indiana University Press, 2013).

24. Foucault, "The Subject and Power," 327.

25. Foucault, "On the Genealogy of Ethics," 262.

26. Nussbaum proposes that Foucault's late work on antiquity "is both mediocre and a departure from views about the inseparability of ideas from social institutions that have been his most valuable legacy to modern philosophy." This judgment appears in her "Affections of the Greeks," *New York Times Book Review* 10 (1985): 13–14.

27. A helpful rejoinder can be found in Amy Allen, *The Politics of Our Selves* (New York: Columbia University Press, 2008), chap. 3. See also Mark Kelly, *The Political Philosophy of Michel Foucault* (New York: Routledge, 2008), 102–4.

28. This has led some commentators to charge Foucault with a muddled, ahistorical deployment of this category. Andrew Thacker, for instance, argues that Foucault "confuses a Greek and post-Kantian sense of the term 'aesthetic.'" See Thacker, "Foucault's Aesthetic of Existence," *Radical Philosophy* 63 (Spring 1993): 13–21.

29. See Timothy O'Leary, *Foucault and the Art of Ethics* (New York: Continuum, 2002), 128.

30. As the opening sections of *The Use of Pleasure* detail, what is at stake are those techniques that "enable individuals to question their own conduct, to watch

over and give shape to it, and to shape themselves as ethical subjects." Michel Foucault, *The History of Sexuality*, vol. 2: *The Use of Pleasure*, trans. Robert Hurley (New York: Vintage Books, 1990), 13.

31. Foucault, *The Use of Pleasure*, 10–11. In a rejoinder to Sartre, Foucault presses this point further: "I would like to say exactly the contrary: we should not have to refer the creative activity of somebody to the kind of relation he has to himself, but should relate the kind of relation one has to oneself to a creative activity." See Foucault, "On the Genealogy of Ethics," 262.

32. Richard Wolin renders this point in characteristically shrill terms. The aestheticized "insensitivity to other values ultimately translates into an insensitivity to other persons qua ends in themselves. They are viewed as the pliable objects of aesthetic fashioning, raw materials to be integrated into a grandiose aesthetic spectacle that is not of their own making. . . . [They] are degraded to the level of fungible extras who are of little intrinsic value when viewed on their own terms." Wolin, "Foucault's Aesthetic Decisionism," 85.

33. Foucault, *The Use of Pleasure*, 25.

34. Foucault, "On the Genealogy of Ethics," 263.

35. For instance, Foucault says that "in the second part of my work, I have studied the objectivizing of the subject in what I shall call 'dividing practices.' The subject is either divided inside himself or divided from others." This passage appears in Foucault, "The Subject and Power," 326.

36. A helpful discussion of this point appears in Alan Milchman and Alan Rosenberg, "The Aesthetic and Ascetic Dimensions of an Ethics of Self-Fashioning: Nietzsche and Foucault," *Parrhesia* no. 2 (2007): 44–65.

37. Take, for instance, the subject who is raised within the fundamentalist norms of a revealed religion, and dedicates him- or herself to this moral framework. This person comes to perform a similar *techne* of the self, that must manage a wide range of temptations, stretching from internet gambling, to a sexualized media sphere, to ideals of conspicuous consumption, all in the aim of managing his or her desires in a manner amenable to the word of the godhead.

38. Michel Foucault, "Technologies of the Self," in *Michel Foucault: Ethics, Subjectivity and Truth*, 225.

39. Foucault, *The Use of Pleasure*, 25–28.

40. Richard Wolin charges that "there is nary a remainder that survives the process whereby the identities of modern subjects are heteronomously fabricated. There is nothing left over that we might call our own." Wolin, "Foucault's Aesthetic Decisionism," 86.

41. These possibilities are sketched in Judith Butler, *The Psychic Life of Power: Theories in Subjection* (Stanford, Calif.: Stanford University Press, 1997), chap. 3.

42. Foucault, "On the Genealogy of Ethics," 271.

43. Foucault, *The Use of Pleasure*, 62. In a 1982 lecture, he expands this point: "the effect, meaning, and aim of taking care of oneself is to distinguish the individual who takes care of himself from the crowd, from the majority, from the *hoi polloi* who are, precisely, the people absorbed in everyday life." Foucault, *Hermeneutics of the Subject: Lectures at the Collège de France, 1981–1982*, ed. Frédéric Gros (New York: Palgrave Macmillan, 2005), 75.

44. Ladelle McWhorter, *Bodies and Pleasures: Foucault and the Politics of Sexual Normalization* (Bloomington: Indiana University Press, 1999), 195.

45. These counter-normalizing possibilities have been noted by a number of commentators. See, for instance, David Halperin, *Saint Foucault: Towards a Gay Hagiography*, 109–11; Benda Hofmeyr, "The Power Not to Be (What We Are): The Politics and Ethics of Self-Creation in Foucault," *Journal of Moral Philosophy* 3, no. 2 (2006): 215–30; Christoph Menke, "Two Kinds of Practice: One the Relation between Social Discipline and the Aesthetics of Existence," *Constellations* 10, no. 2 (2003): 199–210; Johanna Oksala, *Foucault on Freedom* (New York: Cambridge University Press, 2009), chap. 7; and Michael Schwarz, "Repetition and Ethics in Late Foucault," *Telos*, no. 117 (1999): 113–32.

46. For a helpful discussion of this theme within contemporary queer politics, see Michael Warner, *The Trouble with Normal: Sex, Politics and the Ethics of Queer Life* (New York: Free, 1999), 52–61.

47. As Butler poses the question: what are the consequences when "I am led to embrace the terms that injure me because they constitute me socially"? *Psychic Life of Power*, 104. Helpful reflections can also be found in McWhorter, *Bodies and Pleasures*, chap. 1.

48. This passage appears in Wachowski's acceptance speech for the Human Rights Campaign Visibility Award (2012). Accessed online at http://www.hollywoodreporter.com/news/lana-wachowskis-hrc-visibility-award-382177.

49. In a 1982 interview, Foucault says: "If you look at the traditional construction of pleasure, you see that bodily pleasure, or pleasures of the flesh, are always drinking, eating, and fucking. And that seems to be the limit of the understanding of our body, our pleasures. What frustrates me, for instance, is the fact that the problem of drugs is always envisaged only as a problem of freedom and prohibition. I think that drugs must become a part of our culture. . . . We have to study drugs. We have to experience drugs. We have to do *good* drugs that can produce very intense pleasure." This passage appears in "Sex, Power, and the Politics of Identity," in *Michel Foucault: Ethics, Subjectivity, and Truth*, 165.

50. Foucault, "The Subject and Power," 336.

51. This sort of charge runs throughout Rainer Rochlitz, "The Aesthetics of Existence: Post-Conventional Morality and the Theory of Power in Michel Foucault," in *Michel Foucault, Philosopher*, ed. and trans. Timothy Armstrong (London: Harvester Wheatsheaf, 1992), 248–58.

52. This project is helpfully treated by Alexander Nehamas, *The Art of Living: Socratic Reflections from Plato to Foucault* (Berkeley: University of California Press, 1998), 142–45.

53. Michel Foucault, "The Ethics of the Concern for the Self as a Practice of Freedom," 286.

54. Paul Veyne "Foucault Revolutionizes History," in *Foucault and His Interlocutors*, ed. Arnold Davidson (Chicago: University of Chicago Press, 1997), 146–82.

55. These anxieties are particularly evident in Maria Daraki, "Foucault's Journey to Greece," *Telos* 67 (1986): 87–110; Pierre Hadot, "Reflections on the Notion of the 'Cultivation of the Self,'" in *Michel Foucault, Philosopher*, ed. T. J. Armstrong

(London: Harvester Wheatsheaf, 1992), 225–31; James Porter, "Foucault's Antiquity," in *Classics and the Uses of Reception*, ed. Charles Martindale and Richard Thomas (Malden, Mass.: Blackwell, 2006), 168–79.

56. Wolin, "Foucault's Aesthetic Decisionism," 85.

57. Eagleton, *Ideology of the Aesthetic*, 390.

58. Wolin, "Foucault's Aesthetic Decisionism," 85. Likewise, Charles Taylor raises concerns regarding the "unrestrained, utterly self-related freedom that this ideal entails." See Taylor, *Sources of the Self* (New York: Cambridge University Press, 1992), 489.

59. A productive discussion of this indeterminacy can be found in Nancy Fraser, "Foucault on Modern Power: Empirical Insights and Normative Confusions," in *Unruly Practices: Power, Discourse and Gender in Contemporary Social Theory* (Minneapolis: University of Minnesota Press, 1989), 17–34. Or, as Richard Bernstein argues: "Foucault . . . is constantly tempting us with his references to new possibilities of thinking and acting. . . . But the problem is that these references to desirable new possibilities and changes are in danger of becoming empty and vacuous unless we have some sense of which possibilities and changes are *desirable* and why." Richard Bernstein, "Foucault: Critique as a Philosophic Ethos," in *Critique and Power*, 231.

60. The classical source for the charge of "cryptonormativism" is, of course, Jürgen Habermas, *The Philosophical Discourse of Modernity*, 266–93.

61. A helpful overview and response to these challenges appears in Jane Bennett, "How Is It, Then, That We Still Remain Barbarians?" *Political Theory* 24, no. 4 (1996): 653–72.

62. Foucault, "On the Genealogy of Ethics," 256.

63. David Hiley, for instance, fears that Foucault offers only "the binary opposition of individual against society"—or, in stronger terms, a "cult of self." This charge appears in "Foucault and the Question of Enlightenment," *Philosophy and Social Criticism*, vol. 11 (1985): 63–83.

64. Foucault, "The Ethics of the Concern for the Self," 291. See also Nehamas, *The Art of Living*, 178.

65. See Judith Butler, *Precarious Life: Powers of Mourning and Violence* (New York: Verso, 2004); William Connolly, *Identity/Difference: Democratic Negotiations of Political Paradox* (Minneapolis: University of Minnesota Press, 2002); and Stephen White, *The Ethos of a Late Modern Citizen* (Cambridge, Mass.: Harvard University Press, 2009).

66. I have previously treated these debates in Feola, "Fear and Loathing in Democratic Times: Affect, Citizenship and Agency," *Political Studies* 64, no. 1S (2016): 53–69.

67. Lois McNay, *Foucault and Feminism: Power, Gender and the Self* (Malden, Mass.: Polity, 1992), 158. And Wendy Brown asserts more bluntly yet that "there are subjects . . . but not *citizens*" in Foucault's reflections on power and resistance. See Brown, *Undoing the Demos* (Cambridge, Mass.: MIT Press, 2015), 74.

68. Ella Myers, "Resisting Foucauldian Ethics," *Contemporary Political Theory* 7, no. 2 (2008): 134.

69. On this point, see Ella Myers, *Worldly Ethics: Democratic Politics and Care for the World* (Durham, N.C.: Duke University Press, 2013), 48–49.

70. See James Miller, *The Passion of Michel Foucault* (Cambridge, Mass.: Harvard University Press, 1993), 187–93.

71. Michel Foucault, "Interview with Michel Foucault," in *Power*, 280.

72. Foucault, "Interview with Michel Foucault," 294.

73. See particularly Marcuse, *Essay on Liberation.*

74. Michel Foucault, "Useless to Revolt?" in *Power*, 449.

75. Michel Foucault, "Nietzsche, Genealogy, History," in *Language, Counter-memory, Practice* (Ithaca, N.Y.: Cornell University Press, 1977), 148.

76. Michel Foucault, *History of Sexuality, vol. 1: An Introduction*, trans. Robert Hurley (New York: Vintage, 1978), 157.

77. Michel Foucault, "Sex, Power, and the Politics of Identity," in *Michel Foucault: Ethics, Subjectivity, and Truth*, 165.

78. Foucault, *Foucault Live*, 218.

79. Passage cited in Halperin, *Saint Foucault: Towards a Gay Hagiography*, 94.

80. Tom Roach, *Friendship as a Way of Life: Foucault, AIDS and the Politics of Shared Estrangement* (Albany: SUNY Press, 2012), 129.

81. Whitney Davis, *Queer Beauty: Sexuality and Aesthetics from Winckelmann to Freud and Beyond* (New York: Columbia University Press, 2010), chap. 9.

82. Foucault, "Interview with Michel Foucault," 275.

83. On this point, see Brent Pickett, *On the Use and Abuse of Foucault for Politics* (New York: Lexington Books, 2005), 61–63.

84. Foucault, "Sex, Power, and the Politics of Identity," 164.

85. Michel Foucault, "Social Triumph of the Sexual Will," in *Michel Foucault: Ethics, Subjectivity and Truth*, 159–60, 164.

86. McNay, *Foucault and Feminism*, 165.

87. Kennan Ferguson, *The Politics of Judgment: Aesthetics, Identity and Political Theory* (Lanham, Md.: Lexington Books, 1999), 129. See also Myers, *Worldly Ethics*, 32–45.

88. In an oft-cited passage, he goes so far as to insist that "care for others should not be put before the care of oneself. The care of the self is ethically prior in that the relationship with oneself is ontologically prior." For the citizen of the polis, he maintains, it is only by using these techniques to exert mastery over one's desires that one will be able to resist the temptation to dominate or exploit others. See Foucault, "The Ethics of the Concern for the Self," 287.

89. Although McWhorter does not present the point in these terms, it is instructive to read her account of line-dancing in these terms. What she presents as a transformative practice of embodiment likewise depends upon the support and provocation of those who likewise participate within this shared, embodied practice. See McWhorter, *Bodies and Pleasures*, 168–75.

90. As previously cited: "these practices are nevertheless not something invented by the individual himself. They are models that he finds in his culture and are proposed, suggested, imposed upon him by his culture, his society, and his social group." Foucault, "The Ethics of the Concern for the Self," 291.

91. Foucault, *Hermeneutics of the Subject*, 127.

92. See Foucault, *Fearless Speech* (Los Angeles: Semiotext(e), 2001).

93. In another important passage, Foucault tracks the increasing expansion of these projects, from the ranks of the philosophical or religious initiate and into social space more broadly. As he puts it, such a traditional project is "being outflanked, encircled, and challenged by a practice of the self that is a social practice at the same time. The practice of the self links up with social practice or, if you like, the formation of a relationship of the self to the self quite clearly connects up with the relationships of the self to the Other." Foucault, *Hermeneutics of the Subject*, 155.

94. Foucault, "The Social Triumph of the Sexual Will," 159.

95. This strain of the argument has been noted by some of Foucault's more sensitive readers. See Halperin, *Saint Foucault: Towards a Gay Hagiography*, 79–85; Cressida Heyes, *Self-Transformations: Foucault, Ethics, and Normalized Bodies* (New York: Oxford University Press, 2007), 123.

96. In Timothy O'Leary's terms, this reflects how "freedom exists only in the concrete capacity of individuals to refuse, to say 'No.' To say 'No,' for example to being governed in a certain way, or to governing oneself in a certain way. It is this capacity to refuse, a capacity which only exists to a very limited degree in states of domination, that make possible the creative work of both ethics and politics." O'Leary, *Foucault and the Art of Ethics*, 159–60.

97. In Michael Schwarz's terms, "to act otherwise is, in the first instance, to work on oneself anew, to enact a denormalization of who one is." See Schwartz, "Repetition and Ethics in Late Foucault," *Telos* 117 (1999): 126. See also McWhorter, *Bodies and Pleasures*, 195.

98. Foucault, "Sex, Power, and the Politics of Identity," 168.

99. Heyes, *Self-Transformations*, 117.

100. I owe this linkage of illegibility and volence to Judith Butler, *Undoing Gender* (New York: Routledge, 2004), 34–35.

101. For this imperative of world-building, see Ash Amin and Nigel Thrift, *Arts of the Political: New Openings for the Left* (Durham, N.C.: Duke University Press), 1–16.

102. Warner, *The Trouble with Normal*, 177. Or, in a different rendering, Warner offers that a queer counterpublic can "work to elaborate new worlds of culture and social relations in which gender and sexuality can be lived, including forms of intimate association, vocabularies of affect, styles of embodiment, erotic practices, and relations of care and pedagogy." See Warner, *Publics and Counterpublics* (Cambridge, Mass.: MIT Press, 2005), 57.

103. In a late interview, Foucault asks: "How can a relational system be reached through sexual practices? Is it possible to create a homosexual mode of life? This notion of mode of life seems important to me. Will it require the introduction of a diversification different from the ones due to social class, differences in profession and culture, a diversification that would also be a form of relationship and would be a 'way of life'? A way of life . . . can yield a culture and an ethics. To be 'gay,' I think, is not to identify with the psychological traits and the visible masks of the homosexual but to try to define and develop a way of

life." Foucault, "Friendship as a Way of Life," in *Michel Foucault: Ethics, Subjectivity and Truth,* 137–38.

104. This criterion of livability is developed in Butler, *Undoing Gender,* 1–39.

105. On this point, see Robin Kelley, *Freedom Dreams: The Black Radical Imagination* (Boston: Beacon, 2002), 1–12.

106. Warner, *Publics and Counterpublics,* 74–75.

107. Foucault, "Interview with Michel Foucault," 288.

108. Foucault, "The Ethics of the Concern for the Self," 282.

109. In discussing his resistance toward a traditional political language, Foucault says: "We have come to realize that things never happen as we expect from a political program, and that a political program has always, or nearly always, led to abuse or political domination from a bloc—be it from technicians or bureaucrats or other people. . . . Since the nineteenth century, great political institutions and great political parties have confiscated the process of political creation; that is, they have tried to give to political creation the form of a political program in order to take over power. . . . One of the things that I think should be preserved . . . is the fact that there has been political innovation, political creation, and political experimentation outside the great political parties, and outside the normal or ordinary program." See Foucault, "Sex, Power, and the Politics of Identity," 172.

110. See Halperin, *Saint Foucault: Towards a Gay Hagiography,* 56–67; Hayes, *Self-Transformations,* 119–20. As Foucault himself proposes, "the problem is, precisely, to decide if it is actually suitable to place oneself within a 'we' in order to assert the principles one recognizes and the values one accepts; or if it is not, rather, necessary to make the future formation of a 'we' possible by elaborating the question. Because it seems to me that the 'we' must not be previous to the question; it can only be the result—and the necessarily temporary result—of the question as it is posed in the new terms in which one formulates it." Foucault, "Polemics, Politics, and Problematizations," in *Michel Foucault: Ethics, Subjectivity, and Truth,* 114–15.

Chapter 3

1. Riefenstahl's work is a staple in the literature on aestheticization. See, for instance, Paul Gilroy, *Against Race: Imagining Political Culture beyond the Color Line* (Cambridge, Mass.: Harvard University Press, 2000), chap. 4; Sartwell, *Political Aesthetics,* chap. 1.

2. Benjamin, "The Work of Art in the Age of Mechanical Reproduction," 242.

3. Jacques Rancière, *Disagreement: Politics and Philosophy,* trans. Julie Rose (Minneapolis: University of Minnesota Press, 1999), 58.

4. Rockhill, *Radical History & the Politics of Art,* 164.

5. For a short list, see Jacques Rancière, *The Politics of Aesthetics: The Distribution of the Sensible,* trans. Gabriel Rockhill (New York: Bloomsbury, 2004); Jacques Rancière, *The Emancipated Spectator,* trans. Gregory Elliott (New York: Verso, 2009); Jacques Rancière, *The Future of the Image,* trans. Gregory Elliott (New

York: Verso, 2009); Jacques Rancière, *Aesthetics and Its Discontents*, trans. Steven Corcoran (Malden, Mass.: Polity, 2009); Jacques Rancière, *Dissensus: On Politics and Aesthetics*, trans. Steven Corcoran (New York: Bloomsbury, 2010).

6. Jacques Rancière, *Chronicles of Consensual Times*, trans. Steven Corcoran (New York: Continuum, 2010), viii.

7. In Marx's classic formulation, under conditions of ideology "men and their circumstances appear upside-down as in a *camera obscura*." This passage appears in "The German Ideology," in *The Marx-Engels Reader*, ed. Robert Tucker (New York: Norton, 1978), 154.

8. Marx, *The Marx-Engels Reader*, 89.

9. This charge rests at the heart of Herbert Marcuse's *One-Dimensional Man* (Boston: Beacon, 1991).

10. Adorno and Horkheimer, *Dialectic of Enlightenment*, 120–67.

11. Rancière, *The Politics of Aesthetics*, 13.

12. For a helpful discussion of this concept, see Davide Panagia, "'*Partage du sensible*': The Distribution of the Sensible," in *Jacques Rancière: Key Concepts*, ed. Jean-Phillipe Deranty (New York: Routledge, 2014), 95–103.

13. Rancière, *The Politics of Aesthetics*, 12.

14. See, for instance, Kath Woodward, *The Politics of In/Visibility: Being There* (New York: Palgrave Macmillan, 2015), chap. 5.

15. Jacques Rancière "Ten Theses on Politics," in *Dissensus: On Politics and Aesthetics*, ed. Steven Corcoran (New York: Continuum, 2010), 38.

16. Rancière, "Ten Theses," 36.

17. Rancière, *Dissensus*, 50–52.

18. See particularly Jacques Rancière, *The Philosopher and His Poor*, trans. John Drury, Corinne Oster, and Andrew Parker (Durham, N.C.: Duke University Press, 2004), chap. 1.

19. Joseph Tanke offers a terse rendering of this point: "It attempts to naturalize the miscount according to which some are prevented from taking part." Tanke, *Jacques Rancière: An Introduction* (New York: Continuum, 2011), 51.

20. This argument is detailed throughout Jürgen Habermas, *Communication and the Evolution of Society*, trans. Thomas McCarthy (Boston: Beacon, 1979). See also Habermas, *The Theory of Communicative Action*, vols. 1 and 2, trans. Thomas McCarthy (Boston: Beacon, 1984).

21. Cited in Rockhill, *Radical History & the Politics of Art*, 142.

22. If this were the case, then Rancière would have added little to a Gramscian notion of "common sense"—those assumptions and beliefs that justify the contingent arrangements of the world.

23. As Rancière proposes: "Politics is generally seen as the set of procedures whereby the aggregation and consent of collectivities is achieved, the organization of powers, the distribution of places and roles, and the systems for legitimizing this distribution. I propose to give this system of distribution and legitimization another name. I propose to call it *the police*." Rancière, *Disagreement*, 28.

24. A helpful discussion of the "police" in Rancière's thought appears in Tanke, *Rancière: An Introduction*, 45–48. Ayten Gündoğdu likewise stresses the role of the police for understanding Rancière's politics in "Disagreeing with Ran-

cière: Speech, Violence, and the Ambiguous Subjects of Politics," *Polity* 49, no. 2 (2017): 188–219.

25. Rancière, "Ten Theses," 36.

26. As Rancière asserts, "there is a worse and better police. . . . and one kind of police may be infinitely preferable to another." Rancière, *Disagreement*, 30–31.

27. Rancière, *Disagreement*, 22–23.

28. A classic rendering of this exclusionary restructuring of urban space is found in Mike Davis, *City of Quartz: Excavating the Future in Los Angeles* (New York: Verso, 1990), particularly chap. 4.

29. In Brown's terms, "while to be invisible within a local discourse may occasion the injuries of social liminality, such suffering may be mild compared to that of radical denunciation, hystericization, exclusion, or criminalization." Brown, *Edgework: Critical Essays on Knowledge and Politics*, 87.

30. Iris Young develops this point with regard to the "scaling of bodies" as a visual form of hegemonic power. See *Justice and the Politics of Difference* (Princeton, N.J.: Princeton University Press, 1990), chap. 5.

31. This is particularly the case for Axel Honneth, *Disrespect: The Normative Foundations of Critical Theory* (Malden, Mass.: Polity, 2007).

32. Rancière, *Disagreement*, 9.

33. A helpful account of this conceptual transformation can be found in Margaret Somers, *Genealogies of Citizenship: Markets, Statelessness and the Right to Have Rights* (New York: Cambridge University Press, 2008). See also Lisa Duggan, *The Twilight of Equality? Neoliberalism, Cultural Politics and the Attack on Democracy* (Boston: Beacon, 2004); Nancy Fraser and Linda Gordon, "Contract versus Charity: Why Is There No Social Citizenship in the United States?" *Socialist Review* 22 (1992): 45–67.

34. Rancière, *Disagreement*, 22.

35. The locus classicus for Habermas's discourse theory is his "Discourse Ethics: Notes on Philosophical Justification," in *Moral Consciousness and Communicative Action*, trans. Christian Lenhart and Shierry Weber-Nicholson (Cambridge, Mass.: MIT Press, 1980), 43–115. In a symptomatic passage, Habermas renders these conditions as follows: "1) Every subject with the competence to speak and act is allowed to take part in a discourse. 2a) Everyone is allowed to question any assertion whatever. 2b) Everyone is allowed to introduce any assertion whatever into the discourse. 2c) Everyone is allowed to express his attitudes, desires and needs. 3) No speaker may be prevented, by internal or external coercion, from exercising his rights as laid down in (1) and (2)." This passage is found on page 89.

36. For a helpful overview of this argument, see Seyla Benhabib, "Toward a Deliberative Model of Democratic Legitimacy," in *Democracy and Difference*, ed. Seyla Benhabib (Princeton, N.J.: Princeton University Press, 1996), 66–94.

37. Helpful reflections on this point can also be found in Lois McNay, *The Misguided Search for the Political* (Malden, Mass.: Polity, 2014), 140–43.

38. Jacques Rancière, "Dissenting Words: A Conversation with Jacques Rancière," *Diacritics* 30 (Summer 2000): 116, emphasis added.

39. As Jane Mansbridge has detailed, members of certain groups (classed, raced, gendered) have a more difficult time assuming the position of speech

within the operations of deliberative forums; and, when they do, they are more frequently interrupted, their challenges are heard as consent, and their positions are less likely to be taken up by listeners. See Mansbridge, *Beyond Adversary Democracy* (Chicago: University of Chicago Press, 1983).

40. On this point, Rancière reflects a point that has long occupied feminist theory. As Susan Bickford writes: "*what* we are (socially defined categories of race, class, gender, and so on) affects *who* we are (our appearance in the public realm). . . . Patterns of oppression and inequality result in the systematic distortion of some people's appearance and audibility." Bickford, *The Dissonance of Democracy: Listening, Conflict, and Citizenship* (Ithaca, N.Y.: Cornell University Press, 1996), 96.

41. Sara Ahmed, *Willful Subjects* (Durham, N.C.: Duke University Press, 2014).

42. In the words of Mitsuye Yamada, "Not only the young but those who feel powerless over their own lives know what it is like not to make a difference on anyone or anything. . . . we have been trained not to expect a response in ways that mattered. . . . We must remember that one of the most insidious ways of keeping women and minorities powerless is to let them only talk about harmless and inconsequential subjects, or let them speak freely and not listen to them with serious intent." This passage appears in Yamada, "Invisibility Is an Unnatural Disaster: Reflections of an Asian American Woman," in *This Bridge Called My Back: Writings by Radical Women of Color*, 4th edition, ed. Cherríe Moraga and Gloría Anzaldúa (Albany: SUNY Press, 2015), 39–40.

43. Rancière, *Disagreement*, 11. Or as he restates the point: "political activity is always a mode of expression that undoes the perceptible divisions of the police order by implementing a basically heterogeneous assumption, that of a part of those who have no part, an assumption that, at the end of the day, itself demonstrates the sheer contingency of the order, the equality of any speaking being with any other speaking being." Rancière, *Disagreement*, 30.

44. Gabriel Rockhill puts this commitment in the following terms: "Equality, it might be said, is an activity rather than a state of being, an intermittent process of actualization rather than a goal to be attained once and for all." Rockhill, *Radical History & the Politics of Art*, 144. See also Chambers, *The Lessons of Rancière*, 26–27.

45. As Andrew Schaap expresses this insight: "politics paradigmatically entails the enactment of equality in a situation of inequality. The political is constituted when those who are not qualified to participate in politics presume to act and speak as if they are." See Schaap, "Enacting the Right to Have Rights: Jacques Rancière's Critique of Hannah Arendt," *European Journal of Political Theory*, vol. 10 (2011): 35. This active sense of equality is likewise the focus of Todd May's *The Political Thought of Jacques Rancière: Creating Equality* (State College: Pennsylvania State University Press, 2008). For May, this active "taking" of equality is essential for understanding Rancière's distance from a distributive model of politics—where equality is something dispensed to these marginal subjects by elite actors or institutions. As Samuel Chambers has helpfully argued, however, May's text (particularly its strong commitment to anarchist themes) risks "purifying" Rancière's politics of its necessary entanglement with forms of domination. See Chambers,

"Jacques Rancière and the Problem of Pure Politics," *European Journal of Political Theory* 10, no. 3 (2011): 303–26.

46. Rancière, *Disagreement*, 30.

47. As Rancière argues: "Democracy, then, far from being the form of life of individuals dedicated to their private pleasure, is a process of struggle against this privatization, the process of enlarging this sphere. Enlarging the public sphere does not entail, as it is claimed in liberal discourse, asking for State encroachments on society. It entails struggling against the distribution of the public and the private that shores up the twofold domination of the oligarchy in the State and in society." Jacques Rancière, *Hatred of Democracy*, trans. Steven Corcoran (New York: Verso, 2009), 55.

48. Holloway Sparks offers a stimulating reading of how the Rosa Parks case complicates and enriches popular conceptions of democratic citizenship. See her "Dissident Citizenship: Democratic Theory, Political Courage and Activist Women," *Hypatia* 12 (1997): 74–110. For a reading more narrowly tailored toward Rancière, see Todd May's reflections on the "lunch counter" sit-ins in *The Political Thought of Jacques Rancière*, 50–55.

49. As Rancière puts it: "the advances of democracy have always been due to improvisation by unprogrammed actors, by surplus interlocutors: a noisy crowd occupying the street, a silent crowd crossing their arms in a factory and so forth." Jacques Rancière, *On the Shores of Politics*, trans. Liz Heron (New York: Verso, 1995), 103. As Sharon Krause has elaborated, when such spectacles raise claims in ways unrecognized by discursivist theories of politics, they do not simply raise new topics for public consideration, but push back to expose the limitations behind a thinly rationalized construal of how justice claims can be presented and considered. See Krause, *Civil Passions: Moral Sentiment and Democratic Deliberation* (Princeton, N.J.: Princeton University Press, 2008), 118–22.

50. For similar challenges to a deliberative politics, see Margaret Kohn, "Language, Power, and Persuasion: Toward a Critique of Deliberative Democracy," *Constellations* 7 (2000): 408–29; Lynn Sanders, "Against Deliberation," *Political Theory* 25 (1997): 347–76.

51. Such a reading might seem justified by those moments where Rancière proposes that "human beings are tied together by . . . a certain distribution of the sensible which defines their way of being together; and politics is about the transformation of the sensory fabric of 'being together.'" Jacques Rancière, *The Emancipated Spectator*, trans. Gregory Elliott (New York: Verso, 2009), 56.

52. The classic source for this argument is, of course, Guy Debord, *Society of the Spectacle*, trans. Donald Nicholson-Smith (Cambridge, Mass.: MIT Press, 1995).

53. Jacques Rancière, *On the Shores of Politics*, 85.

54. Rancière puts this as follows: "politics is a matter of subjects or, rather, modes of subjectification [*subjectivation*]. By *subjectification* I mean the production through a series of actions of a body and a capacity for enunciation not previously identifiable within a given field of experience, whose identification is thus part of the reconfiguration of the field of experience." Rancière, *Disagreement*, 35.

55. A helpful account of this relationship appears in Chambers, *The Lessons of Rancière*, 100–104.

56. Rancière, *The Emancipated Spectator*, 72.

57. As Rancière proposes: "Political demonstration makes visible that which had no reason to be seen; it places one world in another—for instance, the world where the factory is a public space in that where it is considered private, the world where workers speak, and speak about the community, in that where their voices are mere cries expressing pain." See Rancière, "Ten Theses," 38.

58. This theme is productively explored by Chambers, *The Lessons of Rancière*, 101–4. See also Tanke, *Rancière: An Introduction*, 65–70. In passing, this emphasis on desubjectivization makes it difficult to follow Rockhill's effort to distinguish aesthetics and politics on this terrain: "aesthetics does not truly coincide with politics because it does not produce political subjectivization, that is to say, dissensual acts that disturb the hierarchies of the given police order in the struggle to verify the presupposition of equality through the construction of a *we*. In fact, art—and particularly literature—tends to distance us from politics proper and hinder its development by producing desubjectivization.'" Rockhill, *Radical History & the Politics of Art*, 164.

59. As Rancière argues: "Quite simply, parties do not exist prior to the declaration of wrong. . . . A political subject is not a group that 'becomes aware' of itself, finds its voice, imposes its weight on society." Rancière, *Disagreement*, 39–40.

60. May, *Creating Equality*, 71. The difficulties that attend (and might block or undermine) these efforts are well treated by Gündoğdu, "Disagreeing with Rancière."

61. As Rancière describes the claims of women at the time of the French Revolution who invoked the Rights of Man to bolster their demands for equality, "they acted as subjects that did not have the rights that they had and that had the rights that they had not." This passage appears in Rancière, "Who Is the Subject of the Rights of Man?" in *Dissensus*, 69.

62. For a helpful account of the conditions under which the strike was conducted and for what reasons, see Benjamin Wallace-Wells, "The Plot from Solitary," *New York Magazine*, February 26, 2014, http://nymag.com/news/features/solitary-secure-housing-units-2014-2/. For the conditions of incarceration at Pelican Bay, see Keramet Reiter, *23/7: Pelican Bay Prison and the Rise of Long-Term Solitary Confinement* (New Haven: Yale University Press, 2016).

63. Lisa Guenther, "Political Action at the End of the World: Hannah Arendt and the California Prison Hunger Strikes," *Canadian Journal of Human Rights* 4, no. 1 (2015): 33–56.

64. On these tactics, see Michelle Alexander, *The New Jim Crow: Mass Incarceration in the Age of Colorblindness* (New York: New, 2012), particularly chap. 4; Alexes Harris, *A Pound of Flesh: Monetary Sanctions as Punishment for the Poor* (New York: Russell Sage Foundation, 2016); and Marc Mauer and Meda Chesney-Lind, eds., *Invisible Punishment: The Collateral Consequences of Mass Imprisonment* (New York: New, 2002).

65. Bonnie Honig, *Democracy and the Foreigner* (Princeton, N.J.: Princeton University Press, 2001), 101. See also Chambers, *The Lessons of Rancière*, 118–21.

66. As Cristina Beltrán has argued, such movements disorder not only what it means to speak as a citizen, but also what it means to count as an "immigrant"

(in this case, Latinx), staged as a common subject only through this agitation. See Beltrán, *The Trouble with Unity: Latino Politics and the Creation of Identity* (New York: Oxford University Press, 2010), particularly chap. 5.

67. As Andrew Schaap glosses the point, "the part that has no part is the political actor par excellence since it is through its struggle for appearance that it emerges as an entity that cannot be accommodated within the prevailing social order and yet demands to be." See Schaap, "Enacting the Right to Have Rights," 36.

68. Rancière, "Dissenting Words," 116.

69. Rancière, *Disagreement*, 17.

70. See Peter Hallward, "Staging Equality: Rancière's Theatrocracy and the Limits of Anarchic Equality," in *Jacques Rancière: History, Politics, Aesthetics*, ed. G. Rockhill and P. Watts (Durham, N.C.: Duke University Press, 2009), 140–57. A helpful rejoinder is offered by Beltrán, who (following Wolin and Rancière) challenges the criterion of "sustainability" that mobilizes Hallward's account. See Beltrán, *The Trouble with Unity*, 68–72, 133.

71. Sparks, "Dissident Citizenship."

72. As Myers stresses, "there is very little, if any allowance, in Rancière's work for the possibility that institutions could advance the presupposition of equality, shaping what citizen-subjects do, day in and day out." See Ella Myers, "Presupposing Equality: The Trouble with Rancière's Axiomatic Approach," *Philosophy and Social Criticism* 42, no. 1 (2016): 59.

73. McNay, *The Misguided Search for the Political*, 166.

74. For a helpful rejoinder to this "evental" reading, see Jason Frank, "Logical Revolts: Jacques Rancière and Political Subjectivization," *Political Theory* 43, no. 2 (2015): 249–61.

75. Rancière, *On the Shores of Politics*, 86.

76. Honig, *Democracy and the Foreigner*, 100–104; Schaap, "Enacting the Right to Have Rights"; Samuel Chambers, "A Queer Politics of the Democratic Miscount," *Borderlands* (2009): 1–23; Marina Prentoulis and Lasse Thomassen, "Political Theory in the Square: Protest, Representation and Subjectification," *Contemporary Political Theory* 12 (2013): 166–84; and Davide Panagia, *The Political Life of Sensation* (Durham, N.C.: Duke University Press, 2009), 45–73.

77. Aletta Norval, "'Writing a Name in the Sky': Rancière, Cavell, and the Possibility of Egalitarian Inscription," *American Political Science Review* 10 (2012): 824.

78. Rancière, "Ten Theses," 39.

79. Gabriel Rockhill has also noted questions of reception, though he largely limits this challenge to Rancière's explicit writings on art and the social meaning that artworks might have. See Rockhill, *Radical History & the Politics of Art*, 180–82.

80. Patchen Markell puts the point in Arendtian terms: "whether your activity is a beginning is not wholly under your control: it is, instead, a matter of the character of the responses and reactions it provokes (or fails to provoke) in you and others." See Markell, "The Rule of the People: Arendt, *Arche* and Democracy," *American Political Science Review* 100 (2006): 10. See also Beltrán, *The Trouble with Unity*, 136–37.

81. For instance, Benjamin Barber, *Strong Democracy: Participatory Politics for a New Age* (Berkeley: University of California Press, 2003), particularly chap. 8. For a reading that takes more seriously the role of agonism and conflict in democratic listening, see Susan Bickford, *The Dissonance of Democracy*, chap. 1; and Andrew Dobson, *Listening for Democracy: Recognition, Representation, Reconciliation* (New York: Oxford University Press, 2014).

82. Danielle Allen, *Talking to Strangers: Anxieties of Citizenship since Brown v. Board of Education* (Chicago: University of Chicago Press, 2006). Allen's reflections upon democratic "sacrifice" are particularly fruitful here.

83. As Antonio Vazquez-Arroyo has charged (albeit in a different context), such an approach runs the risk of subordinating the noise of democracy to a patrimonial logic of "permission" granted by privileged agents. See Vazquez-Arroyo, "Agonized Liberalism: The Liberal Theory of William E. Connolly," *Radical Philosophy* 127 (2004): 14–16. Such questions must likewise be asked of Nikolas Kompridis's intervention, cited in the opening chapter: a position where much of the action seems to be on the side of the recipient. See Kompridis, "Receptivity, Possibility and Democratic Politics."

84. Panagia, *The Political Life of Sensation*, 11, emphasis in original.

85. Rancière, *The Emancipated Spectator*, 13.

86. To my eye, this is the question that Norval does not address when she claims that greater receptivity toward these marginal subjects hinges upon a "change in *ethos*." Where this reflexive moment is important, the argument does not sufficiently explore the *social* dynamics of disqualification at the heart of Rancière's diagnosis—nor how such changes in *ethos* could be inaugurated by those who indict, trouble, and implicate the subject at stake. See Norval, "'Writing a Name in the Sky,'" 819–23.

87. The classic instance is located in Kant's "The Contest of the Faculties," in *Kant: Political Writings*, ed. Hans Reiss (New York: Cambridge University Press, 1991), 176–91.

88. Alexander Hirsch, "Walking Off the Edge of the World," *Humanities* 5, no. 3 (2016): 6.

89. See Jay Bernstein, "Confession and Forgiveness: Hegel's Poetics of Action," in *Beyond Representation: Philosophy and Poetic Imagination*, ed. Richard Eldridge (New York: Cambridge University Press, 1996), 47.

90. On this tendency, see also Rockhill, *Radical History & the Politics of Art*, 180–82.

91. The logic of this rejoinder is, of course, a staple of Derridean reading. See, for instance, Jacques Derrida, *Limited Inc*, trans. Samuel Weber and Jeffrey Mehlman (Evanston, Ill.: Northwestern University Press, 1977).

Chapter 4

1. G. W. F. Hegel, *Phenomenology of Spirit*, trans. A. V. Miller (New York: Oxford University Press, 1977), 9.

2. Here I draw from Sharon Krause's incisive challenge to an abstract, practical rationalism—where moral commitments and evaluations are ultimately *felt* at the level of sensibility. And sensibility, by extension, must be viewed as a site of moral formation and response. See Krause, *Civil Passions: Moral Sentiment and Democratic Deliberation*, 27–76.

3. Helpful reflections on this linkage of feeling, reason, and evaluation are found in Cheryl Hall, *The Trouble with Passion: Political Theory beyond the Reign of Reason* (New York: Routledge, 2005); George Marcus, *The Sentimental Citizen: Emotion in Democratic Politics* (University Park: Pennsylvania State University Press, 2002).

4. Meg McLagan and Yates McKee, eds., *Sensible Politics: The Visual Culture of Nongovernmental Activism* (Cambridge, Mass.: MIT Press, 2012), 9.

5. On the connection between (a) affect and (b) the opening (or closing) of fields of agency, see Deborah Gould, *Moving Politics: Emotion and ACT-UP's Fight Against AIDS* (Chicago: University of Chicago Press, 2009).

6. Hannah Arendt, *The Human Condition* (Chicago: University of Chicago Press, 1958), 198–99.

7. In a well-known passage, Arendt describes the "privative" sense of private life as follows: "To live an entirely private life means above all to be deprived of things essential to a truly human life: to be deprived of the reality that comes from being seen and heard by others, to be deprived of an 'objective' relationship with them that comes from being related to and separated from them through the intermediary of a common world of things, to be deprived of the possibility of achieving something more permanent than life itself. The privation of privacy lies in the absence of others; as far as they are concerned, private man does not appear, and therefore it is as though he did not exist. Whatever he does remains without significance and consequence to others, and what matters to him is without interest to other people." Arendt, *The Human Condition*, 58.

8. This is the core argument of Arendt's *Lectures on Kant's Political Philosophy*, ed. Ronald Beiner (Chicago: University of Chicago Press, 1992).

9. See, for instance, Richard Wolin, *The Politics of Being: The Political Thought of Martin Heidegger* (New York: Columbia University Press, 1990), 191. Where Wolin attempts to assimilate Arendt to a broadly Heideggerian framework, a more strongly Arendtian (and ultimately more faithful) reading is offered by Dana Villa, *Arendt and Heidegger: The Fate of the Political* (Princeton, N.J.: Princeton University Press, 1996).

10. See, for instance, Kim Curtis, *Our Sense of the Real: Aesthetic Experience and Arendtian Politics* (Ithaca, N.Y.: Cornell University Press, 1999); Dana Villa, "Beyond Good and Evil: Arendt, Nietzsche and the Aestheticization of Political Action," *Political Theory* 20, no. 2 (1992): 274–308; and Linda Zerilli, "We Feel Our Freedom: Imagination and Judgment in the Thought of Hannah Arendt," *Political Theory* 33, no. 2 (2005): 158–88.

11. As suggested in the previous chapter, however, Arendt suggests an important corrective to any one-sided, bottom-up approach to political action: such new beginnings entail a dependency on one's fellow citizens—whether they will

take up this opening, refuse it, push it further, pursue it in new directions, or whatever. These spectators (in both politics and aesthetics) are not simply objects of instruction or viewers of interventions that would remain the same regardless of their response, but rather co-participants in what these gestures will mean or whether they will happen at all.

12. This trope, for instance, repeatedly occurs through Jason Hill, *Civil Disobedience and the Politics of Identity: When We Should Not Get Along* (New York: Palgrave Macmillan, 2013). Invisibility here characterizes the situation of a wide range of marginalized subjects, stretching from veiled Muslim women to queers to the colonized.

13. Ralph Ellison, *Invisible Man* (New York: Random House, 1995), 3.

14. See, for instance, Iris Young, *Justice and the Politics of Difference* (Princeton, N.J.: Princeton University Press, 1990), 19–20.

15. This position is developed throughout Larry Gross, *Lesbians, Gay Men and the Media in America* (New York: Columbia University Press, 2001).

16. A variety of perspectives on the contemporary deportation state are found in *The Deportation Regime: Sovereignty, Space and the Freedom of Movement*, ed. Nicholas de Genova and Nathalie Peutz (Durham, N.C.: Duke University Press, 2010). See also Gregoire Chemayou, *Manhunts: A Philosophical History*, trans. Steven Rendall (Princeton, N.J.: Princeton University Press, 2012), 134–48.

17. This point is treated in Susan Star and Anselm Strauss, "Layers of Silence, Arenas of Voice: The Ecology of Visible and Invisible Work," *Computer Supported Co-Operative Work* 8, no. 1–2 (1999): 9–30.

18. See, for instance, Teo Ballvé, "The Mask of 'Anarchy,'" *Territorial Masquerades*, November 7, 2011, http://territorialmasquerades.net/the-mask-of-%E2%80%98anarchy%E2%80%99/. For broader reflections on the mask within the Zapatista context, see Jeff Conant, *A Poetics of Resistance: The Revolutionary Public Relations of the Zapatista Insurgency* (Oakland: AK, 2010), 119–75. Useful reflections are also found in Sophie Nield, "Tahrir Square, EC4M: The Occupy Movement and the Dramaturgy of Public Order," in *The Grammar of Politics and Performance*, ed. Shirin Rai and Janelle Reinelt (New York: Routledge, 2015), 121–33.

19. A helpful discussion of Arendt on this point is found in Marieke Borren, "Towards an Arendtian Politics of In/visibility: On Stateless Refugees and Undocumented Aliens," *Ethical Perspectives: Journal of the European Ethics Network* 15, no. 2 (2008): 213–37.

20. This echoes a point by Slavoj Žižek with regard to what Foucault (ostensibly) overlooks in his account of social marginality: "the 'excluded' are, of course, visible, in the precise sense that, paradoxically, *their exclusion itself is the mode of their inclusion*: their 'proper place' in the social body is that of exclusion (from the public sphere)." This passage appears in Žižek, *First as Tragedy, Then as Farce* (New York: Verso, 2009), 101. Similar reflections are offered by Yamada, "Invisibility Is an Unnatural Disaster."

21. This phrase is taken from Judith Butler, "Bodies in Alliance and the Politics of the Street," in *Sensible Politics: The Visual Culture of Nongovernmental Activism*, ed. Meg McLagan and Yates McGee (New York: Zone Books, 2012), 117.

22. Judith Butler, "Endangered/Endangering: Schematic Racism and White Paranoia," in *Reading Rodney King/Reading Urban Uprising*, ed. Robert Gooding-Williams (New York: Routledge, 1993), 17.

23. A significant literature has recently addressed this point, in response to a wave of recorded incidents of police violence against black citizens. See Tommy Curry, "Michael Brown and the Need for a Genre Study of Black Male Death and Dying," *Theory & Event* 17, no. 3 (2014); Ange-Marie Hancock, "Trayvon Martin, Intersectionality and the Politics of Disgust," *Theory & Event* 15, no. 3 (2012).

24. Judith Butler, *Precarious Life* (New York: Verso, 2004), 32. See also Butler, *Frames of War.*

25. For a helpful account of the political work of this unnameability, see Moya Lloyd, "Naming the Dead and the Politics of the 'Human,'" *Review of International Studies* 43, no. 2 (2017): 260–79.

26. For more extended reflections on the possibilities and limits of this argument in Butler's thought, see my "Norms, Vision and Violence: Judith Butler on the Politics of Legibility," *Contemporary Political Theory* 13, no. 1 (2014): 130–48. For a creative application of these themes, see Lisa Marie Cacho, *Social Death: Racialized Rightlessness and the Criminalizatin of the Unprotected* (New York: New York University Press, 2012).

27. Achille Mbembe offers similar reflections on the visual economy of colonialism: "looking and seeing have in common the fact that they solicit judgment, enclosing what is seen or the person who is not seen in inextricable networks of meaning—the beams of history." This passage appears in *Critique of Black Reason*, trans. Laurent Dubois (Durham, N.C.: Duke University Press, 2017), 111.

28. See Sara Ahmed, *The Cultural Politics of Emotion* (New York: Routledge, 2004), 62–81. I have treated this question previously in Feola, "Fear and Loathing in Democratic Times."

29. Franz Fanon, *Black Skin, White Masks*, trans. Richard Philcox (New York: Grove, 2008), 89–96.

30. George Yancy, *Black Bodies, White Gazes: The Continuing Significance of Race in America* (New York: Rowman and Littlefield, 2016), 19.

31. This line of argument finds incisive voice in the work of William Connolly—who has persistently interrogated how social dynamics of feeling both form and deform the possibilities of democratic citizenship. See, for instance, Connolly, *The Ethos of Pluralization* (Minneapolis: University of Minnesota Press, 1995); Connolly, *Identity/Difference: Democratic Negotiations of Political Paradox* (Minneapolis: University of Minnesota Press, 2002); and Connolly, *Pluralism* (Durham, N.C.: Duke University Press, 2005).

32. The canonical articulation of this position is offered by Debord, *Society of the Spectacle.*

33. See Thomas Keenan, *Democracy in Question* (Stanford, Calif.: Stanford University Press, 2003), 1–4, 180–82. Or, as Colin Crouch puts this, "public electoral debate is a tightly controlled spectacle, managed by rival teams of professionals expert in the techniques of persuasion, and considering a small range of issues selected by those teams. The mass of citizens plays a passive, quiescent,

even a pathetic part, responding only to the signals given them." See Crouch, *Post-Democracy* (Malden, Mass.: Polity, 2004), 4.

34. Here, the literature draws not only on the forms of power that Foucault identified within the act of surveillance, but also on the reifying power of "the gaze" to capture and fix the seen object. For some canonical examples, see Laura Mulvey, "Visual Pleasure and Narrative Cinema," in *Visual and Other Pleasures* (New York: Palgrave Macmillan, 1989), 14–28; Jean-Paul Sartre, *Being and Nothingness: A Phenomenological Essay on Ontology*, trans. Hazel Barnes (New York: Washington Square, 1956), 340–400.

35. The phrase is borrowed from Lilie Chouliaraki's probing account in *The Ironic Spectator: Solidarity in the Age of Post-Humanitarianism* (Malden, Mass.: Polity, 2013), 26–53.

36. For such an argument, see Luc Boltanski, *Distant Suffering: Morality, Media and Politics*, trans. Graham Burchell (New York: Cambridge University Press, 2004).

37. See, for instance, Didier Fassin, *Humanitarian Reason: A Moral History of the Present*, trans. Rachel Gomme (Berkeley: University of California Press, 2012), 1–20. Similar questions are likewise raised by Moya Lloyd in "Naming the Dead," 272–73; Miriam Ticktin, *Casualties of Care: Immigration and the Politics of Humanitarianism in France* (Berkeley: University of California Press, 2011).

38. I have previously addressed these arguments and the critical rejoinder in "The Body Politic: Bodily Spectacle and Democratic Agency," *Political Theory* 46, no. 2 (2018): 197–217.

39. For a helpful recounting of these symbolic forms, see Douglas Crimp, ed., *AIDS DemoGraphics* (Bay, 1990); see also Alisa Solomon, "AIDS Crusaders Act Up a Storm," in *Radical Street Performance: An International Anthology*, ed. Jan Cohen-Cruz (New York: Routledge, 1998), 42–51.

40. A productive discussion of this event appears in Douglas Crimp, "Portraits of People with AIDS," in *Melancholia and Moralism: Essays on AIDS and Queer Politics* (Cambridge, Mass.: MIT Press, 2002), 87–108.

41. On this point, see Joseph Todd, "Occupations, Assemblies, and Direct Action—a Critique of 'Body Politics,'" *Red Pepper*, August 22, 2016, http://www.redpepper.org.uk/occupations-assemblies-and-direct-action-a-critique-of-body-politics.

42. John Gilliom, "Resisting Surveillance," *Social Text* 23, no. 2 (Summer 2005): 78. See also Gilliom's longer treatment of this theme in *Overseers of the Poor: Surveillance, Resistance, and the Limits of Privacy* (Chicago: University of Chicago Press, 2001).

43. Dean Spade, *Normal Life: Administrative Violence, Critical Trans Politics, and the Limits of Law* (Durham, N.C.: Duke University Press, 2015), 119–20.

44. See Dora Apel, "'Hands Up, Don't Shoot': Surrendering to Liberal Illusions," *Theory & Event* 17, no. 3 supplement (2014).

45. On this point, see Coates, *Between the World and Me* (New York: Spiegel & Grau, 2015); Ange Marie Hancock, *The Politics of Disgust: The Public Identity of the Welfare Queen* (New York: New York University Press, 2004); and Loic Wacquant, *Punishing the Poor: The Neoliberal Government of Social Insecurity* (Durham, N.C.: Duke University Press, 2009).

46. Hannah Arendt, "Reflections on Little Rock," *Dissent* 6, no. 1 (1959): 45–56.

47. Similar challenges have been raised by Peggy Phelan, *Unmarked: The Politics of Performance* (New York: Routledge, 1993).

48. Luckily, there is already a considerable literature on how activists increasingly turn to theatrical means as an essential feature of their politics. For a brief list, see Jan Cohen-Cruz, ed., *Radical Street Performance* (New York: Routledge, 1998); Bradford Martin, *The Theater Is in the Street: Politics and Public Performance in Sixties America* (Amherst: University of Massachusetts Press, 2004); and T. V. Reed, *The Art of Protest* (Minneapolis: University of Minnesota Press, 2005). See also Graham St. John, "Protestival: Global Days of Action and Carnivalized Politics in the Present," *Social Movement Studies* 7, no. 2 (2008): 167–90; Pnina Werbner, Martin Webb, and Kathryn Spelkman-Poots, eds., *The Political Aesthetics of Global Protest* (Edinburgh: Edinburgh University Press, 2014); and Shirin Rai and Janelle Reinelt, eds., *The Grammar of Politics and Performance* (New York: Routledge, 2015).

49. As Amy Gutmann and Dennis Thompson argue, these "nondeliberative" activities (e.g., "antiwar marches, sit-ins and workers' strikes") can be justified *if* they help to achieve deliberative aims. And this qualified endorsement is qualified further: "deliberative processes . . . are generally more valuable than are nondeliberative means, and they are also more likely to aid victims of injustice." Gutmann and Thompson, *Why Deliberative Democracy* (Princeton, N.J.: Princeton University Press, 2004), 144. For a critical rejoinder, see Krause, *Civil Passions*, 118–19, 152–53.

50. Gutmann and Thompson, *Why Deliberative Democracy*, 51.

51. Butler, "Bodies in Alliance," 124.

52. John Dryzek, *Deliberative Democracy and Beyond: Liberals, Critics, Contestations* (New York: Oxford University Press, 2000), 51–52.

53. As Karin Fierke proposes: "the act is so spectacular and so outside the everyday that it disrupts or causes a rupture in the fabric of the everyday . . . the act of speech is an inversion of the speech act. . . . The sacrifice speaks louder than words, without using words, through the suffering of the body." See Fierke, *Political Self-Sacrifice: Agency, Body and Emotion in International Relations* (New York: Cambridge University Press, 2012), 83–84. Throughout this section, my account bears a debt to Iris Young's rejoinder to canonical deliberative positions. To channel the activist complication for democratic theory, she argues "the activist believes it is important to continue to challenge these discourses . . . and often he must do so by nondiscursive means—pictures, song, poetic imagery, and expressions of mockery and longing performed in rowdy and even playful ways aimed not at commanding assent but disturbing complacency. One of the activist's goals is to make us *wonder* about what we are doing, to rupture a stream of thought, rather than to weave an argument." See Young, "Activist Challenges to Deliberative Democracy," *Political Theory*, 29, no. 5 (2001): 687.

54. I owe this excellent point to Banu Bargu. For an incisive account of the politics of lip-sewing (particularly in relation to a politics of speech), see Bargu, "The Silent Exception: Hunger Striking and Lip-Sewing," *Law, Culture,*

and the Humanities (2017). Advance online publication, https://doi.org/10.1177/1743872117709684. For broader reflections on silence as a form of agency, see Kennan Ferguson, "Silence: A Politics," *Contemporary Political Theory* 2, no. 1 (2003): 49–65.

55. See Feola, "The Body Politic," where I offer a greatly expanded account of how bodily spectacle can generate political claims—particularly bodies that subject themselves to public undoing (e.g., die-ins, self-immolation, etc.). Judith Butler has helpfully detailed this claiming of public space in the occupation movement. See Butler, "Bodies in Alliance."

56. Martin Luther King Jr., *A Testament of Hope*, ed. James Melvin Washington (San Francisco: Harper San Francisco, 1991), 291, emphasis added.

57. This insight is also at the heart of Panagia, *The Political Life of Sensation.*

58. Martin Luther King Jr, *Why We Can't Wait* (New York: Penguin, 2000), 24. Emphasis added.

59. With this qualifier, I mean to suggest that there are good reasons to press on some of these standard conclusions. As Martin Berger has argued, the legacy of civil rights photography cannot simply be taken as an unvarnished, unmediated "eye from the street." Rather, the visual culture of the movement reflected a series of significant choices by both black and white newspapers as to *which* pictures would be chosen—what they would show (or not show)—and how they would be captioned. As Berger convincingly demonstrates, the image choices of white media outlets ultimately reflected significant white anxieties over black agency. See Berger, *Seeing Through Race: A Reinterpretation of Civil Rights Photography* (Berkeley: University of California Press, 2011).

60. For a helpful account of the significant training that many such activists undertook in order to maintain discipline in the face of provocation, see Susan Leigh Foster, "Choreographies of Protest," *Theatre Journal* 55, no. 3 (2003): 397–403.

61. This point is made in various ways by Paul Lawrie, "The Tragic Action and Revolutionary Intent of Black Lives," in *Truth in the Public Sphere*, ed. Jason Hannan (New York: Lexington Books, 2016), 63–78; Randy Martin, "Toward a Kinesthetics of Protest," *Social Identities* 12, no. 6 (2006): 796–98; and Joel Olson, *The Abolition of White Democracy* (Minneapolis: University of Minnesota Press, 2004), particularly chap. 2.

62. Passage cited in Jenny Edkins and Veronique Pin-Fat, "Through the Wire: Relations of Power and Relations of Violence," *Millennium: Journal of International Studies* 34, no. 1 (2005): 2.

63. The clearest instance is, of course, Guy Debord, *Society of the Spectacle.* See also Raoul Veneigem, *The Revolution of Everyday Life*, trans. Donald Nicholson-Smith (Seattle: Left Bank Books, 2003).

64. Jonathan Crary, *24/7: Late Capitalism and the Ends of Sleep* (New York: Verso, 2014).

65. Perhaps the clearest example in the critical theory tradition is the work of Herbert Marcuse, particularly *An Essay on Liberation* (Boston: Beacon, 1969). See also Ash Amin and Nigel Thrift, *Arts of the Political: New Openings for the Left* (Durham, N.C.: Duke University Press, 2013).

Index